D1031736

The Politics
of Presidential
Appointments

The Politics
of Presidential
Appointments

G. Calvin Mackenzie

THE FREE PRESS
A Division of Macmillan Publishing Co., Inc.
NEW YORK

Collier Macmillan Publishers
LONDON

The Free Press
A Division of Macmillan Publishing Co., Inc.
866 Third Avenue, New York, N.Y. 10022

Collier Macmillan Canada, Ltd.

Library of Congress Catalog Card Number: 80-1029

Printed in the United States of America

printing number

1   2   3   4   5   6   7   8   9   10

Library of Congress Cataloging in Publication Data

Mackenzie, G. Calvin
  The politics of Presidential appointments.

  Includes bibliographical references and index.
    1.   United States—Officials and employees—
Appointment, qualifications, tenure, etc.
  2.   Presidents—United States.   3.   United States.
Congress. Senate.   I.   Title.
JK736.M33   353.001'32   80-1029
ISBN 0-02-919670-1

*For my mother
and my father*

Contents

List of Tables and Figures

Acknowledgments

For the flaws of this book, I bear full responsibility. For whatever qualities it possesses, I must share the credit with many friends, colleagues, and critics, who generously bore my requests for help.

In their various permutations, portions of the manuscript benefited from the close reading and thoughtful comments of Eugene Declercq, Hugh Heclo, Paul Lenchner, Sandy Maisel, Clark Norton, and Stephen Wayne. To Paul Quirk I owe an enormous debt both for his rigorous criticisms and for his constant encouragement to bring this effort to fruit.

While a graduate student, I was blessed with the opportunity to study and work with Prof. Samuel H. Beer of Harvard. Like a generation of political scientists similarly blessed, I have tried to emulate the model of vigorous scholarship that emerges from his words and his work. If I have not fully succeeded, it is not for want of inspiration from this grand and generous man.

Other practitioners of my profession have had a significant, though indirect, impact on the way this book was conceived and executed. I was able, because they were so well marked, to follow the intellectual trails already blazed by Graham Allison, Joseph Cooper, Richard Fenno, Ralph Huitt, John Manley, Dean Mann, Richard Neustadt, Warner Schilling, and Aaron Wildavsky. I simply could not have proceeded with this project had they not gone first.

Much of the information and interpretation in the pages that follow were gleaned from discussions I held with individuals who have participated in the appointment process. Their willingness to make themselves available to me, to share their views and explain their roles, often in bold candor, has contributed greatly to my ability to write about a process in which I never took part. In spite of their demanding schedules, my requests for interviews were never turned down, my phone calls were returned, and my letters were answered. For that I am keenly appreciative. I do not wish to understate the contributions of any of these people, but I do want to express a particular debt of gratitude to Dan H. Fenn, Jr., and to Frederic V.

Malek, who responded patiently and thoughtfully to repeated requests for information and explanations.

The burden of preparing this book was lightened considerably by the assistance I received from several very able people. For help with the research and logistics I am indebted to Linda Fisher, Ellen Grant, and John Kiminski. Mrs. Patricia Kick typed the manuscript with much more efficiency and good cheer than my frequent revisions and illegible handwriting warranted. Helen Ketcham, a most remarkable young woman, was uncanny in her ability to track down "unavailable" information. Her industry and insights were an indispensable source of aid and enlightenment.

For financial support for this project, I am grateful to Harvard University, to the Graduate School of Arts and Sciences at George Washington University, to the Social Science Research Grants Committee at Colby College, and to the Lyndon Baines Johnson Foundation.

In a way that belies my efforts to express it, the most profound obligation I owe is to Arthur Maass. His initiative started me thinking about this topic. His perceptive warnings and tough criticisms kept me from pursuing a number of fruitless lines of inquiry. The high standards of scholarship that he imbued in me have become my most reliable navigational aids. I am grateful to him for all of that. And for introducing me to Sam Scolla.

Nancy and Andrew and Peter succeeded where I would have failed in preventing this book from totally interfering with the most important things in our lives. I only hope they know how much I ached to be with them in the adventures they undertook while I was holed up in the study. To Nancy particularly, I owe more than I can repay. Had it not been for her sense of perspective and priorities, the last few years could not possibly have been as delightfully pleasant as she has made them.

G.C.M.

Waterville, Maine

Introduction

The process of choosing a President of the United States is the quadrennial focal point of American politics. No sooner is one election over than we begin to follow the strategies and events and interactions that lead to another. Through the caucuses and the primaries and the conventions, candidates come and go, issues emerge and fade. In the last few months every word, every turn of phrase becomes an object of scrutiny. On Election Day the ballots are cast and counted. The winner is determined. The process of choosing a President is over.

But the process of choosing a new administration has just begun. And, in American politics, these are separate processes. One occurs in the center ring, the other is a sideshow. One is the subject of reams of attention from journalists and prolific analysis from political scientists. The other gets only scant attention from journalists and almost none from political scientists. As a result our accumulation of knowledge on how Presidents are chosen vastly exceeds our knowledge of how administrations are chosen.

Most of what passes for common knowledge about the appointment process is more shibboleth than substance. Statements like "The President always finds jobs for his friends" or "The Senate is just a rubber stamp" are part of the common litany of American politics. Their validity is widely accepted but rarely tested. They provide a kind of shorthand explanation of the appointment process, but it is a shorthand that too often lacks a sound empirical base or a broad theoretical perspective.

This should not surprise us. The appointment process commands little public attention, save for those exceptional and dramatic cases that occur very rarely in each administration. Of the few substantial scholarly efforts that have been made to study the appointment process, most have focused on those dramatic cases.[1] Little attention has been given to the hundreds of routine appointment decisions that compose the bulk of the appointment process and shape its character.

That is too bad. For these routine decisions reveal a great deal more about the way administrations are constructed than do those few

atypical appointment controversies that penetrate the public consciousness. Studying routine decisions tells us little about extreme
behavior but a great deal about normal behavior. It helps us to identify behavior patterns, to discern motives, and to get a sense of the
strategies that participants in a decision employ to influence its outcome. The problem in studying only controversial cases is that the
picture they produce is often distorted. What they reveal is more
interesting than instructive. They rarely provide us with an adequate
basis for generalizing about the normal process from which they vary.

The assumption that pervades this book is that one can begin to
understand and assess the appointment process only after examining
all of its contours. Those who turn these pages looking only for descriptions of recent appointment controversies will be disappointed.
They will find those controversial appointments mentioned here only
when they help to illustrate points that apply more broadly to the full
range of appointment decisions. The purpose of this book is to look at
the appointment process not as a series of interesting though idiosyn-
cratic case studies, but rather as a coherent and revealing channel of
government activity.

Each year the President of the United States submits between
fifty thousand and seventy thousand nominations to the Senate for its
approval. Not all of these are of great consequence by any means. The
vast majority are initial appointments or promotions in the armed
forces, the Foreign Service, or the Public Health Service. Though he
is the formal appointing authority, the President plays no active role
in filling these positions. His attention, or at least that of his staff, is
concentrated instead on the selection of people to fill those positions
at the highest levels of the federal government: Cabinet and subcabinet officers, the heads of independent agencies, the members of
regulatory commissions, the directors of government corporations,
ambassadors, and federal judges.

These major appointments are the topic of this book, but even
some of them are examined here only peripherally. I shall have little
to say, for instance, about minor ambassadorships. Most of these are
handled within the State Department and rarely generate much
interest in the White House or in the Congress. I shall also have less
to say about the appointment of federal judges than their importance
merits. This is because the process by which federal judges are appointed has been the subject of much scholarship, and the literature
on that topic is comprehensive and revealing.[2] There is a brief discussion in this book of "senatorial courtesy," and a few Supreme Court

appointments are used to illustrate Senate concerns in the confirmation process. But there is no systematic treatment here of judicial appointments. Instead, I have concentrated on those appointments in the executive branch and in the regulatory commissions that normally command the direct attention of the White House and the Senate.

In describing the subjects of this study, I shall frequently use the terms "major appointments" or "important appointments." These words are not intended to imply any value judgment. They are terms of exclusion, used to help differentiate those appointments to which individual attention is usually given by the White House and the Senate from that far larger body of appointments that are treated as routine and pro forma. Table I-1 indicates the number of these major appointments confirmed by the Senate in recent Congresses.

The manner in which these important federal offices are filled is governed by Article II, Section 2 of the United States Constitution:

> [The President] shall nominate and by and with the advice and consent of the Senate, shall appoint Ambassadors, other public Ministers and Consuls, Judges of the Supreme Court, and all other officers of the United States, whose appointments are not herein otherwise provided for, and which shall be established by law: but the Congress may by law vest the appointment of such inferior officers, as they think proper, in the President alone, in the courts of law, or in the heads of departments.

This constitutional language requires that the appointment power be shared by the President and the Senate. In effect, it creates a decision-making process with two stages. The first—"the selection process"—is the decision on whom to nominate and is dominated by the President. The second—"the confirmation process"—is the decision on whether to confirm the President's nominee and is dominated by the Senate. Together they compose what I shall subsequently refer to as the "appointment process," the principal stages of which are outlined in Figure I-1.

Because the initial objective of this project was to explore the contemporary appointment process, the research has concentrated almost entirely on the period since World War II. The examination of the selection process begins in 1945 and ends at the beginning of 1978. The year 1945 is not an important line of demarcation in the historical development of the selection process; that occurs in the early 1960s. Beginning this study with 1945, however, creates an

Table I-1.   Presidential Appointments Confirmed by the Senate, 1961–1978

| | MAJOR NOMINATIONS BY CATEGORY | | | | | | |
YEAR	EXECUTIVE OFFICE OF THE PRESIDENT	CABINET DEPARTMENTS [a]	INDEPENDENT AGENCIES	REGULATORY COMMISSIONS [b]	FEDERAL JUDGES [c]	ALL OTHER NOMINATIONS	TOTAL NOMINATIONS CONFIRMED
1961	6	133	32	18	60	48,712	48,961
1962	8	61	15	16	54	51,626	51,780
1963	6	44	37	9	15	66,492	66,603
1964	5	38	12	11	18	53,514	53,598
1965	11	90	21	21	29	54,404	54,576
1966	10	70	16	13	60	66,120	66,289
1967	5	77	16	15	35	68,934	69,082
1968	4	57	32	14	24	49,018	49,149
1969	12	205	30	18	27	72,343	72,635
1970	6	40	18	9	65	61,024	61,162
1971	7	43	26	16	63	48,700	48,855
1972	2	46	10	11	25	65,960	66,054
1973	5	129	17	22	22	66,622	66,817
1974	4	69	20	18	34	64,292	64,437
1975	4	91	30	22	17	71,112	71,276
1976	4	61	16	20	31	59,970	60,102
1977	16	214	53	10	25	65,313	65,631
1978	4	68	25	21	39	58,785	59,099

[a] Includes ambassadors.
[b] Includes Atomic Energy Commission, Civil Aeronautics Board, Commodities Futures Trading Commission, Consumer Product Safety Commission, Equal Employment Opportunity Commission, Federal Communications Commission, Federal Elections Commission, Federal Maritime Commission, Federal Power Commission, Federal Reserve Board, Federal Trade Commission, Interstate Commerce Commission, Nuclear Regulatory Commission, Securities Exchange Commission.
[c] Includes only appointments to the Supreme Court, the Circuit Courts, and the District Courts.
SOURCES: *Daily Digest of the Congressional Record* and *Congressional Quarterly Almanacs.*

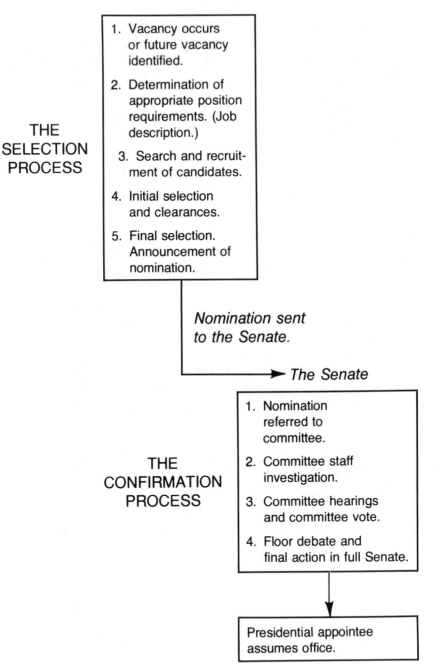

The White House

THE
SELECTION
PROCESS

1. Vacancy occurs
   or future vacancy
   identified.

2. Determination of
   appropriate position
   requirements. (Job
   description.)

3. Search and recruit-
   ment of candidates.

4. Initial selection
   and clearances.

5. Final selection.
   Announcement of
   nomination.

*Nomination sent
to the Senate.*

The Senate

THE
CONFIRMATION
PROCESS

1. Nomination
   referred to
   committee.

2. Committee staff
   investigation.

3. Committee hearings
   and committee vote.

4. Floor debate and
   final action in full Senate.

Presidential appointee
assumes office.

Figure I-1. The Appointment Process.

opportunity to examine the White House role in the appointment process before the onset of the significant changes of the 1960s. This makes it easier to identify those changes and to assess their impact.

Necessity has imposed a different time frame on my examination of the Senate confirmation process. Much of the analysis for this section is based upon interviews with Senate staff members and a close reading of Senate confirmation hearings (see the Appendix for a description of this research). Because there are a great many of these hearings and because it was exceedingly difficult to locate Senate staff members who were involved in or remembered much about the confirmation process before the mid-1960s, the decision was made to limit the examination of the confirmation process to the period for which there was an abundance of adequate and reliable source material, that is, from 1964 through 1978. This period was short enough to allow close scrutiny of several hundred confirmation decisions, but long enough to permit the formulation of reasonable generalizations about Senate reactions to the nominees of four different Presidents, two Republican and two Democratic.

As the research for this book got under way, it quickly became apparent that this would not be simply a story about the White House and the Senate. The appointment process is a substantial enterprise; it touches virtually every aspect of the governing process in the United States. The President and the members of the Senate are the main actors in the appointment process, but they are not its sole participants or the only sources of influence over its outcomes. There are at least five other discrete sets of individuals who take a frequent interest and often play an active part in appointment decisions.

The first of these is the White House staff. We shall see in the pages ahead that recent Presidents have made it a practice to assign operational responsibility for the selection of their nominees to a group of full-time personnel aides. The size of this group has varied from less than a dozen to more than fifty, and in the years after 1960 it came to play an important part in structuring the selection process and in defining the criteria that would govern the President's choices. The training and the goals of the people who served as personnel advisers to the postwar Presidents have had a very substantial effect on the character of the appointment process.

The political executives and the career personnel in the departments and agencies compose a second group of interested observers and frequent participants. Who, after all, is more likely to be directly affected by an appointment to a position in a Cabinet department than the people who are already there—the Secretary, the subcabinet officers, and the career civil servants? The Secretary wants to have some control over the selection of his subordinates. The subcabinet officers want to ensure that their colleagues in office share their fundamental views about policies and priorities. The career employees of the department want to be certain that their new boss will be sympathetic to what they do and the way they do it, and that he will be an effective advocate for their needs and interests. In making their decisions on appointments, the President and the Senate rarely have to wonder for long about a department's feelings toward a suggested candidate for a vacancy within that department. The people within the department will usually make every effort to express their feelings and to do so with vigor.

Interest groups also have a profound interest in appointment decisions and strong incentives to try to influence their outcomes. It is not uncommon for a national interest group to feel that its treatment by policy-makers, administrators, and judges will be strongly conditioned by the attitudes that those people bring with them when they take office. Thus their vigilance over the appointment process stems from a desire to ensure that their views will be given adequate consideration and fair treatment when major decisions that affect their interests are made.

Political parties are a fourth set of actors who pay persistent attention to the appointment process. Their concerns are most commonly expressed by the leaders of the state and national party organizations. From their point of view, the appointment process is, or should be, a patronage process. If their party controls the White House, they will want to make sure that party activists and loyal party supporters are well represented among the President's major appointments. The state and national organizations will produce long lists of candidates for appointments. They will pass political judgment on those the President is considering. And they will constantly remind the President that his support within the party is affected in no small measure by his willingness to appoint his co-partisans to federal offices.

A final set of concerned actors comprises the members of the House of Representatives. The House has no formal role in the appointment process, but its members, like those of the other groups listed here, often have a direct interest in appointments to individual offices. A subcommittee chairman wants to influence the selection of the agency head he will be dealing with, members from wheat-producing states want a Secretary of Agriculture who understands the particular problems of their constituents, party leaders in the House want to enlarge their influence with their colleagues by helping them secure favorable appointment decisions. The House is no indifferent bystander in the appointment process. That its members lack a formal role only means that they must work harder to develop informal avenues of influence.

This book is about the *politics* of the appointment process. It needn't have been, of course. One could just as well study the history of the appointment process or the formalities of it. But ultimately one can effectively describe and explain the appointment process in no other way than by examining its politics. The range of participants in this process is broad. Their interests vary. As a result, appointment decisions are conflictive, often highly so. The Secretary of the Interior may have a candidate to head the Geological Survey. So too does the chairman of the House Interior Committee. The mining engineers have a third. All try to persuade the President that their candidate is the best choice for this office. If they fail with the President, they redirect their persuasive efforts toward the Senate committee that must pass on the nominee's qualifications. This sort of disagreement is common in the appointment process. Few nominations escape it. This is the politics of the appointment process.

But it is not a shapeless politics. Disagreements over appointments rarely turn into open hostility. Conflict occurs routinely in the appointment process, but conflict is channeled and controlled. The participants disagree with each other, but they rarely fight. They rarely fight for two reasons. First, fighting is counterproductive to the maintenance of permanent and useful relationships. Some participants may be woefully unhappy with a particular nomination. But they usually recognize that once the nomination is made their chances of changing it are slim. It is best to admit defeat in lost causes and save one's influence and resources for the next important appointment decision. Once in a great while, a nomination will strike some of the regular participants in the appointment process as so egregiously awful that they feel compelled to fight it, to testify vigorously in opposition at committee hearings, to lobby senators and committee staff intensively, to pore over a nominee's record for some hint of damning evidence. When they do this, however, they usually make life unpleasant for the President and uncomfortable for senators. If they do it often, they will soon find themselves shut out of appointment decisions entirely. When they lose their direct access to the decision-making process, their influence wanes.

A second reason why disagreement in the appointment process rarely turns into visible hostility is that over time the participants in the process have developed several effective techniques for conflict avoidance and conflict resolution. The President rarely announces a nomination without first assessing the sentiments of those individuals and interests most likely to be affected by the nomination. The Senate uses the confirmation process not simply as an opportunity to reject or support a nominee, but also to identify the areas in which its members disagree with the nominee and to attempt to narrow those areas of disagreement so that it can feel comfortable in confirming him. Explaining these techniques for conflict avoidance and conflict resolution will be an important task of this book. Without them, the appointment process would be far more vitriolic and far less workable than it is.

Conflict occurs regularly in the appointment process for a very simple reason. Appointments matter. Were that not the case, presidential administrations would not have several dozen White House aides devoting full time to appointment decisions; Senate committees would not hold hundreds of hours of confirmation hearings; interest groups, agencies, political parties, and members of the House would not spend their time or resources trying to shape appointment decisions. Yet they all do these things, and they do them because they think it makes a difference who gets appointed to serve in particular federal offices.

The dynamics of the appointment process become clearer to us when we pursue this point further. Why do these participants in appointment decisions think appointments matter? In what sense do they matter? The answer is that appointments are important in several ways.

They are important, first of all, as jobs, as patronage. The universal spoils system died long ago, but administration jobs are still regarded by many participants in the political process as an important part of the rewards system. They are important to those who get the jobs, but also to those who give them or procure them. For the former, an appointive position is a recognition of past services or perhaps a credit toward future considerations. For the latter, influence over appointment decisions is a measure of importance or political clout.

Appointments are also important for their symbolic value. By appointing members of a certain group or representatives of certain interests to positions in his administration or in the judicial branch, a President can enlarge the sense of involvement and participation in the national government. The appointment of a person who is black to the Supreme Court or the Cabinet, for instance, may have little real effect on the social or economic progress of black citizens. But it does provide explicit demonstration that black leaders have some influence with the President or that he personally wants blacks to be represented in the highest councils of government. The symbolic importance of such appointments may equal or even outweigh their impact on practical politics. Lyndon Johnson believed this about his path-breaking appointments of blacks to major political offices.

> Distinguished black men and women had assumed their rightful places in the highest offices in the land—the Supreme Court, the Cabinet, the foreign service, the Federal Reserve Board, the mayorship of Washington, D. C., the chairmanship of the Equal Employment Opportunity Commission. I had chosen these people—Thurgood Marshall, Robert Weaver, Andrew Brimmer, Patricia Harris, Walter Washington, Clifford Alexander—and many others for their competence, wisdom, and courage, not for the color of their skin. But I also deeply believed that with these appointments Negro mothers could look at their children and hope with good reason that someday their sons and daughters might reach the highest offices their government could offer.[3]

Whatever their patronage or symbolic value, however, the importance of appointments is registered most clearly in their impact on public policy. The driving force in the appointment process, its fundamental dynamic, is the widely held assumption that who you get *in* government directly affects what you get *out* of government. The significance of the relationship between the character of presidential appointments and the shape of public policy has been given emphatic recognition by students of the governing process and by participants in it. Frederic V. Malek, for instance, who held several high-level federal offices, has written:

> In today's government, the Cabinet and the White House staff exert powerful influence on the direction of an administration, and most decisions that are credited to a President are actually made at the staff level with only pro forma approval from the President. The people

around the chief executive are the ones who actually run the agencies, sift through the issues, identify the problems, and present analyses and recommendations for the chief's decision. It is they who give shape to the administration's governing strategy and transform vague party platforms to hard policies and legislative proposals.[4]

Hugh Heclo, a perceptive student of executive politics, has echoed the same point: "In affecting the everyday work of the government, these hundreds of personnel selections add up to a cumulative act of choice that may be at least as important as the electorate's single act of choice for president every four years."[5]

The importance of this point cannot be understated. Other concerns appear in the appointment process, and they will be noted throughout this book. But the operational principle that shapes political behavior and directs political action in the appointment process is the notion that all of its participants share: that appointment decisions are important because they have a significant effect on the outcome of policy decisions.

Notes

1. See, for example, Joseph Harris, *The Advice and Consent of the Senate* (University of California Press, 1953); James N. Rosenau, *The Nomination of "Chip" Bohlen* (Holt, 1958); Louis C. James, "Senatorial Rejection of Presidential Nominations to the Cabinet: A Study of the Constitutional Customs," *Arizona Law Review*, Vol. 2 (1961).
2. See, for example, William J. Burris, *The Senate Rejects a Judge: A Study of the John J. Parker Case* (University of North Carolina Press, 1962); David J. Danelski, *A Supreme Court Justice Is Appointed* (Random House, 1964); Richard Harris, *Decision* (Ballantine Books, 1971); Henry J. Abraham, *Justices and Presidents: A Political History of Appointments to the Supreme Court* (Oxford University Press, 1974); and Harold W. Chase, *Federal Judges: The Appointing Process* (Minnesota University Press, 1972).
3. Lyndon B. Johnson, *The Vantage Point* (Popular Library edition, 1971), p. 179.
4. Frederic V. Malek, *Washington's Hidden Tragedy* (The Free Press, 1978), p. 63.
5. Hugh Heclo, *A Government of Strangers* (Brookings, 1977), p. 88.

I

The Selection Process

1　The Personnel Selection Function

The first and most formidable of the tasks facing a new President is the problem of finding men and women to fill the most important positions in his administration. In the earliest days of the Republic this was not terribly difficult. The government was small, and a new administration faced only a handful of vacant positions. These could be filled by drawing on a small band of public servants whose reputations and abilities were well known to the President. George Washington filled the Cabinet positions in his first administration with Thomas Jefferson, Henry Knox, Edmund Randolph, and Alexander Hamilton. He sent Thomas Pinckney to serve as Ambassador to Great Britain and Gouverneur Morris to France. John Jay was nominated to serve as Chief Justice of the United States. These constituted the bulk of Washington's major appointments. And none of these men were strangers to him. He knew them all personally and could well gauge their abilities and the likelihood of their loyalty to him on the basis of this personal knowledge. That was a simpler age.

But times have changed. A contemporary President faces two problems in making important personnel decisions that were unknown to the early Presidents. First, the government has grown to such proportions that a President cannot possibly know a broad enough range of qualified people to permit him to choose as his appointees only those with whom he is personally familiar. He is forced to look beyond his own circle of friends and acquaintances to select people he has never met and about whom he knows very little.

This would be an easier burden for the President to bear if he had sufficient time to invest in the selection process, if he could carefully review the qualifications of and conduct personal interviews with all of those he nominates to positions of responsibility. But his second problem is that he doesn't have this time. Between his election and his inauguration, he has less than eighty days to fill the top posts in his administration. But even in that period only a small portion of his time can be devoted to personnel decisions. Other issues clamor for his attention. He has to put together budget recommendations to go to the Congress shortly after he takes office. He must begin to shape a legislative program. And inevitably he will be drawn into dozens of courtesy meetings with the heads of important national interest groups, the leaders of Congress, and visiting foreign dignitaries. Time is scarce and the flow of decisions is awesome. Even those Presidents with a strong desire to involve themselves personally in selection decisions rarely have the opportunity to do so to any substantial extent. After inauguration day the burdens of office accelerate, and direct presidential involvement in selection decisions becomes increasingly difficult.

Inevitably, then, modern Presidents have been forced to delegate some of their responsibility for personnel selection to the White House staff and, in some cases, to other agencies, individuals, and organizations as well. In the period since World War II, the process of finding and recruiting people to serve in high-level executive and judicial positions has become a corporate enterprise. In this chapter, I shall explore the manner in which postwar administrations have organized the management of the personnel selection function. I shall also identify the criteria and priorities that have been most important in shaping the outcomes of presidential selection decisions in each of those administrations.

As indicated earlier, the President has technical responsibility for several hundred thousand personnel appointments throughout the government. The total of those that are of sufficient importance to command White House attention is substantially smaller, though still considerable. The number of these significant positions has grown gradually in recent years, as Table 1–1 indicates, and is now slightly in excess of 1,500. This overstates the actual number of major appointments a President can make, however, because many of these positions have a term of office that is not coincident with his. Judges, for instance, have life tenure, and a President may nominate new judges only as vacancies occur. The number of important personnel decisions facing a new President therefore usually numbers in the vicinity of five hundred or six hundred, about half of which require Senate confirmation.[1]

Presidential Considerations

At the beginning of a new administration, several salient concerns color the selection process. The most important of these is that

Table 1-1.   Major Appointive Positions Subject to Senate
Confirmation, Selected Years[a]

LOCATION	YEAR		
	1952	1969	1977
Executive Office of the President	3	22	17
Cabinet departments [b]	574	616	659
Independent Agencies	243	266	304
Legislative Branch	4	4	5
Judicial Branch	336	481	544
Total	1160	1389	1529

[a] This table does not include positions in the uniformed military services, Foreign Service, postmasters, etc., a number of which are (or were) presidential appointments subject to Senate confirmation.

[b] Includes ambassadors (State Department) and U.S. Attorneys and Marshalls (Justice Department).

SOURCES: U.S. House of Representatives, 94th Congress, 2d Session (1976), Committee on Post Office and Civil Service, *United States Government, Policy and Supporting Positions.*

Office of Management and Budget, *Budget of the U.S. Government, Fiscal Year 1979: Appendix* (GPO, 1978).

"6500 Patronage Jobs Open to Nixon Administration," *Congressional Quarterly Weekly Report,* January 3, 1969.

Joseph P. Harris, *The Advice and Consent of the Senate* (University of California Press, 1953).

the new President is in debt. He is in debt to those groups and individuals who contributed to his victory with their efforts, their dollars, and their votes. They will not hesitate to seek appointive positions in the new administration as a due reward for their support, and the President will feel some responsibility for treating their claims with favor. Some of his initial nominations, therefore, will go to people from those groups that helped him get to the White House.

But initial selection decisions normally reflect other considerations as well. Three of these are most common: symbolism, politics, and managerial needs. In making his initial personnel selections, the President has a rare opportunity to establish the character and direction of his administration. At no time is the selection process more visible than during the transition period and the early months of a new administration. In the absence of other clear evidence, early personnel selections are seized upon as significant indicators of the priorities and intentions of a new President.

In the short run, at least, the symbolism inherent in these early personnel decisions is very important. This is most apparent in the selection of a President's first Cabinet. His choices for individual positions and the collective make-up of the Cabinet are thus subject to very close scrutiny. In his comprehensive study of presidential Cabinets, Richard Fenno wrote:

> The presidential decisions leading to the composition of a new "official family" are taken during the peak period of public interest which attends the national election campaign. As executive decisions go, they are pre-eminently concrete and visible. Among the earliest of presidential moves, they are treated as symbolic acts of considerable significance.[2]

These initial selections are also important because they provide the President with a chance to lay the groundwork for political relationships that will directly affect the future success of his administration. Not only do they allow him to reward those who have supported him in the past, they also permit him to broaden his base of support within his own party, with organized interest groups, and in the Congress. These opportunities, however, are not boundless. Presidents seem never to have enough available appointments to satisfy all the demands and suggestions they encounter. Inevitably some of those seeking appointments for themselves or for their friends will be disappointed. William Howard Taft's lament that "every time I make an appointment I create nine enemies and one ingrate" still holds. Hence the selection process, particularly in the early stages of a new administration, is governed by scarce resources and multiple, competing demands. Opportunities exist for gaining some political advantage from these early personnel choices, but, if used unwisely, those opportunities are easily squandered.

A third criterion affecting early selection decisions is the President's managerial needs. As the federal government has grown in size and in the breadth of the functions it performs, it has become increasingly difficult for Presidents to serve as the central creative and directive force in the executive branch. Among the instruments available to a President for coping with this responsibility, the appointment power is widely regarded as one of the most important.[3] Thus in selecting the heads of Cabinet departments and large independent agencies the President is forced to concern himself with the managerial and administrative abilities of potential candidates for these offices. This concern is most compelling in selecting the leaders of large conglomerate departments like Defense and HHS or multifunction agencies like the Office of Economic Opportunity or the Veteran's Administration. As we shall see, however, this criterion is often given a lower priority in early selection decisions than is the case later in a President's term. In part this results from the early importance of symbolic and political criteria, and in part it results from the inability of an administration to assess its managerial needs clearly before it takes office.

In examining the selection process, it is important to keep in mind the distinction between nominations made at the beginning of a new administration and those made in-term. Personnel selection responsibilities are ongoing. They do not end when the transition period is over. Normal patterns of tenure and turnover require a President to continue to make major personnel decisions throughout his administration. Figure 1-1, for example, illustrates tenure patterns in Cabinet positions in the period from 1945 through 1977. The median term of service for a Cabinet Secretary in that period was 2.1 years, and more than 40 percent stayed in place for less than two years. Turnover at the subcabinet level and in the independent agencies is

Figure 1-1. Tenure of Cabinet Secretaries, 1945–1977 (N = 126)

Percent of all Cabinet Secretaries, 1945–1977

25%   21.4% 23.0% 23.0%
20%
15%   13.5%
10%   9.5%
5%   1.6% 2.4% 5.6%
0

Length of tenure in years: 0–.9 1–1.9 2–2.9 3–3.9 4–4.9 5–5.9 6–6.9 7–8

Median length of service, all Cabinet Secretaries, 1945–1977 = 2.1 years comparable.[4] The result is that the selection process is endless. Resignations occur regularly, and there are always important positions to be filled.

But the conditions and considerations that govern these in-term selection decisions are often different from those that prevail at the beginning of a new administration. Public and media attention in the selection process begins to fade, electoral debts are paid off or forgotten, and the President's attention turns to the task of setting and accomplishing substantive objectives. The symbolic importance of personnel selections gradually diminishes, and practical considerations are given larger priority in selection decisions. Those practical considerations are of several types.

For one thing, a President's nominees are the primary link between him and the millions of men and women in the federal bureaucracy. Most of these men and women are located in the executive branch of government and technically work for the President. But he has little power to hire and fire them, he cannot control their political loyalties, and he lacks the time and resources to supervise their activities. His executive appointees must act as his surrogates in dealing with the bureaucracy. The quality and character of the people he chooses to serve in executive positions will have a strong impact on the ability of his transient administration to direct and control the permanent government.

Successful accomplishment of presidential objectives also requires support from the Congress, and selection decisions have a bearing on that as well. In making those decisions, an administration can do two things to help its relations with the Congress. First, it can emphasize among its selection criteria the importance of appointing people who are sensitive to the special problems of dealing with an institution like the Congress. Careful attention to this in the selection process can save a lot of ruffled feathers in future interaction between the two branches.

A second way in which an administration can use the selection process to foster good working relations with the Congress is to pay some heed to the expressed interests of the members of Congress in making selection decisions. Important senators and representatives are often eager participants in the selection process. In some cases they will propose candidates of their own; in others they will have strong negative feelings about a candidate they know to be under consideration. Often congressional interest in appointments can be used as the basis for policy-related bargaining between the President and strategically placed members of Congress. The willingness of a committee chairman or party leader to support a presidential policy initiative can often be encouraged by deferring to that congressman in filling a position in which he has a particular interest.

So it is characteristic of in-term selection decisions to reflect the President's concerns in dealing with the executive establishment and with the Congress. The selection process itself also undergoes some changes after an administration settles into office. The intensity of the early rush of decisions slows to a pace that permits more deliberation and the establishment of routine and more rational decision-making procedures. An administration has more time to consider its needs carefully, to search out and recruit a candidate who seems to meet those needs, and then to assess the likely reaction to that candidate among those who will be affected by the actions he will take once in office. In-term personnel selections thus often become a central part of an administration's political and administrative strategies for accomplishing its policy objectives.

While the concerns outlined here are common to all administrations, no two administrations treat them in exactly the same fashion. Each has to adjust its selection procedures and criteria to its own distinctive set of objectives, constraints, and priorities. Hence there is considerable variety across administrations in the way the selection process is organized, in the manner in which selection decisions are made, and in the aggregate character of personnel choices. The remaining chapters in Part I look at the characteristics of the selection process that are distinctive to each of the postwar administrations and at the patterns and procedures that are common to them all.

Notes

1. Most of those which do not require Senate confirmation are positions on the White House staff or in the Executive Office of the President.
2. Richard F. Fenno, Jr., *The President's Cabinet* (Vintage Books, 1958), p. 51.
3. See, for example, Louis W. Koenig, *The Chief Executive*, 3d Ed. (Harcourt Brace Jovanovich, 1975), chapter 8.
4. A study of the tenure of under secretaries and assistant secretaries covering the period from 1961 through 1972 found that one-fifth served less than twelve months and fewer than half served more than two years. See Arch Patton, "Government's Revolving Door," *Business Week*, September 22, 1975, p. 12.

In 1974 John Cushman, the executive director of the Administrative Conference of the United States, indicated that the average tenure of independent regulatory commissioners is less than three years. See "Nixon Legacy: Many Long-term Appointments," *Congressional Quarterly Weekly Report,* 32(August 24, 1974): 2282

2   Selection and Recruitment, 1945–1977

Harry S. Truman

Most Presidents, upon coming to the White House, have to form a government. Harry Truman inherited one. That fact dominated the executive selection procedures of his administration.

The administration that Harry Truman took over had been in place for twelve years. It had been tested by two of the great calamities in American history. Truman knew most of its executives and on major policy matters was in essential agreement with them. And while it soon became clear to him that he would eventually want to fill the major government offices with his own appointees, there was little compulsion on his part to look very far beyond Washington in finding those he would ultimately select. With little need to "capture" the government or to redirect it significantly, Truman was able to make a large percentage of his executive nominations from his own circle of acquaintances and from among individuals whose actions and reputations he had been able to observe at close range.

The process of personnel selection was not elaborately structured during the Truman years, though Truman was the first President to have an aide whose primary responsibility was to review candidates for appointive positions. The aide so charged was Donald Dawson, a lawyer from Kansas City and a close associate of the President. Dawson served as a personnel generalist, dealing with patronage matters, fending off jobseekers, and overseeing the search for executive vacancies. Despite the uniqueness of Dawson's responsibilities, however, little effort was made within the White House Office to separate the personnel selection function from the great variety of other duties carried out by the President's assistants.

By all accounts, Harry Truman took a keen personal interest in appointment decisions. In part, no doubt, this resulted from the fact that his personal attention was required because there was no specialized White House staff to handle personnel matters. But it also reflected a personal predilection. Truman liked dealing with people directly. He made a habit of calling his nominees to the White House for a personal meeting to inform them of their nominations. That is a practice that only Lyndon Johnson among subsequent Presidents attempted to duplicate.

Truman's personnel selections were governed by two criteria predominantly: loyalty to the President and his programs, and prior experience in government and politics.

The first criterion was important because of the circumstances under which Truman came to power. The government he inherited was a Democratic government, and he was a good Democrat. But many of those in high-level posts in 1945 were Roosevelt loyalists who found it difficult to transfer the full intensity of their allegiance to Truman. The new President wasted little time in seeking or accepting the resignations of those carryover officials who faced this problem.[1] Eight of the ten Cabinet members he inherited left office within the first ten months of Truman's presidency. And as the President undertook the process of replacing those who left, he sought to ascertain that their successors would be personally loyal to him and would vigorously support his programmatic goals. He justified the selection of Lewis Schwellenbach as Secretary of Labor, for example, by saying, "We saw right down the same alley on policy."[2]

Truman's reliance on government experience in picking his subordinates was rooted in his own broad reading of history and in the lessons of his years in politics. He felt that there was an immutable relationship between politics and government, that success in the latter depended upon experience in the former. He stated this explicitly in remarking on his first wave of Cabinet replacements:

> At this time [mid-July 1945] my Cabinet was made up of men who had government experience and most of whom had had political experience along with it.
>   I consider political experience absolutely necessary, because a man who understands politics understands free government. Our government is by the consent of the people, and you have to convince a majority of the people that what you are trying to do is right and in their interest. If you are not a politician, you cannot do it.[3]

Because Truman emphasized loyalty and experience in making personnel selections, he chose a larger percentage of his political appointees from within the government than did any of his successors. This tendency was reinforced by several of the circumstances that conditioned his selections. Since the government had been administered by Democrats for twelve years, Truman had a sizable body of experienced co-partisans from which to choose. Cabinet and agency heads had had abundant opportunitites to identify and advocate the appointment of talented individuals working under them, including many who had started their careers as civil servants. Federal employees provided Truman with a ready body of available, experienced, and well-tested candidates for appointive positions.

Truman's unusually heavy reliance on people in the federal service was not simply a matter of personal preference. In many cases he had little choice. He was limited in the range of potential nominees available to him from outside the government because, after four years of wartime mobilization, there was considerable reluctance among talented Americans to seek or accept public service opportunities. The war years had forced most of these people out of their careers, and there was little eagerness after the war to prolong that interruption. Truman was further hemmed in by his own limited contacts among people in business, in the professions, and on university faculties. Ultimately the bulk of his personnel selections were made from among those with whom Truman was best acquainted and to whom he had greatest access: government employees.

In an interesting study of the appointment process using a sample of 108 political executives, Dean E. Mann found that 65 percent of the Truman appointees were people already serving in the public sector at the time of their selection.[4] Twenty-two percent of his choices were noncareer executives whom he promoted; 35 percent were promoted from the career service; and 8 percent were political appointees who were transferred from one agency to another.[5] The Truman appointees had much more extensive prior administrative service (median = 5.2 years) than did those of Roosevelt (3.3 years) or Eisenhower (2.0 years).[6]

This heavy reliance on those already in the public service is not surprising when one examines Mann's data on the process by which these people were selected. The primary selection criterion for 54 percent of the Truman appointees whom Mann investigated closely was "general experience in the area of responsibility." In 24 percent of the cases, the prime criterion was "general experience plus political factors." Hence Mann found that experience was a central factor in 78 percent of Truman's selection decisions.[7] The search for political executives, whether conducted by the White House itself or by the heads of departments and independent agencies, was far less likely to extend beyond the friends and associates of the individual making the final decision than was true under subsequent administrations. Mann found, for instance, that in 75 percent of his sample of cases in which the agency head made the final selection decision, the search had been limited to his own close friends and associates, and in only 11 percent of the cases had an effort been made to broaden the search beyond the range of personal acquaintances.[8]

In the Truman years the practice of personnel selection was carried on much as it had been since the turn of the century. The one notable innovation was the designation of a single member of the White House staff to serve as a central clearance point for personnel and patronage decisions. Personnel selection procedures remained relatively primitive in the Truman years primarily because of the absence of any overarching personnel policy. Selection decisions were only occasionally related to broad administrative objectives.[9] More often they were the product of ad hoc policy considerations, of presidential friendships,[10] or of convenience. With no consistent plan to guide its personnel choices, the Truman administration had little need for a specialized staff or rigorous procedures to control and direct the selection process.

Dwight D. Eisenhower

Dwight Eisenhower came to the White House under circumstances very different from those that surrounded Truman's accession. Truman took command of a government that had been under the control of his own party for twelve years. Eisenhower, on the other hand, was the first Republican President in twenty years. Truman had been in Washington for a decade prior to the time he became President, and he was personally familiar with many of the people he would later ask to join his administration. Eisenhower, however, had not been in Washington for any extended period since before the war and had limited acquaintanceship among those people most likely to serve as political executives. Eisenhower's party had been out of power for a generation; there was no Republican "government in exile" waiting only for him to sound the call for their return to Washington. For him the problems of personnel selection were vastly different from those that confronted Truman.

There was a significant difference as well in the way the two men came to the presidency. Truman had grown up in the Byzantine organizational politics of Missouri in the 1920s and 1930s. He had served in local offices and had been affiliated with the Pendergast machine, which dominated the state's public affairs during that period. He had gone to Washington as a loyal New Deal Democrat in 1934 and had come into prominence as the head of a Senate committee that investigated the management of the war effort. His experience outside of politics, in farming and retailing, had been notably unsuccessful. Eisenhower, on the other hand, had no experience in elective politics and no particular fondness for it. Having spent a long career in military staff positions, however, he came to Washington with fixed opinions about administrative management. He sought immediately to make changes in the way the White House was run, to adapt it to his own sense of order and responsibility:

> For years I had been in frequent contact with the Executive Office of the White House and I had certain ideas about the system, or lack of system, under which it operated. With my training in problems involving organization it was inconceivable to me that the work of the White House could not be better systematized than had been the case during the years I observed it.[11]

Eisenhower's early efforts at administration building were shaped by the coalescence of three factors. First, the President needed to look beyond those already in government and beyond his circle of associates in order to fill the major positions in his Cabinet and in the departments and agencies. Second, having been out of power for two decades, Republicans were intensely interested in these selection decisions, and they were unremitting in their efforts to influence them.[12] And, third, Eisenhower had a strong and fundamental desire to impose a sense of order and hierarchy on decision-making procedures in the White House, including those involving personnel decisions. Hence in its early stages the Eisenhower selection process was governed by the need to recruit extensively in the private sector, to cope with the demands of a patronage-starved party, and to follow a structured decision-making routine.

To organize his initial selection effort, Eisenhower called on two close and trusted friends, Herbert Brownell and General Lucius Clay. Brownell had been a central figure in Eisenhower's campaign, was a former Republican National Chairman, and had close contacts with the "Dewey wing" of the Party. His political experience and his political contacts were far broader than Eisenhower's, and he was well suited for the personnel responsibilities delegated to him. Although Clay, like Eisenhower, was a military man, he had extensive political and administrative experience. The President-elect recognized Clay's proven talent for accomplishing a mission and highly valued his ability to judge people.

Planning for the job of recruiting a new administration began after the Republican Convention in 1952, when Harold E. Talbott, an Eisenhower supporter and New York businessman, hired the consulting firm of McKinsey and Company to carry out a study of executive recruiting in the event of an Eisenhower victory. The firm produced a report that identified the top 915 positions of policy-making importance and set up a schedule of priorities to guide the new administration in filling them.[13] The McKinsey consultants also generated a list of names of several thousand potential appointees, drawn primarily from the recommendations of state party organizations.[14] By the end of January 1953, nominees had been selected for about one-fifth of the positions identified by the report as most important to the new administration.[15]

The first officials chosen by the Eisenhower selection team were the cabinet secretaries. All of these had been designated within a month of the election, an unusually rapid pace as Table 2-1 indicates.

In making these choices so quickly, however, the new administration had failed to observe some of the normal courtesies and clearances in the selection process. A particularly grievous error was committed in not maintaining closer contact with the Republican

Table 2-1. Time Required for Selection of Initial Cabinets, 1952–1976[a]

	EISENHOWER	KENNEDY	NIXON	CARTER
Date elected	Nov. 4	Nov. 8	Nov. 5	Nov. 2
First Cabinet selection announced	Nov. 21	Dec. 2	Dec. 11	Dec. 4
Last Cabinet selection announced	Dec. 2	Dec. 18	Dec. 11	Dec. 23
Total elapsed time: election to last announcement	28 days	40 days	36 days	51 days

[a] Does not include Presidents Johnson and Ford, who originally took office without benefit of an election.

members of Congress and with the party leadership at the Republican National Committee. Most of the Cabinet nominees had come from the moderate wing of the badly factionalized Republican Party. One, Martin Durkin, a union leader selected to be Secretary of Labor, had been an open and avowed Stevenson supporter. Only Ezra Taft Benson, the Secretary of Agriculture designate, had the explicit approval of Senator Robert A. Taft, the Republican leader in the Senate.[16] These developments , in Sherman Adams's words, "created quite a stir in Washington."[17]

Senator Taft had been Eisenhower's principal opponent for the nomination and had elicited a pledge from Eisenhower during the campaign that Taft's supporters would not be discriminated against in the formation of a new administration.[18] When it became clear in the period between the election and the inauguration not only that Taft was being excluded from consultation in selection decisions, but that he wasn't even being informed of Eisenhower's choices prior to their public announcement,[19] he made it clear that he considered this an inappropriate way to treat the leader of the President's party in the Senate. On January 12, 1953, Taft led a delegation of Republican Senators to Eisenhower's headquarters at the Commodore Hotel in New York. They complained to the President-elect that their suggestions on appointments had been disregarded and that the clearances that Senators had come to view as a normal courtesy often had been forgotten by the Eisenhower staff.

Eisenhower defended his right to name his own Cabinet nominees, but he agreed to allow members of Congress to negotiate directly with the departments and agencies in the selection of subordinate officials.[20] The "Commodore Agreement" did not bring about changes in the selection process that were entirely satisfactory to congressional Republicans, but it did reveal to the new President some of the unhappy consequences that could result from continued disregard of what Senators viewed as their personal prerogatives. The Senators tried to convince him that, with narrow majorities in both houses of Congress, he simply could not afford to depoliticize the executive recruitment process despite his apparent desire to do so.

The events of the transition period set the tone for the development of personnel selection procedures in the Eisenhower administration. But the direction that development took was conditioned as well by the President's personal feelings about executive recruitment and by his desire to reorganize the White House Office. Eisenhower had little personal relish for the complexities of personnel selection.

He participated actively in the choice of high-level officials—Cabinet secretaries, Supreme Court justices, and important ambassadors— but he chose to remain essentially aloof from the selection process for subcabinet and patronage positions.[21] He noted in his diary on January 5, 1953, after participating in the selection of a lower-level administrative officer:

> My experience in this case has generated in me the profound hope that I will be compelled to have little to do, during the next four years, with the distribution of federal patronage. Having been fairly successful in late years in learning to keep a rigid check on my temper, I do not want to encounter complete defeat at this late date.[22]

Sherman Adams also noted that the pressures engendered in making these lower-level appointments were "a constant annoyance" to Eisenhower and that "he wanted no part of it."[23]

As a consequence, several steps were taken to ensure that personnel selection decisions for all but the most important positions could be finalized without active presidential involvement. This not only satisfied Eisenhower's desire to separate himself from a function he did not enjoy, it also fitted into the pattern of delegated responsibility that he sought to impose on his administration. The first step was to grant Cabinet secretaries and agency heads the power to select their own subordinates. In operational terms, the scope of this delegation varied from department to department. Some of the new Cabinet members relied heavily on White House suggestions in filling positions in their departments. Others, especially those against which special interest groups made proprietary claims, acted more independently in making subcabinet decisions.[24]

The second step was to redirect the patronage requests that flooded into the White House by designating the Republican National Committee, chaired by Leonard Hall, as the major clearinghouse on patronage matters. In a Cabinet meeting on June 5, 1953, Eisenhower made it clear that Hall had his full support in placing well-qualified Republicans in lower-level positions.[25] This helped to resolve what Sherman Adams called "the most worrisome headache of the President's office."[26]

But the Eisenhower White House had no desire to dissociate itself totally from the business of personnel selection. It was Eisenhower's goal to create a mechanism in the White House Office that would allow him to maintain quality control over appointments without actually attending to all the details of executive selection and recruitment. The responsibility for organizing this task fell largely to Sherman Adams and to his assistant, Charles F. Willis, Jr. Under Willis's direction, a systematic effort was undertaken to compile rosters of positions outside the civil service in which vacancies were anticipated and to develop lists of potential candidates to fill them. He and Adams, later with the assistance of Robert Gray and Robert Hampton, adopted a set of procedures for executive recruitment that remained in effect for the remainder of the Eisenhower administration.[27]

These procedures were more a formalization of the traditional steps in the selection process than a qualitative change in the nature of that process. They were designed to serve several purposes: to hasten the replacement of Democrats with Republicans, to ensure that the appropriate political clearances were conducted, and to avoid the nomination of security risks.[28] The one significant change instituted by the Eisenhower selection staff was the requirement that all potential appointees by subject to extensive background investigations conducted by the Federal Bureau of Investigation. The President himself demanded this, largely in response to the national emphasis on internal security in the early years of his presidency. FBI checks had been undertaken sporadically in the past, but this was the first administration in which they were required for all nominees.[29]

The FBI check normally took place in the later stages of the selection process. Prior to that time, Adams and Willis would draw up a list of names of potential candidates for a particular vacancy. After choosing the candidate they deemed best qualified, they would clear his nomination with the Republican Senators from the state in which the candidate resided or, if there were no Republican Senators from that state, with the Republican governor or state party organization. In many cases, candidates would be cleared as well with the Republican National Committee.[30] Opposition at some stage in the clearance process did not necessarily mean that the candidate would be dropped, only that negotations would take place between the White House and those who opposed him. If the home state Senators or the party organization could not be persuaded to give their support, then in all likelihood a new nominee would be sought, and the process would begin again. Eisenhower, for example, had intended to nominate Val Peterson, a former Governor of Nebraska, as Ambassador to India. But Nebraska's two Republican Senators, Butler and Griswold, refused to go along, and the nomination was never made.[31]

After the political clearance and the FBI check had been success-fully completed, a firm offer would be made to a candidate. Adams or Willis usually performed this task rather than Eisenhower himself. The administration thought it unfair to put the candidate in the posi-tion of possibly having to say no to the President of the United States, and they chose to avoid the embarrassment to the President and his office that might accrue from having such an offer turned down.[32]

In selecting personnel for his administration, Eisenhower and his aides never defined very precise criteria for determining the kinds of individuals they were seeking. They did employ some position-related criteria, however. Eisenhower wanted as Secretary of Labor "no one who had evidenced extreme views in labor–management rela-tions."[33] We wanted the Defense Department to be "directed by experts."[34] He sought a Secretary of the Interior who, following tradi-tion, would be "a man familiar with the needs, history, and thinking of the West."[35] The Eisenhower administration was most specific in setting criteria for the selection of candidates for the federal judiciary. The President demanded that they have the advance approval of the American Bar Association, that they be in good health, that they have no "extreme legal or philosophic views," and that they be no more than sixty-two years of age.[36] For Supreme Court nominees he added the criterion of previous judicial experience.[37]

But specific criteria such as these were applied to only a small proportion of the appointive positions under the President's control. For the bulk of the remaining offices, little central guidance was provided. Eisenhower mentioned "ability" and "harmony of views" as important considerations,[38] but little effort was made to specify par-ticular types of ability or to harden the meaning of "harmony of views." Eisenhower directed his personnel aides to pay attention to a candidate's "past record, reputation, and standing in his commu-nity,"[39] and he advised them that he was not much interested in nominating to executive positions anyone who was "a seeker after a political post."[40] But he chose not to apply a strict test of loyalty in his personnel selections.[41] The only criterion he consistently imposed regarding the policy views of nominees was that they not be extreme in any direction.

The Eisenhower administration initiated personnel selection procedures that, while still rudimentary, were more systematic than those of its predecessors. But the administration never really de-veloped a "personnel plan" for selecting political executives. It was fully aware of the potential political significance of personnel selection, but it never sought to centralize the selection process in order to harness and shape those consequences to its own ends.[42] After leaving office, Eisenhower was asked by an interviewer whether he had "ever sort of turned the screw on Congress to get something done . . . saying you'll withhold an appointment or something like that?" He answered: "No, never. I took very seriously the matter of appointments and qualifications . . . Possibly I was not as shrewd or as clever in this matter as some of the others, but I never thought that any of these appointments should be used for bringing pressure upon the Congress."[43]

For most of his first term Eisenhower was under constant criticism from Republican Party leaders and Republican members of Congress for failing to make effective (i.e., partisan) use of his appointment powers.[44] The opportunity that personnel selection provided for reducing the effects of the factional conflict within his own party was never fully grasped. Too much of the President's control over personnel was delegated to subordinates in Cabinet departments and executive agencies. Executive competence, party consolidation, and policy goals were never fully reconciled in the selection process, nor is there much evidence that such a reconciliation was ever attempted. Eisenhower's personal indifference to personnel decisions and their potential utility is ironic for one who so vigorously professed a desire to improve the management of the executive branch. His administration made some changes in the procedural oganization of the selection process, but those changes were never fully aligned with a carefully prepared program for optimal use of the appointment power. Eisenhower saw personnel decisions as a problem to be delegated away. His successors saw them as an opportunity to be used more effectively for broader political and administrative purposes.

John F. Kennedy

Elections are the cleansing ritual of American politics, the benchmark for new directions and new hopes. Never was this more clearly reflected than in the burst of enthusiasm and optimism with which the Kennedy administration came to Washington in 1961. Kennedy had campaigned on the promise that he would "get the country moving again," that his would be an administration marked by youth, vigor, and action. And from the day of his election to the day of his inauguration, finding the people to help him deliver on that promise became the dominant concern of the President-elect and his close circle of advisers.

Several objectives governed the initial search for Cabinet officers and other top-level officials. Pre-eminent among these, as Kennedy professed, was a desire to find men and women of superior ability.[45] The manner of Kennedy's campaign for both the Democratic nomination and the presidency itself had not, in his view, deeply indebted him to any single faction or individual within his party. He thus felt no strong compulsion to include in his Cabinet any national party figures, as Woodrow Wilson had felt compelled to do with William Jennings Bryan or Roosevelt with Cordell Hull. Initially, at least, Kennedy felt a substantial measure of freedom to make Cabinet choices in which ability was a primary criterion. As Theodore Sorensen later wrote of this period, "Kennedy wanted a ministry of talent."[46]

But it was not quite that simple. Other objectives conditioned these early selection decisions as well. Kennedy had been elected by one of the narrowest margins in history. Large segments of the population and indeed of his own party had withheld their votes from him. Necessity, therefore, required that his early selection decisions be made with an eye both to consolidating his narrow victory and to broadening the base of his political support. A corporation president was chosen to be Secretary of Defense. A Republican who had contributed handsomely to Richard Nixon's campaign was selected to head the Treasury Department. Adlai Stevenson was nominated to be U.S. Ambassador to the United Nations, and the post was upgraded to Cabinet status. These selection decisions and others like them were a visible part of the Kennedy effort to overcome the handicap of a slender mandate.

A third factor in these early personnel choices was a consideration that occurs whenever there is a change in the party controlling the White House. Kennedy, like Eisenhower eight years earlier, was concerned about the task of redirecting the efforts and reinvigorating the energies of the civil servants in the executive branch. He wanted Cabinet secretaries and agency heads who would support the President and his programs and vigorously carry that support into their departments and agencies, people who would not become simply the instruments or mouthpieces of the organizations they were appointed to lead. As Arthur Schlesinger, Jr., noted, the problem was both persistent and familiar:

> The permanent government [had] developed its own stubborn vested interests in policy and procedure, its own cozy alliances with the committees of Congress, its own ties to the press, its own national constituencies. It began to exude the feeling that Presidents would come and Presidents go but it went on forever. The permanent government was, as such, politically neutral; its essential commitment was to doing things as they had been done before. This frustrated the enthusiasts who came to Washington with Eisenhower in 1953 zealous to dismantle the New Deal, and it frustrated the enthusiasts who came to Washington with Kennedy in 1961 zealous to get the country moving again.[47]

There was as well the standard concern in the Cabinet selection process with the matter of balance and representativeness. Kennedy's first Cabinet, as is the norm, drew its ten members from both parties, from all sections of the country, from each of several religious backgrounds, and from a wide range of occupations and professions. Though Kennedy sought to create an administration that was young, fresh, aggressive, and eager to act, he did not let this interfere with the more traditional concerns for geographical, religious, and political balance.

The job of filling positions in the executive branch was rather quickly complicated by two developments that had by then become a common accompaniment to a shift in party control of the White House. The first was that the President and his coterie of close friends and advisers soon came to realize that they could not adequately fill all of these positions without enlarging their search for candidates beyond the scope of their own acquaintance. The problem was not simply that there were several hundred such jobs to fill, but that many of them required skills and talents that were alien to the experience of the President or his aides. The President and his staff had backgrounds predominantly in politics, law, and business. None of them was very familiar with mining engineers, fish and wildlife specialists, or experts in Indian affairs. The number of jobs that had to be filled and the range of qualified people required to fill them soon made it apparent that some means would have to be found, and found quickly, for broadening the personnel selection process.

An equally pressing problem was the fact that the Kennedy victory had loosed an avalanche of job requests and job recommendations. Having waited out eight years of Republican ascendancy, Democrats in the Congress and in the state and national party organizations began to clamor for appointments for their friends or themselves. The problem was at once both political and logistical. On the one hand, there were great mounds of paper to be processed. On the other, there was the constant danger of failing to make the right response to some strategically located politician who had loyally supported Kennedy in the past or who, if properly treated, might loyally support him in the future. So, from this perspective too, the need for a more systematic organization of the selection process became eminently clear.

To cope with these problems in the transition period and its immediate aftermath, Kennedy's aides created what came to be known as the Talent Hunt.[48] The Talent Hunt was at all times a fluid operation, never very rigid in its organization or procedures. It did, however, add a modicum of logic and order to the personnel selection process.

The Talent Hunt was divided into two functional operations. One group, headed by Lawrence O'Brien, Ralph Dungan, and Richard Donahue, concerned itself primarily with the political side of the selection process. This group organized a roster of individuals who had given the new President significant political support and sought to find positions that these candidates were qualified to fill. It was also their responsibility to screen, evaluate, and organize the steady flow of job recommendations and applications. As one participant noted, "names began to accumulate, in letters, in notes of telephone conversations, on the backs of envelopes, accompanied by descriptions ranging from a vague phrase through an acute thumbnail sketch to a full resume. The need for a system to catalogue the information became acute."[49]

Another group, directed by Sargent Shriver and including Adam Yarmolinsky, Harris Wofford, Louis Martin, and Thomas Farmer, attacked the personnel task from the opposite direction. It began by identifying positions that could be filled by presidential appointment and then sought out candidates to fill them. Identifying all the available appointive positions was a more difficult chore than it should have been, and the Shriver group came to rely heavily on a list of these offices that had been compiled by the House Post Office and Civil Service Committee.[50] Having identified what it thought to be the most important policy-making positions, this group then began to develop lists of potential candidates through consultation with trusted figures in the business, professional, and university communities. As its task expanded, the Shriver group sought the assistance of volunteer consultants, mostly Washington lawyers, who focused their efforts on particular departments or functional areas.

The Talent Hunt sought to institute some systematic means of locating and choosing candidates. A personnel specialist from the IBM Corporation, brought in as a consultant, proposed as a test of excellence the rate at which a man's salary or the number of people he supervised had increased. Sorensen at one time suggested the use of a point system based on the strength of an individual's support for Kennedy during the campaign. None of these tests was of much help to the recruiters, and all fell into nearly immediate disuse. In their place, the Talent Hunt substituted a series of broad attitudinal criteria against which it attempted to measure potential nominees. These included "judgment," "toughness," "integrity," "ability to work with others," "industry," and "devotion to the principles of the President-elect." The nonspecific nature of these criteria allowed a good deal of subjective latitude on the part of the recruiters. Their primary usefulness was in providing a common checklist that could be used in soliciting information when discussing candidates with administration contacts around the country. Lists of potential nominees were also scrutinized to determine the political impact that each might have on the standing of the administration in the nation or in the nominee's community or professional group. As a final step prior to suggesting a candidate to the President-elect, a judgment would be made regarding his fitness and preparation for the specific job for which he was being considered.

The division of functions and the operating procedures employed by the Talent Hunt were never quite as fixed or as formal as described here. In operation, there tended to be a good deal of overlap between the two groups. Standardized application of criteria and commensurability in evaluation were difficult, often impossible, to achieve. Ultimate selection decisions were as often based on subjective inferences—the influence of an agency head, presidential suggestion, or political exigencies—as on objective assessments. The Talent Hunt was short of time, short of help, and short of preliminary analysis. It was never as systematic in operation as in intent.

The President-elect was an active participant in the Cabinet selection process and the early stages of the Talent Hunt. He often made phone calls to friends and acquaintances around the country in pursuit of penetrating assessments of potential candidates for important positions in his administration. He personally interviewed many of the candidates himself. And he jealously guarded the right to make final decisions on his nominees to the fifty or so positions that he deemed most important to the success of his administration.

As inauguration day approached, Kennedy's attention was increasingly diverted away from personnel matters. He refused, however, to follow Eisenhower's precedent of delegating the selection of people for subordinate positions in the agencies and departments to the Cabinet secretaries or agency heads. Instead he and his staff participated fully in these decisions. Those agency heads in whom Kennedy had great faith or regarding whose programs Kennedy had little interest or knowledge were given considerable latitude in staffing their own agencies. In a number of cases, however, Kennedy and his staff played the leading role in filling these second-level posts. Kennedy, for example, nominated G. Mennen Williams to be Assistant Secretary of State for African Affairs and offered the position of Ambassador to the U.N. to Adlai Stevenson before he made the final selection of Dean Rusk as Secretary of State.

In general, the relationship between the President-elect's staff and the newly designated department and agency heads was a cooperative one. A member of the Talent Hunt was assigned to work with each of the Cabinet members in filling the important appointive positions in the departments. And the appointment pattern in each department reflects a mix of individuals, some selected and recruited primarily by the secretary-designate, others on the recommendation of the Talent Hunt. There is no evidence that this approach to the selection process produced any significant measure of conflict or tension between the President-elect's staff and his Cabinet nominees.

Personnel selection in the transition period between administrations is a relatively sheltered activity. Though there are abundant pressures on the newly elected President to make "political" appointments, those pressures are more easily deflected in the period before the inauguration than in the days that follow. There are several reasons for this. The fact that the Congress is not in session for most of this period diminishes its institutional visibility. The President-elect and his closest advisers usually remain away from Washington and thus away from direct contact with those who are most insistent in making personnel demands. And, perhaps most important, the new President's legislative program is still on the drawing board, and the relationship between congressional support for that program and personnel selections has not yet fully developed. Personnel recommendations emanating from members of Congress take on a larger importance only later, when it appears that a favorable response may be useful in greasing the skids for the President's legislative proposals.

The Kennedy administration experienced this change in environment rather quickly after the inauguration. The staff of the Talent Hunt soon began to find its efforts circumscribed by strong assertions of interest from members of Congress and the state and national Democratic Party organizations. Personnel decisions began to gravitate to the White House staff, and by the end of January 1961 the Talent Hunt was essentially out of business.

In the next few months, personnel responsibilities became the province of Ralph Dungan, who was appointed special assistant to the President. But Dungan had other responsibilities as well and was unable to devote his full attention to personnel questions. After an unhappy experience in selecting a new Chairman of the Securities and Exchange Commission, Dungan came to recognize that the selection process would be a continuing concern.[51] In the summer of 1961, he asked Dan H. Fenn, Jr., a faculty member at the Harvard Business School, to come to Washington and set up a more permanent and systematic personnel operation than then existed. On the recommendation of Civil Service Commission Chairman John Macy, Fenn brought David Jelenek into the White House to assist in this effort, and they were later joined by John Clinton, Edward Sherman, Richard Barrett, and others. This group, never numbering more than five professionals, reported to Dungan and formed the nucleus of the White House personnel staff for the bulk of the Kennedy administration.[52]

Upon arriving in Washington, Fenn took a look at the personnel procedures then in effect and described them with the acronym BOGSAT, meaning "a bunch of guys sitting around a table" asking each other, "Whom do you know?"[53] With its emphasis on screening applicants rather than aggressive recruiting, it was, in Fenn's view, a limited and unsophisticated method for filling the most important political offices in the land.

Fenn had a relatively free hand in setting up a system for filling personnel vacancies. His staff concentrated on the approximately 250 major presidential appointments in the executive branch. The so-called patronage or honorary posts (short-term assignments, advisory commissions, special overseas delegations, etc.) were handled by a small staff headed by Dorothy Davies.

The personnel operation that Fenn established was quite unlike anything that had ever existed before. It was different primarily in two ways. First, Fenn sought to develop a mechanism for centralizing the selection process in the White House. This was to be more than the simple clearinghouse that had developed under Truman and Eisenhower. The objective was to permit the White House to retain the ultimate authority in the selection process for major presidential appointments throughout the administration, to institutionalize the President's involvement in those selection decisions. Fenn strongly felt that constant attention to personnel decisions was a *sine qua non* of good management. Because of the importance of the work done by his appointees to major positions, Fenn believed, the President ought to retain final control in determining who filled those positions. The purpose here was not to strip agency heads of the opportunity to select their own subordinates, but rather to ensure that the selection process was one in which the agency and the White House participated as partners, with the White House always the senior partner. Sometimes a selection would result from an agency initiative, sometimes from the initiative of Fenn's group. But the important point, from the White House perspective, was to guarantee that the President's concerns were a constant factor in these decisions.

For the most part, the Kennedy White House made a conscious effort not to interfere in nonpresidential appointments, respecting the right of agency heads to make their own selections. Adherence to this policy was not perfect, however. The White House would sometimes involve itself in the choice of appointees to lower-level positions in which the President's personal policy interests were directly involved (AID mission chiefs, for example). In 1962 Fenn and John Macy undertook a program to encourage the agencies to find visible positions (mostly Schedule C) for blacks. This was done both to prepare blacks for future appointments at higher levels and to provide models for younger blacks who might be skeptical about the availability of significant jobs for minorities in the public service. Macy and Fenn had also planned to urge and to help the agencies to develop their own personnel offices so that they too would have the kind of professional personnel support operation that had developed in the White House. This effort, however, was cut short by the Kennedy assassination.[54]

The second unique component of the personnel operation in the Kennedy White House was the development of a capacity for active recruiting. A principal objective of the personnel system that Fenn established was to allow the President to draw from the best talent available in the country in staffing his administration. One of Fenn's first steps was to undertake the development of a network of well-placed individuals in a wide range of occupations and professions, people who could be called upon to suggest and evaluate potential appointees.

Fenn and his staff worked with the Brookings Institution to set up this network. This was done with some care because of a strong predisposition in the White House to rely primarily on advice from individuals whose judgment was known to be trustworthy. Like most Presidents, Kennedy was uncomfortable with recommendations solicited from strangers. He and the personnel staff found it hard to evaluate a recommendation without first being able to evaluate the source.[55]

The network that Fenn set up had two components: a general contact list and a number of special contact lists. The latter were used for appointments in specific substantive areas like science or education. These lists, however, were only one source of information about potential candidates. The personnel staff also frequently solicited or received references from people already serving in the agencies, from the White House staff, and occasionally from interest groups and members of Congress.

Some effort was made during the Kennedy years to set up a "talent bank," a sort of permanent roster of highly qualified people who might be called upon when a vacancy occurred. The talent bank idea was not a major preoccupation of the personnel staff, however, and never became a primary source of appointees. As Ralph Dungan has pointed out, "It was so crude, I am almost embarrassed to talk about it. But it was at least a step toward systematizing the headhunter process."[56]

With the rudiments of a personnel system in place, the selection process began to follow a set of routine procedures. The personnel staff would try to identify upcoming vacancies as far in advance as possible in order to give themselves some lead time in finding replacements. The process usually began with discussions among the personnel staff, the agency people, and others in the administration to determine what kind of person was needed for a particular position at a particular time. The President might suggest some possibilities, though that was not often the case in the initial stages. Members of the White House staff would often propose names of people with whom they were familiar. There were frequent suggestions from members of Congress and from those interest groups to whom a particular position was especially important. Very often more names were generated by the personnel staff drawing on its lists of contacts around the country. A most important source in nearly every case was the agency in which the vacancy would occur. And, of course, there were always people who were happy to recommend themselves.[57]

From this list, the personnel staff would cull the names of the most promising candidates. More checking with references would ensue, and eventually the list would be reduced to just a few names. Their credentials were rechecked, the reaction of the relevant department or agency was determined, and the candidates' willingness to accept the nomination if offered was ascertained. The political acceptability of these candidates would also be examined at this stage, usually by Dorothy Davies's office.[58] Whenever possible, Fenn sought to carry out this search procedure without the knowledge of the candidates being considered.[59] This avoided both the incitement of unwanted pressure from the hopefuls and the arousal of feelings of disappointment and perhaps enmity among the unselected.

At this point, two or three names were sent to the President along with background information on each. In most cases, one of these was specifically recommended by the personnel staff. When the President had made his decision—which most of the time was a ratification of the personnel staff's recommendation—several more steps followed before the nomination was formally announced. The FBI would conduct an investigation of the selected candidate. If nothing derogatory developed from this (as was usually the case), the candidate would then be contacted by the personnel staff to determine definitely that he would accept the nomination. This was done before it was firmly offered to avoid the embarrassment to the President of having an invitation to join his administration publicly turned down. As a final step, the nomination would be formally announced.

The criteria guiding this selection process were never very clearly or specifically defined during the Kennedy administration. In part this resulted from the fact that the President's direct involvement in the selection process, except in ambassadorial appointments, was rarely very intense after the transition period. He never provided much guidance to his personnel staff in terms of general criteria, although he would sometimes provide guidance on criteria for specific vacancies. For Fenn and his staff, the primary objective was to find nominees who could meet the test of being "our kind of guy."[60] Instead of looking for individuals with specific sets of policy views, Fenn sought people who shared the President's orientation to the role and responsibilities of government and who could work well with the bureaucracy and the Congress. He wanted people who, in Theodore

Sorensen's words, possessed, "an outlook more practical than theoretical and more logical than ideolological; an ability to be precise and concise; a willingness to learn, to do, to dare, to change; an ability to work hard and long, creatively, imaginatively, successfully."[61]

The personnel system established during the Kennedy administration was by no means inviolable. Indeed, it is probably safe to say that no two selection decisions ever followed exactly the same path. So much variation occurred in terms of the needs of the President, the willingness of individuals to serve, and the pressures applied by the Congress, the agencies, the press, and the special interests that efforts to systematize the process were always doomed to frustration. The primary reason for this was that Kennedy himself never became wedded to the personnel system his advisers established. His personal interest in personnel decisions was neither consistent nor comprehensive. Sometimes the personnel staff would begin to search for a candidate only to find that the President already had the man he wanted firmly in mind.[62] He permitted, in some cases even encouraged, circumventions of his own personnel operation. As a result the selection process was never as systematic in operation as in design. It remained, as Fenn has noted, "highly serendipitous."[63]

In spite of their inconsistencies, however, the selection procedures established during the Kennedy administration were a turning point in the development of a modern and rational personnel function within the White House Office. An important instrument of presidential leadership and control was operated less haphazardly and with more central direction than had ever previously been the case.[64] For the first time, there began to appear the nascent outlines of a personnel plan. The procedures of recruitment were integrated with the goals of recruitment. Planning, standards, contacts, agency relations, and clearances were coordinated and centrally organized in a way that significantly improved the President's opportunities to use his appointment powers as a more effective tool for administrative management and political leadership. For the administrations that followed, there would be no turning back from these important developments.

Lyndon B. Johnson

The jarring suddenness with which Lyndon Johnson became President left him little time to think about the problems of staffing his administration. He asked nearly all of the Kennedy appointees to stay on, at least until the 1964 election, and most agreed to do so. For the year following Johnson's assumption of office, personnel selection procedures remained much as they had been before Kennedy's death. Dan Fenn had left the White House to accept an appointment to the Tariff Commission in 1963, but the personnel operation he established was left intact and continued to function under the day-to-day direction of John B. Clinton.

After the 1964 election, however, the President no longer thought of himself as a caretaker, and his growing urge to put his own stamp on the executive branch was reflected in the procedures and criteria that came to govern his personnel choices. Ralph Dungan, who had nominal responsibility for personnel recruitment and selection in the previous four years, was appointed to serve as Ambassador to Chile. And instead of replacing Dungan with a White House staff member, Johnson sought the help of John W. Macy in administering the process of filling the top positions in his administration.

Macy was quite unlike the individuals to whom other Presidents had designated responsibility for personnel selection. Most of his career had been spent in the federal service. He was not "political" in the conventional sense; he had little experience in elective politics and was not a protégé of any major political figure. He was a professional personnel specialist with many years of service on the staff of the Civil Service Commission and, at the time Johnson became President, was Chairman of that Commission.

Johnson's selection of Macy for this job grew out of a relationship that had developed between them when the former was Vice President and chaired the President's Committee on Equal Employment Opportunity. Through this and several other activities, the two men, in Macy's words, "struck up an association that was unusual in terms of the Vice-President and the Chairman of the Civil Service Commission."[65] Johnson had been slow to fill executive vacancies during his first year in office, but after the election he was ready to move quickly to get his administration up to strength and to fill it with people of his own choosing. He knew and trusted Macy, and he asked him to assist the White House in the immediate task of finding qualified and talented people to fill the two hundred or so vacancies that had accumulated by the end of 1964. Macy did not initially regard this as a permanent assignment, and he retained his position as Chairman of the Civil Service Commission. Permanent it was, however, and Macy continued to wear two hats for the rest of Johnson's term in office.

Few Presidents have come to office with a wider range of friends and contacts upon whom to draw in making appointments than Lyndon Johnson. But even Johnson harbored no illusions about his ability to staff his administration solely with friends and acquaintances. He recognized from the outset that he would need to develop and maintain a personnel support staff within the White House Office. Johnson chose Macy to head this staff because he wanted the selection process to be wide-ranging, professional, and systematic, and he thought Macy's experience in identifying talent within the civil service would be helpful in undertaking this task for exempted positions.[66]

Macy regarded executive selection as essentially a two-step process. The first step required a careful definition of the nature of the position to be filled. Macy and his staff wrote position profiles for each executive vacancy before they began their search for a candidate. But this was a complicated task since job descriptions in executive positions are rarely static. A position that seems to need a first-rate administrator at one time may require a sensitive politician or a conciliator or an inspirational leader at another. Macy describes some of the complexities of this:

> [I]f there was a vacancy as Assistant Secretary of Commerce [for example] it wasn't enough to see whether or not there was some kind of statutory prescription for that particular job. It was a matter of having that and then looking at the job in the context of that particular department at that particular time. What did the chemistry need to be with the secretary? What was important in that particular position? Was it effectiveness in dealing with Congress on legislation? Was it effectiveness in answering interrogation about a particular problem that has come up? Was it a matter of gaining support among interest groups? Was it the need for a high degree of professional specialization in a particular field? Was it need for someone who had a strong administrative background?[67]

In seeking answers to these questions, the personnel staff frequently found it useful to solicit the views of outside experts, of other White House aides, and, most important, of people in the relevant departments and agencies. And in most cases they tried to project the likely requirements for a position several years into the future.

Once a position profile was created, the search for a qualified candidate began. It was in this area that the Kennedy personnel operation had been most successful in improving procedures. Under Fenn, and later under John Clinton, the Kennedy staff had established extensive files of potential candidates and a national network of prominent individuals capable of assessing those candidates and identifying others. Contrary to tradition, these resources were not removed from the white House immediately after the Kennedy assasination.[68] In fact, they were melded into the Johnson files and remained there for the rest of the Johnson administration.

Both Johnson and Macy admired the procedures that had been initiated during the Kennedy administration. They sought, however, to expand the personnel operation and to develop it further to fit Johnson's particular needs. The personnel staff grew somewhat in size during the Johnson years, and this enabled Macy to establish a division of labor. Kennedy's personnel aides had dealt with all kinds of appointments as vacancies occurred; there was little staff specialization. But Macy was able to divide his staff into two groups, one responsible for appointments to domestic positions and the other for positions dealing with international affairs. Each group had a desk officer, and each desk officer had his own assistant. Macy noted that this procedure "allowed the two teams to concentrate their energies and gain in-depth experience in two distinctly different kinds of executive recruiting."[69]

In hiring his staff, Macy looked for people who had worked in the federal service and who had an intuitive sense of the requirements for a wide range of positions. Most of the people who worked with Macy thus came from the Foreign Service, the Bureau of the Budget, and the Civil Service Commission. Few remained on the personnel staff for more than two years, largely because Macy believed it important to have a team that was freshly familiar with the agencies and departments it was charged with staffing.

As the presidential personnel operation grew in size and scope, the problem of information management became more pressing. This was the case most notably with the candidate files that composed what was often referred to as the "talent bank." The files contained some two thousand names in 1964; by the time Johnson left office in 1969 the number had grown to thirty thousand.[70] It was no longer possible for the personnel staff to recollect fully or accurately the contents of those files. To cope with this, the staff created an Executive Biographic Index, which allowed them to list and cross-reference information about the qualifications and background characteristics of those whose names were on file. To help in matching candidates with jobs, they also indexed and cross-referenced information about positions: the skills required, the history of recent incumbents, and the likelihood of vacancies. Representatives of leading computer manufacturers

were asked to assist in automating this information storage and re-
trieval effort, though ultimately computer support for the personnel
operation was provided by the Office of Emergency Preparedness.

Macy and his staff also made changes in the contact network they
had inherited from the Kennedy administration. The list of contacts
grew from two hundred to six hundred people in the Johnson years.
The list was in constant flux as the personnel staff was better able to
assess the quality of advice it was getting from the individuals in the
networks. If a particular contact seemed to be providing evaluations
that were either inaccurate or simply not very helpful, the personnel
staff would stop calling on him. One of the limitations of the contact
network was that many of those it included were not people whom the
President knew personally. Macy soon discovered that Johnson was
reluctant to nominate candidates without some evaluation from an
independent source with whom he was acquainted. Thus, after making its initial evaluations, the personnel staff often had to find someone who knew both the President and the candidate and obtain that
person's assessment of the candidate's capabilities.

In searching for a candidate to fill an executive vacancy, the
Johnson administration drew primarily on three sources. One was the
White House talent bank, described above. It was not true, as some
contemporary reports maintained, that jobs were filled simply by
feeding information into the computer and nominating the people
whose names it spewed out. In fact, the computer really did little
more than provide ready access to the files. It was often the case that
an appropriate candidate could not be found in the White House files,
and the search had to extend elsewhere.

A second source was the contact network. The contact network
included individuals in a wide range of professions and was, in Macy's
words, "a cross section of what Time Magazine calls a leadership
community."[71] When the administration was attempting to fill a position in the area of economic affairs, for instance, the personnel staff
could call on its contacts in the financial community—bankers, ac-
countants, and economists—for recommendations and advice. Often
names were generated by these contacts that were included in the
candidate files for later consideration.

A third, and highly important, source of potential candidates for
appointive positions was the career service. The President, believing
that government was becoming an increasingly specialized profession, wanted his administration staffed by experienced hands. Macy
and Johnson had spent the bulk of their working lives in Washington,

and both sensed that there was a large untapped resevoir of executive talent already employed in government, much of it in the career service. One of the principal goals of their personnel recruitment effort was to locate and use that talent and experience. In a memorandum to the President late in 1968, Macy pointed out with some satisfaction that more than 44 percent of Johnson's appointees to executive positions had been individuals who had spent the majority of their professional careers in the federal service.[72]

Once the staff had winnowed its list of potential candidates down to the most promising half-dozen or so, a memorandum was prepared for the President. This memorandum outlined the nature of the position and current considerations in filling it. If the position was one on a collegial body like a regulatory commission, the names of the other members of the commission would be listed and the current balance of attitudes or ideologies indicated. Then the staff would identify the potential candidates and give a capsule sketch of each.[73] Also included would be some indication of who was supporting each candidate and the advantages and disadvantages of nominating each. In most cases, the staff recommended the candidate it thought most qualified. The memorandum then ended with a ballot on which the President could choose one of the candidates on the list, ask for more information about one or several, or reject them all and require that the search continue.

The most distinctive characteristic of executive selection procedures in the Johnson administration was the high level of personal involvement by the President. No other Chief Executive in recent times had taken as active and intensive an interest in his personnel appointments as Lyndon Johnson. The memoranda that Macy's staff prepared were included in the President's night reading and, with few exceptions, were returned the next day with his comments and decisions. While he often followed the staff's recommendations in making a selection, he nearly always reserved the final decision for himself.[74] But Johnson's interest in appointments involved more than merely making final decisions. In fact, he participated at every stage of the selection process. Macy's comments illustrate Johnson's role in this process:

> [T]he President had many associates on the outside with whom he discussed appointments. He had a high interest in appointments himself. He was deeply involved in a large number of appointments. He had a fantastic memory and he could recall some detail on a summary

we would send to him, months and months afterwards, and would frequently enjoy challenging me on whether I could remember as well as he could what those particular details were.[75]

[E]very time he was talking to anyone, every time he was involved in a meeting, he had in one part of his active mind an evaluative film rolling that was recording his impressions with respect to people. And very frequently he would send me a note or have somebody call me or call me himself, saying "Now did you notice so-and-so who made that presentation at the cabinet meeting? That is somebody we need to keep an eye on."[76]

Once the President had made his choice, the personnel staff followed up by setting in motion the FBI full field investigation. There were usually checks as well to ensure that the candidate had paid his income taxes and that he was not encumbered by potential conflicts of interest. If the candidate cleared all these checks, then the personnel staff would determine, as obliquely as possible, whether he would accept the nomination if offered. All of this was carried out with the maximum degree of secrecy. The President had a passion for surprise, and nothing angered him quite so quickly as to have the name of a nominee leak out before he could announce it publicly. It is reported, in fact, that he would sometimes delay action on a nomination when he had been deprived of this element of surprise.[77]

Johnson relied very heavily on his personnel staff in selecting candidates for executive positions. Though Macy was the first to admit that he was not the exclusive talent scout for the administration, he doubted that more than 3 to 5 percent of Johnson's important executive appointments came from outside the selection process he administered.[78] Johnson's reliance on his personnel staff not only served his needs, it also protected his interests. Macy's operation provided him with a buffer against the pressures that Presidents constantly receive from those who want to influence their selection decisions. When someone outside the administration made a personnel suggestion, Johnson could simply refer him to Macy, telling him that Macy would give consideration to the proposed candidate. If the person so referred did not fit into the administration's plans, Johnson could blame Macy for not making the nomination. Macy indicated that

. . . a number of times it was reported back to me that somebody would come in and complain about a particular appointment that the President had made and he was quoted as having said, "Well, don't blame me. It's that God damn Macy. He insists on having merit." And that tended to terminate the conversation as far as the complainant was concerned.[79]

As might be expected, given his personal interest in the appointment process, Johnson went farther than most Presidents in stating and clarifying the criteria he wanted to apply to selection decisions. When he first talked to Macy about taking charge of the selection process, he told him that "he was interested in having the very best people we can get across the country for these jobs."[80] Publicly, the President declared that he wanted to conduct "a continuing talent search, in all professions and in all parts of the country, to discover the best people available."[81]

The first thing the President looked for in a potential appointee was intelligence. "He is convinced," said Macy, "that we must have people with demonstrated intellectual capacity. He is very much interested in whether a person who is being considered is a Phi Beta Kappa or graduated summa cum laude, or where he was in his law school class, or how long it took him to get his Ph.D., or whether he was a Rhodes Scholar or a Wilson Scholar or a Marshall Scholar."[82]

Johnson placed a definite emphasis as well on people who were relatively young, people in the age bracket from thirty-five to fifty whose careers were still on the rise. Johnson was also looking for individuals who had begun to establish a reputation in a particular field for which they were being considered. "If we are looking for a man in the fish and wildlife area," said Macy, "we want someone who has a reputation in conservation—either academically or in some form of public life. Or if we are looking for the chief counsel for the Internal Revenue Service, we want someone who has had a successful career in tax law."[83]

The President had a special interest in expanding the number of women and minority group members serving in the government. He took great pride in nominating the first black Cabinet member and the first black Supreme Court Justice.[84] In fact, he appointed more blacks, more Mexican–Americans, and more women to important positions than any of his predecessors. His 107 appointments of blacks to executive, judicial, and part-time positions were more than twice the number appointed by Kennedy.[85] He was further convinced, as one of his aides later wrote, that "the country was not using sufficiently the talent represented by its women."[86] As a result, he often pressed his personnel staff to seek out talented women for positions in his administration. For reasons that reflect personal convictions as well as political considerations, Johnson was determined to use his appointment powers to provide greater opportunities to those groups that had traditionally been underrepresented at the highest levels of government.

The administration also applied a test of loyalty in picking its candidates, although the nature of this test changed over time. Initially Johnson professed little interest in the political party identification of his nominees.[87] In fact, he bragged about not knowing that John Gardner was a Republican until just a few minutes before he announced his nomination to be Secretary of HEW.[88] What was important was loyalty to the President and to his policies. About this Johnson felt most strongly. In discussing a potential appointee with an aide, he once said, "I don't want loyalty. I want *loyalty*. I want him to kiss my ass in Macy's window at high noon and tell me it smells like roses."[89]

Increasingly, however, loyalty came to mean loyalty to the President's Vietnam policy. The more criticism the war engendered, the more concerned Johnson became that his appointees support his war policies. The effect of his concern was to narrow the range of people from which executive selections were made. It is a normal development for executive recruiting to become more difficult in the later stages of an administration than in the early days. The bloom is off the rose. The most important policy initiatives have been undertaken. Enemies have been made. Time is short, and good people are unwilling to interrupt their private careers for a public service job with an uncertain future. The natural curve of attractiveness declines over the course of an administration. Lyndon Johnson's passion about Vietnam, however, and his near-paranoid concern about loyalty exacerbated the decline of the curve. Over the last two years of his administration, Johnson turned more and more to familiar figures to man the major posts in his administration: to Texans and to those already serving in subordinate positions. As the attacks on his Vietnam policies escalated, support for those policies became an even more important criterion in presidential selection decisions.[90]

The Johnson administration was a continuing link in the chain of development that characterizes the personnel selection function in the White House after World War II. In one important sense, however, it was also an aberration. Many of the practices employed by John Macy and his personnel staff were an extension of the initiatives taken during the Kennedy years. Macy's primary innovations were the application of significantly improved techniques of information management and the enlargement and increased specialization of the personnel staff. The personnel operation established by Macy was ultimately more sophisticated and comprehensive than the one he inherited.

But the single most important characteristic of the personnel selection process during the Johnson years was the President's high level of reliance upon it and involvement in it. Indeed, it is quite probably because of his involvement in the selection process that Johnson felt so free to rely on the system that Macy established. He could trust that system because he constantly monitored it, participated in it, orchestrated it. The personnel operation became the central conduit for selection decisions because Lyndon Johnson nurtured and protected it. With rare exceptions, he required those with personnel suggestions to go through John Macy and his staff; he had little tolerance for circumventions of the process. In that regard the Johnson personnel operation was unique. No other President in the postwar period has given so much control over the flow of selection decisions to his personnel staff. But then, too, no other President has been so active a participant in the work of that staff.

Richard M. Nixon

Richard Nixon came to Washington in 1969 with fewer assets and more liabilities than any President since World War II. Only 43 percent of the participating electorate had voted for him. He was the titular head of a minority party. He faced a Congress that had opposition majorities in both houses. And he had to direct an executive branch that had been under Democratic leadership for the previous eight years and for twenty-eight of the previous thirty-six. Whatever policy objectives and administrative innovations he pursued would have to be achieved in spite of these handicaps.

Nixon and his staff, like Eisenhower and Kennedy and their staffs, had had no time during the campaign to make preparations for the personnel selection task that would face them in the immediate aftermath of the election. Only after the results were in did some semblance of an organized recruitment effort begin to take shape. The first priority was the selection of a Cabinet, and this effort was directed primarily by Nixon's law partner, John Mitchell, and a Wall

Street banker named Peter M. Flanigan. Their "crash program," as Flanigan called it, resulted in the selection of a complete Cabinet within the first five weeks after the election. On December 11, 1968, the President-elect went before a national television audience to introduce the twelve men he had selected to serve in his initial Cabinet. He said then that "there has to be an extra dimension which is the difference between good leadership and superior or even great leadership," and he declared that each of his Cabinet designees possessed that extra dimension.

The process of selecting the Nixon Cabinet was governed by the typical mixture of motives and constraints. Several of its members were long-standing personal friends of the President-elect (Mitchell, Robert H. Finch, and William P. Rogers). There were three Republican governors (Walter J. Hickel, George W. Romney, and John A. Volpe), a Member of Congress (Melvin Laird), two academics (George P. Shultz and Clifford N. Hardin), and several representatives of the business community (David M. Kennedy, Winton M. Blount, and Maurice Stans). As usual, the Secretary of the Interior was a Westerner, the Agriculture Secretary was from the Midwest and had an agricultural background, and the Secretary of the Treasury was a banker.

In some ways, however, this was an atypical Cabinet group. Especially unusual, given the closeness of Nixon's victory, was the absence of Democrats from the Cabinet. Historically, most initial Cabinets have included at least one member from the defeated party. Nixon's first Cabinet also had no one with a labor union background and no blacks, women, or Jews. All of its members were prosperous white male Republicans. The selection process seems to have been guided by little more than the desire to follow convention, to pay off some personal and electoral debts, and to surround the new President with people who seemed to share his political outlook.

While Mitchell and Flanigan were concentrating their attention on the selection of Cabinet and other top-level officials, another recruiting effort was going on for people to fill other appointive positions. This operation was headed by Harry S. Flemming, a twenty-eight-year-old businessman who had previously served on the staff of the Republican National Committee. Flemming was given a dual task: first, to fill the large number of administrative positions below the very top and, second, to lay the groudwork for a continuing personnel selection system to remain in place after the transition period. His initial activities focused on the job of finding candidates for the several thousand subcabinet, agency, and patronage positions that the new administration had to fill.

Flemming had no experience in personnel administration, and this was no small task. Yet he was left largely on his own, with little guidance or oversight from the President or his senior staff. As part of an effort to develop a broad range of candidates from which to make personnel selections, Flemming devised the tactic of writing form letter to all of the eighty thousand people listed in *Who's Who in America*. Recipients of these letters were asked to recommend individuals for service in the Nixon administration. This mailing produced an avalanche of replies (more than sixty thousand by one count),[91] and each recommended candidate was then sent a letter asking for a resumé.

This episode engendered a good deal of amused criticism. Skeptics wondered who might have been recommended by people like Elvis Presley and Casey Stengel. One observer referred to the product of this mass mailing as "a flood of low-quality paper."[92] While some appointments did apparently result from the *Who's Who* experiment, it was not a notable success. It added enormously to the work of an already overburdened personnel staff and raised the false expectations of many individuals who did not receive administration jobs.[93] Even Harry Flemming later admitted that it was a "mistake."[94] If nothing else, however, it did indicate the nature of the problem he faced in trying to broaden the base from which the administration could fill its personnel needs.

Flemming's was not the only personnel operation at work during the transition period. The early selection process, in fact, was marked by an unusual degree of fragmentation. Flanigan in New York shared responsibility with Flemming in Washington. But other Nixon aides were also working on personnel matters, usually autonomously. John Ehrlichman was involved in a number of selection decisions;[95] Leonard Garment headed a search for black, Puerto Rican, and Mexican–American candidates;[96] and Robert Ellsworth hunted for potential nominees for positions on the regulatory commissions and in the smaller executive agencies.[97] This was a confusing arrangement, and, not surprisingly, it produced some curious personnel choices and some hurt feelings among those whose recommendations were neither followed nor acknowledged.

The selection process began to take on more clarity after the inauguration. Peter Flanigan joined the White House senior staff and took overall control of the personnel function. Harry Flemming, who reported to Flanigan, handled most of the day-to-day details. The personnel staff they managed was larger than that of any previous administration, numbering more than fifteen people. The procedures it followed were not substantially different from those employed during the Kennedy and Johnson administrations. A concerted effort was made to establish a talent bank and the computerized Executive Biographic Index was retained.[98] Search procedures followed the normal course: Qualified candidates were identified; references were contacted for assessments of those candidates; the list was narrowed to the most promising few; these were cleared with the appropriate people in the party, the Congress, and the administration; a selection was made; the chosen candidate was subjected to final security and political clearances; and the nomination was announced.

The criteria that guide the selection of presidential nominees are rarely as clear as White House personnel staff would like them to be. In varying degrees this is a problem in every administration. In the early days of the Nixon administration, however, the absence of clearly articulated selection criteria was a handicap of considerable proportions. Richard Nixon had talked from time to time, both publicly and privately, about the kind of people he wanted in his administration. In a campaign speech, for instance, he had said:

> I don't want a government of yes-men, but one drawn from the broadest possible base—an administration made up of Republicans, Democrats and independents, and drawn from politics, from career government service, from universities, from business, from the professions—one including not only executives and administrators, but scholars and thinkers.
>
> Only if we have an administration broadly enough based philosophically to ensure a true ferment of ideas, and to invite an interplay of the best minds in America, can we be sure of getting the best and most penetrating ideas.[99]

Nixon personally told Flemming only that he wanted his administration to include a "broad selection of Americans."[100] This vague criterion was not easy for the personnel staff to operationalize or implement.

Beyond this general desire to bring a cross-section of talented Americans into the administration, personnel selection policies seemed to be guided, at least rhetorically, by the President's perceived need to take firm command of a federal bureaucracy from which he expected very little sympathy or loyalty. In their subsequent testimonies before several congressional committees, some of the individuals who served as personnel aides to Richard Nixon spoke of this consuming desire to "get control of the government."[101]

It is ironic, therefore, that an administration so committed to using its appointment powers to get control of the government was so poorly organized to do it. In the first eighteen months of the Nixon presidency, the structure of the personnel operation and the procedures of personnel selection were not well fitted to the primary task of imprinting the President's stamp on the federal executive branch. Indeed, in some ways the personnel operation interfered with, rather than facilitated, the accomplishment of that objective.

A fundamental problem was the President's personal indifference to and dissociation from the selection process. In this regard, he and Lyndon Johnson were polar opposites. Nixon rarely suggested possible candidates for vacant positions, consistently delegated final selection authority to his chief of staff, and almost never took the time to meet with his nominees before their names were sent to the Senate.

No President, of course, has sufficient time to oversee all aspects of the selection process. Much of that responsibility must be delegated to a personnel staff, and this accounts for the development of these staffs that has taken place since World War II. Presidential interest and involvement at certain stages of the process, however, can be an important factor in keeping selection decisions aligned with administration objectives. Regular interaction between the President and his personnel staff serves two functions. First, it emphasizes the importance of their work by demonstrating the President's interest in what the personnel staff is doing. It can be a source of encouragement, even inspiration, to those involved in filling administration positions. Second, regular interaction with the President allows the personnel staff constantly to hone its sense of the kind of people he wants in particular positions. These discussions frequently help to clarify the qualifications and disqualifications that are most salient to a Chief Executive. As Frederic Malek, who was to become the President's special assistant for personnel, later wrote, "The President can exert great leverage over the Federal Government by strengthening his management control over non-career personnel. Fully capitalizing on this potential requires the personal leadership of the President."[102]

Presidential involvement in the selection process can also have a desirable effect on the people who become presidential appointees.

When the President takes the time to meet with new members of his administration before they take office, he can help add a personal dimension to their relationship. Malek noted that "such meetings strengthen the appointee's loyalty to the President as a personal leader rather than as a dignitary read about in the newspaper."[103] And if the President wishes to convey a few words of encouragement or guidance to a new appointee, this kind of meeting provides an appropriate opportunity to do so. Most appointees long remember their initial discussions with the Presidents they have been chosen to serve.[104]

But Richard Nixon kept his distance from both the selection process and the nominees it produced. In so doing, he constrained the ability of his personnel staff to clarify the criteria he deemed most important and lost the opportunity to imbue his new appointees with his own order of priorities and objectives. In the long run, this course of action weakened his administration's efforts to "get control of the government."

Nixon interfered with the accomplishment of this objective in another important way. At one of their meetings early in 1969 the President and his Cabinet engaged in a discussion of administration personnel policies. Nixon was unprepared to talk about this matter and in an expansive moment stated to those present that the primary responsibility for filling positions in each of the departments belonged to the Cabinet officers themselves. He further specified that these jobs should be filled on the basis of ability first and loyalty second. This was a significant, if impulsive, delegation of personnel selection authority that members of the Cabinet would not soon or easily surrender. Nixon recognized almost immediately that in granting this discretion he had made an error in judgment. As he left the Cabinet room after the meeting, he is reported to have said to an aide, "I just made a big mistake."[105]

The immediate result was that it was exceedingly difficult for the White House personnel operation to centralize the selection process in a way that permitted systematic control of administration appointments. Tensions developed between the President's personnel staff and personnel officers in the departments, and this required Harry Flemming to devote a lot of time to the task of reestablishing the right of his staff to approve the nominations recommended by department heads.[106] The White House thus lost much of the initiative in the selection process in the first year of the Nixon administration.

The combination of an inexperienced personnel staff, ambiguous selection criteria, presidential noninvolvement, conflicts with the departments, and an opposition Congress constituted a nest of trouble for the White House personnel operation. The external view—that it simply didn't work very well—soon became the White House view as well. Dissatisfaction developed on several fronts.

Congressional Republicans were the most vociferous in their complaints. They objected to the fact that Democrats were not being replaced fast enough. They objected to the failure of the personnel staff to recognize the normal courtesies in acknowledging congressionally generated recommendations and in clearing prospective nominees with the congressional delegations from their home states. But most vehement of all were the criticisms that resulted from the administration's failure to find enough jobs for the favored candidates of congressional Republicans. After eight years of waiting for a President of their own party, Republicans expected more than they received. Republican Senator Robert Dole of Kansas voiced this criticism. He suggested that his GOP colleagues include this line in their letters of recommendation to the White House: "Even though Zilch is a Republican, he's highly qualified for the job." And he lamented his inability to get a single Kansan placed in the new administration. "There must be a spot for one between now and 1976," he said. "A janitor maybe?"[107]

The personnel staff also made some curious, in some cases even embarrassing, choices in the first year and a half of the Nixon presidency. The President was opposed to the policy of busing schoolchildren to achieve racial integration. But his first Commissioner of Education had been the principal architect of such busing plans in New York State. The administration's first nominee to serve as Ambassador to Venezuela was strongly opposed to American importation of oil; yet Venezuela is a major exporter of petroleum to the United States. The administration's first designee as Director of Consumer Affairs had a highly visible conflict of interest that forced her resignation within days of the announcement of her appointment.

But it was neither the complaints from congressional Republicans nor the weight of repeated blunders that led to a reexamination of the personnel operation in 1970. The real problem, in the view of senior White House aides, was that the personnel staff had not succeeded in finding and recruiting nominees who were loyal enough and tough enough and adept enough to take command of the agencies they headed and to bring their operations into line with presidential policy objectives. In the middle of 1970, that fundamental goal of "getting control of the government" remained unfulfilled.

Nixon's chief of staff, H. R. Haldeman, had grown increasingly disenchanted with Flemming's personnel operation. He thought that too heavy an emphasis was placed on patronage considerations and the quality of presidential appointments was not up to what it should be. In the late summer of 1970 Haldeman called Frederic Malek, then Deputy Under Secretary of HEW, and asked him to give some thought to the White House personnel operation. Malek submitted a memo about this, and a few days later Haldeman asked him to come to work at the White House. Malek accepted the offer, and in September, at Haldeman's direction, he and his assistant, William Horton, began what amounted to a consultant's study of the White House personnel operation. By December, they had produced a forty-five page report on the selection process as it then existed, including a number of recommendations for improvement. The report began with this statement:

> In the two years of the Nixon Administration, the difficulty in effectively managing the Federal Government has become increasingly apparent. The Executive Branch has not galvanized sufficiently as a team implementing Presidential policy. In some cases, Presidential directives have not been carried out, and counter-productive efforts have taken place within a number of Departments.
> While the causes of this problem are varied and complex, the President can do much to solve it by increasing his direct management control over appointees to non-career positions in the Executive Branch. Such management control can be achieved by attracting the best qualified individuals who are philosophically compatible with and loyal to the President and placing them in leadership positions, motivating them by recognizing and promoting outstanding performers, and removing any whose performance is poor. At the same time, personnel decisions should be made and announced to maximize political benefit and minimize political costs.[108]

The report went on to note that the existing White House role in the selection process was largely reactive, that most personnel choices were initiated by the departments, subject only to White House clearance.[109] It further identified the diffusion of responsibility for selection decisions within the White House staff and noted the problems that sometimes resulted from this diffusion.[110] To deal with each of these areas of difficulty, the report recommended the centralization of all responsibility for coordinating personnel decisions in a central office to be called the White House Personnel Operation

(WHPO). The WHPO would be more assertive than the Flemming operation had been at exercising "greater management control across the range of personnel activities."[111] The report suggested a table of organization for the WHPO and a series of procedures to be followed in making personnel selections. These suggestions became the basis for presidential personnel operations over the ensuing several years.

With Flemming's departure from the administration and the President's approval of the Malek report, Malek took charge of the WHPO and quickly reorganized it. The personnel operation was divided into three sections. The first, responsible for executive recruiting, was under Malek's direct control. He hired a staff of professional recruiters, primarily from the private sector, and assigned responsibilties for certain types of appointments to each. Some sought out candidates to deal with specific aspects of domestic or international affairs. Others attempted to identify and recruit women or members of minority groups. Malek had argued the importance of creating an effective White House recruitment capability in his report:

> [E]stablishing an executive search capability would enable the White House to exercise considerably more influence than is presently possible over the substantive and political qualifications of candidates. . .
>
> In addition, there are three other advantages to establishing an executive search capability in the White House. First, it could assist in seeking candidates for Regulatory Commissions and Agency Head positions. Secondly, a wider scope from the White House viewpoint would provide greater opportunities to match skills with job requirements for top-level people. Last, an executive search capability at the White House would make it easier to achieve a desired mix of appointees within the Administration, e.g., by geographic region, type of training and experience, educational background, sex, ethnic characteristics, etc.[112]

The ability to reach out and find its own candidates was essential to the White House, because it rarely found the kind of people it sought among those job applications and recommendations that came in "over the transom" each month. As Malek put it, "Typically, the kind of person we want is not looking for a government job. He's happy where he is, doing something constructive, making more money than we can offer him and has great advancement potential. Many are in their mid-30s and earning six-figure incomes."[113]

The executive recruiting staff focused primarily on the most important policy-making positions within the administration. Their job was to broaden the range of candidates from which the administration could make its selections. They maintained contacts with individuals across the country who generated the names of potential candidates and provided evaluations of the capabilities of those being considered for particular positions. They also handled the difficult task of persuading successful individuals to make the financial and career sacrifices that were often inevitable in coming to work for the federal government.

A second component of the White House Personnel Operation was the so-called personnel administration section. This part of the operation was initially headed by Malek's senior aide, Daniel T. Kingsley. Its function was to maintain liaison with the departments and agencies and to handle appointments to lower-level and patronage positions. It sought to monitor these appointments, to supervise political clearances, and to screen the several hundred requests for jobs that were received each month at the White House. Kingsley's group was also involved in setting up orientation programs for new appointees and in maintaining a system of rewards and incentives for government employees.

The third component of the reorganized personnel operation, referred to as the special projects section, was headed by William Horton. It carried out a kind of management consulting or evaluation function for the personnel operation. In Malek's view, it was not enough merely to try to appoint the right people to administrative positions. It was equally important to review their activities once in office and to identify administrative problem areas. The task of the special projects section was to conduct studies of the organization and operations of individual departments and agencies, with primary attention to the handling of personnel matters. "If an operation is not running up to expectations," said Malek, "our job is to analyze it and assist in improving it."[114] These studies by the special projects section often led to the reorganization of staff functions in an agency or, in some cases, to the reassignment or dismissal of administrative personnel.

The personnel management system that Malek put into effect was more specialized, more centralized, and more professional than any of its predecessors. The procedures that were followed in selecting nominees were similar to those that had been in use since the Kennedy administration, although the improvement in its resources and capabilities allowed Malek's staff to search more widely and systematically for executive candidates than had previously been possible. In the initial phase of the talent search as many as fifty names might be generated as potential nominees. Further research and evaluation would reduce the list to around fifteen. Security clearances were then conducted on this group, and these were followed by the normal array of political clearances, which narrowed the list to a half-dozen candidates or less. Their names and pertinent information about them were circulated around the White House and, where appropriate, to department and agency officials for a final clearance. Malek's staff would indicate the candidate it thought best qualified on the list of names sent to the White House chief of staff. On some occasions information on the leading candidates, along with memos indicating staff and departmental recommendations, were sent to the President for a decision. In most cases, however, the final determination was made by the chief of staff.

A prime objective of the personnel operation established by Malek was to protect the President's appointment powers from outside forces. Malek recognized that all Presidents are constant targets for Congressmen, interest groups, agency heads, and even members of the White House staff who have friends or "clients" for whom they would like to procure administration jobs. In Malek's view, the creation of a system that permitted the White House to divert all but the most important of these external pressures was essential to bringing the President's appointment powers into full alignment with administration objectives. The centralization of personnel decision-making in the White House Personnel Operation was an important step in that direction. But Malek went even farther by designing a coding system that permitted the personnel staff to screen job recommendations and applications and to assign each a number that indicated its political value to the administration. For the most part the numbers were based on the importance of a candidate's sponsor and the staff's evaluation of the sponsor's interest in seeing a particular candidate placed.

The coding system for political evaluations tended to follow this outline:

1. "Must"—must be corresponded to, interviewed, and offered position.
2. "High Priority"—must be corresponded to, interviewed, and offered opportunity to compete for position. Approximately 50 percent of these should be placed.
3. "Courtesy Political Referral"—must be corresponded to, and in some cases, offered an opportunity to interview. If equal in other respects should be offered the position over other candidates.

4. "Nonpolitical"—would be given routine processing through government channels.
5. "Political Problem"—signal to White House Personnel Operation to hold all action pending resolution of dispute or uncertainty regarding candidate.
6. "Politically Undesirable"—no action.[115]

In addition to the political rating, the personnel staff also employed a substantive rating that divided candidates into two categories:

A. Possible candidate for high-level position, or non-Presidential Executive level.
B. All others

These ratings were not often used in the selection of nominees for major policy-making positions since most of these candidates were recruited through the initiative of the personnel staff. The ratings were widely used, however, in dealing with candidates whose names came in unsolicited.

In July 1972 Malek left the personnel office and joined the Committee to Re-Elect the President. He was succeeded as head of the White House Personnel Operation first by Daniel Kingsley and later by Jerry H. Jones and David J. Wimer. After the President's reelection in 1972, a number of changes began to occur in the work and in the concerns of the White House Personnel Operation. Some of these were extensions of efforts begun by Malek and Kingsley, others were substantial changes in direction.

Early in 1971 Malek had sought to focus the attention of the WHPO on presidential and other executive-level appointments, that is, to move away from the emphasis on patronage that had prevailed during Flemming's tenure. The WHPO ceased to perform clearances or to provide "go/no-go" decisions on each noncareer supergrade appointment in the agencies. These responsibilities were delegated to the agencies themselves and only monitored by the White House. After the 1972 election the WHPO again became more actively involved in these decisions, attempting with renewed vigor to ensure the loyalty and responsiveness of appointees to these positions and to derive maximum political value from their selection.

The postelection efforts of the WHPO were composed of several parts. In a number of agencies it sought to set up personnel offices that would work closely with the White House to make sure that the political and administrative concerns of the Nixon administration would be a constant factor in personnel actions within those agencies. These political personnel officers (whom some in Washington called "proconsuls" or "political commissars") were charged not only with expeditiously handling referrals from the White House but also with overseeing the hiring, firing, promotion, and transfer of all noncareer appointees and, in some cases apparently, of individuals in the competitive career service as well.[116]

To help organize the efforts of the political personnel officers, Kingsley temporarily hired a man named Alan May, who had developed something of a reputation within the administration both for his skill in organizing departmental personnel efforts and for his passionate distrust of the career bureaucracy. May authored a manual that was distributed to the agency political personnel officers. It explained the political priority coding system, instructed them in ways to apply that system to the administration's advantage, and provided them with advice in dealing with unresponsive career personnel. The manual declared that the goal of the departmental personnel officers should be "to insure placement in all key positions of substantively qualified and politically reliable officials with a minimum burden on line managers in achieving that goal. The objective of that goal is firm political control of the department or agency, while at the same time effecting good management and good programs."[117] May also conducted seminars for the political personnel officers to help them sharpen their skills in dealing with "insimpatico" career employees. One participant at these seminars described them as instructions in the "legal way to commit murder."[118]

While some who served in the WHPO at the time sought to characterize its efforts in late 1972 and 1973 as a "decentralization," it was a most peculiar kind of decentralization. No grants of autonomy were involved here; in fact, the desired result was just the opposite. The WHPO sought to expand the influence of departmental personnel officers, but only so that they could more effectively and comprehensively impose White House interests on departmental personnel actions. In reality, its intention was to expand, not decentralize, control over personnel decision-making.

The vigor of this effort soon diminished, largely because other concerns intervened. As the cloud of Watergate began to shadow other aspects of presidential politics, the personnel staff seemed to pay increasing attention to patronage pressures, particularly those emanating from Capitol Hill. Selection decisions were considered as carefully for their political value as for their impact on what was still regarded as a hostile federal bureaucracy. Recruiting of talented people became more difficult as the image of the administration darkened.[119] And more and more deference was paid to those congressional supporters who were the President's last hope of staving off impeachment.[120] The twin goals of earlier Nixon personnel efforts— to use appointments to improve the President's managerial control of the bureaucracy and to enlarge his political support—gave way to a burgeoning obsession with political survival.

In the short history of formal personnel staffs in the White House, the Nixon personnel operation is distinctive in several ways. The first is its size. From 1969 through 1974, the size of the White House personnel staff grew steadily. Neither Kennedy nor Johnson had ever had as many as a dozen people working on personnel matters at any one time. Yet Nixon's personnel staff grew from sixteen under Harry Flemming to thirty-three under Malek, and finally, at its peak, to sixty under Jerry Jones.[121] As the functions of the WHPO grew broader and more elaborate, a persistent need was felt to expand the personnel staff.

The Nixon personnel operation stands out as well for its sophistication. After Harry Flemming's departure in 1970, the personnel staff was headed by a succession of people with backgrounds in management. For the most part they shared a desire to create and maintain a personnel operation that would strengthen the President's "management control over key positions in the executive branch."[122] To carry this out, the WHPO was created. Under Malek's direction, it came to encompass several separate functional units; its staff was composed largely of management and personnel professionals; and its operating procedures grew increasingly rigorous and systematic. The WHPO became more than just a personnel referral office in the White House. Its outreach capacity was greatly expanded; it took a larger part in executive-level and subcabinet personnel decisions; and it developed a capacity for evaluating administration personnel in order to reward those who performed well and to replace those who did not. No other administration in our history has established a personnel operation in the White House that could match Richard Nixon's in size or in scope of activities.

Despite the legitimacy of many of its objectives, however, and the intelligent and dedicated efforts of a number of talented presidential aides in pursuing those objectives, the Nixon personnel operation persistently fell short of its goal of enabling the President to "get control of the government." There are, perhaps, several reasons for that.

One of these was the President's desire to avoid participation in most selection decisions and to refrain from meeting his nominees when they joined the administration. The personnel staff made occasional efforts to bring the President into closer contact with groups of his appointees, but it never fully succeeded in overcoming his personal unconcern with most aspects of the selection process, and he continued to keep his distance, in some cases even from appointments to his own Cabinet. The advantages of presidental involvement in selection decisions were discussed earlier in this section. Richard Nixon's noninvolvement negated most of these.

Another flaw in the Nixon personnel operation was its occasional lapses into insensitivity. These were invariably counterproductive, increasing the enmity of agency and departmental personnel rather than winning their loyalty and support. New but unnecessary positions were created to facilitate "must" placements. Hiring freezes were selectively violated. Appointees were fired or transferred with little notice. Perhaps no incident so clearly demonstrated the Nixon administration's capacity for insensitive treatment of its members as did its demand that all Nixon appointees submit their resignations one day after Richard Nixon had won reelection by the largest margin in American history. Chairman Robert Hampton of the Civil Service Commission echoed the prevailing reaction to this demand for en masse resignations. "It was incredible," he said, "to build a team over four years and then ask everyone to quit."[123]

Ultimately the Nixon personnel effort became the victim of its own convictions. In its technical aspects, the personnel process that Malek established provided the President with professional and effective support in making presidential appointments. After mid-1972, however, and particularly in the heady months following Nixon's overwhelming reelection, the WHPO sought to expand it functions beyond the principal task of recruiting highly qualified presidential appointees. As part of a broad effort by the Nixon White House to solidify its control over the executive branch, the WHPO expanded in size and attempted to extend its influence beyond presidential appointments to other noncareer and even to some career appointments in the agencies and departments.

Eventually, perhaps inevitably, the territorial aggressiveness of the postelection WHPO began to get out of control. Political criteria were applied to appointments to competitive positions in the civil service. A variety of ingenious ways to circumvent the merit system were developed and employed (some of them, it should be noted, learned from previous administrations). Subsequent investigations by congressional committees, journalists, and grand juries uncovered abundant evidence of agency, departmental, and White House efforts to subvert civil service merit hiring procedures for political purposes. It is ironic that none of these efforts seemed to contribute much to the administration's pursuit of better control of the bureaucracy or to improved relations with the Congress.

In large part that is so because many of these efforts were built on the faulty assumption that the White House can effectively control administrative operations within federal departments and agencies if only it has staff and persistence enough to pursue that objective. But it can't. It can't because its resources can never be adequate to the task. And it can't because the people in the departments and agencies and their friends in Congress will not stand for it. In fact, their resistance usually grows in proportion to the vigor they perceive in White House efforts to control them. The more the WHPO sought to influence personnel actions in the agencies, the less support it got from departmental secretaries and agency heads, from the career personnel officials in the agencies, from the bureaucrats, and from agency sympathizers in Congress. The effort floundered because Watergate made its further pursuit impractical. But in all probability it would soon have sunk from its own weight even without Watergate.

This is not to suggest that the White House should not employ its appointment powers in an effort to make the executive branch more responsive to administration objectives, or even that they are not a useful tool for that purpose. It is only to indicate that there are limits on the effective reach of the President's appointment authority. If he truly wants loyalty and creative support from the executive branch, he is best served by working assiduously to fill positions *at the top levels* with people who will be responsive to his policy objectives and who, through the resourceful administration of their own departments and agencies, will be capable of inspiring this kind of responsiveness in the subordinates they appoint and in the career bureaucrats. When the White House tries, as the WHPO tried after 1972, to extend its control well down into the administrative hierarchy of executive agencies, it only incites the determined resistance of the career personnel and undermines the authority of the presidential appointees. The personnel operations of Flemming and Malek seemed to function with this understanding, but those of their successors did not.

All Presidents, as we have noted before, face the task of developing working relationships with the permanent government. The

Nixon administration took a novel approach to this task. Instead of trying to make its peace with the bureaucracy, it made war. From day one, the bureaucracy was regarded (and treated) as the enemy. One attempt after another was made to infiltrate and capture it. The administration's belief that the bureaucracy was a hostile force eventually became a self-fulfilling prophecy. Hostility arose because friendship and trust were rarely sought or offered. Where previous and subsequent administrations attempted to deal with the "problem" of the permanent government by working out accommodations, by cultivating support, and by honoring loyal and creative civil servants, the Nixon administration all too often sought to employ the levers of presidential authority to command a loyalty it hadn't effectively attempted to win. Aggressive implementation of presidential appointment powers could not fully overcome, and ultimately may even have exacerbated, the inadequacies of other aspects of the administration's personnel management policies.

The Nixon administration created the most sophisticated personnel operation of our time. It dedicated more concentrated effort and manpower to the traditional concerns with bureaucratic responsiveness and congressional relations than any administration before or since. But its achievements in both areas were incomplete, its objectives unfulfilled. If the personnel system was a good one—and there is much in it to commend—it was still only a system. And as one student of personnel administration has pointed out, "Systems do not manage; people manage."[124] The Nixon personnel operation, for all its strengths, never fully overcame the absence of presidential involvement, the insensitivity of senior White House staff, the unrestrained antics of some of its agressive implementers, or its flawed perception of White House capabilities for administrative personnel management. The system worked, but the grand design collapsed.

Gerald R. Ford

Staffing a presidential administration is more than just a mechanical process. The ability of a President to attract talented people to his administration is often affected by conditions over which he has no control. As this discussion of the postwar experience has indicated, the task is least difficult when a President comes into office after winning an election, particularly if his victory also forces a change of party at the White House. The election victory creates a contagion of enthusiasm that helps to diminish some of the normal disincentives to public service. The campaign has permitted the new President to test and assess many of the people who will serve in his administration. The transition period gives the President-elect an opportunity to focus his attention on the selection process. And those who are offered places in the administration can usually look forward to at least four years in which to make a mark on the policies and operations of the government.

Most of these recruiting advantages were lost to Gerald Ford. The personnel difficulties his administration faced are perhaps best documented by comparing the experiences of the Ford and Kennedy administrations. Kennedy's term in office was only eleven weeks longer than Ford's. Yet personnel selection in the Kennedy administration took place under much more favorable conditions than was the case during Ford's presidency. Kennedy's accession followed a vigorous and stimulating campaign, Ford's did not. Kennedy's party had been out of the White House for eight years; Ford's had held the White House through one of the darkest chapters in American history. Kennedy's appointees could look forward to a full term of service; Ford's could not. And while Kennedy's nominees were subject to confirmation by a Senate controlled by his own party and operating under a tradition of acquiescence to presidential nominees, Ford's nominations were considered by a Senate in which the opposition party had a large majority and the tradition of acquiescence was rapidly deteriorating. The prospects for personnel selection in the Ford administration were not, therefore, altogether rosy.

The swiftness of the events surrounding Richard Nixon's resignation left Gerald Ford little time to prepare for his own presidency. Hence not until several months after he took office did the structure and personnel of the Ford administration begin to take shape. The first personnel changes took place in the White House itself. These were followed closely by changes in the departments and agencies. The President's personnel staff during this initial changeover period was headed by William N. Walker, a lawyer who had served in several posts in the Nixon administration but who had little direct experience in personnel matters. In the White House chain of command, Walker reported to Donald Rumsfeld, a senior presidential assistant. He had access to the President, however, and often dealt with him directly on personnel matters.[125]

Walker initiated several changes in the structure and operation of the personnel staff he inherited from the Nixon administration. The term "White House Personnel Operation" was discarded and replaced with the less officious sounding "Presidential Personnel Office" (PPO). Within the first few months after Ford became President, there was a 50 percent turnover in the staff of the PPO. Walker also sought to move away from the emphasis that Malek and his successors had placed on the use of professional executive recruiters. His intention was to put personnel decisions back into the hands of people with substantive government experience:

> The most important role of this office is to be able to bear judgment on the capability of candidates to undertake public policy responsibilities they will be called upon to discharge. Professional recruiters have mechanical skills but not the background in government to make the sort of judgments we are called upon to make . . . We are deliberately seeking out people who are not personnel specialists but those who have experience and competence in substantive areas.[126]

Ten weeks after taking office, Ford announced the nomination of Andrew E. Gibson to be Federal Energy Administrator. A few days later, however, the *New York Times* revealed that Gibson had a ten-year employment separation contract with a corporation that operated oil tankers and was half-owned by Cities Service, a large oil company. The terms of the contract provided that Gibson would receive $88,000 a year for ten years from his former employer. The potential conflict of interest was so patently clear that the President soon felt compelled to withdraw the Gibson nomination.

This incident had an important effect on the role of the PPO during the Ford presidency. The Gibson nomination had not been handled by the PPO, and none of the normal background investigations had taken place before it was announced. Because of the President's desire to replace the incumbent energy administrator with Gibson, the normal selection process was circumvented. The reaction on the part of the President and his senior aides was a resolve to do no more shortcutting, to make full and consistent use of the PPO.[127] The embarrassment of the Gibson nomination thus enlarged and fortified the role played by the PPO in selection decisions for the remainder of the Ford administration.

Andrew Gibson's nomination was not the only personnel problem encountered by the Ford administration in its first few months in office. In fact, it suffered an unusually large number of setbacks in its efforts to win the appointment of its personnel choices. The President was forced to withdraw several ambassadorial nominees, and a number of his other nominations were not confirmed by the time the 93d Congress adjourned. Senate scrutiny was growing more intense during this period, and there was a growing bipartisan chorus of complaints in Congress about the qualifications of the Ford nominees and the administration's failure to observe the expected courtesies and consultation with members of Congress before these nominations were submitted.[128]

In April 1975 William Walker was nominated to serve as the President's deputy special trade representative. He was replaced as director of the PPO by Douglas P. Bennett, who had been working in congressional relations and whose selection to head the PPO was based in part on his experience in dealing with the Congress.[129]

It was Bennett's firm belief that an effective personnel office had to be well managed. The President's personnel advisers, in his view, had to be able to anticipate executive vacancies, to have appropriate candidates ready when they occurred, and to cope with the complex set of political pressures and relationships that surround each major selection decision. To achieve this degree of managerial effectiveness, Bennett reorganized the PPO shortly after becoming its director in the spring of 1975. The staff, which normally numbered around thirty-five during the Ford administration, was divided into four jurisdictional areas: economic affairs, national security affairs, natural resources, and human resources. In each area there was an associate director, an assistant director, a staff assistant, and several secretaries. Peter M. McPherson, Bennett's deputy, oversaw the day-to-day operations of the office.

Selection procedures during Bennett's tenure at the PPO were broadly similar to those that had been in effect since the initial establishment of a White House personnel office by Dan Fenn during the Kennedy administration. Bennett did, however, make a few innovations. For one thing, he shared William Walker's view that, while professional executive recruiters were not essential to the task of finding people to serve in presidential administrations, many of their techniques were. He, too, wanted his staff to be composed of people capable of evaluating the political and substantive qualifications of potential nominees; he thought this required a unique blend of experience and knowledge that most professional executive recruiters did not necessarily have.[130]

Bennett also worked very hard to establish amicable and effective relations with the departments and agencies. He thought it essential that the director of the President's personnel office work closely with the departments in the search for subcabinet nominees. "Strong personal relationships with the Cabinet," he has said, were a "very important factor" in his ability to do his job well.[131] Whenever possible, he made sure that at least the top two officials in each department had an opportunity to interview and evaluate potential nominees for positions in their departments before a recommendation went to the President.

Bennett also established the practice of relying heavily on members of the White House staff for assistance during the selection process. When the PPO was looking for a nominee in a particular substantive area, presidential assistants with experience in that area would often be called in to interview prospective candidates. Bennett also called on other substantive experts throughout the executive branch to conduct interviews of this sort. This practice was particularly helpful to the PPO in three ways. First, it enhanced the personnel staff's ability to assess the strengths and weaknesses of individual candidates. Second, it permitted the people who would have to work directly with the President's nominees to have some input into their selection. Third, it provided the President with a set of evaluations from trusted sources when it was time for him to make a final evaluation.

The PPO under Bennett also minimized its reliance on talent banks and computers. No effort was made, as there had been in the two previous administrations, to create a permanent file of individuals qualified for executive positions. Because it was hard to keep them current, and because ad hoc considerations play such a large role in selection decisions, these talent banks had never become a central component of the selection process.[132] Bennett did not think the utility of a talent bank warranted the staff time and attention necessary to maintain it.

Several criteria governed personnel decisions during the Ford administration. In their early discussion, Ford had especially emphasized to Bennett his desire to have an administration that was "representative of the United States."[133] He wanted geographical balance in his appointments and an adequate representation of the principal groups in American society, such as women, minorities, and young people. The strength of this concern was such that, when attempting to fill a particular job, the PPO often looked specifically for someone from a certain part of the country or a certain population group.[134]

In the wake of Watergate, the PPO also took special care to ensure that Ford's nominees possessed untarnished reputations. In the first few months of Ford's presidency, the White House often required the Watergate Special Prosecutor to clear prospective nominees of any involvement in the Watergate scandal.[135] The Ford PPO also subjected administration job candidates to searching conflict of interest checks. Bennett maintained that 15 percent of those subjected to these checks could not subsequently be nominated because they were unwilling or unable to take the necessary steps to mitigate a potential conflict of interest.[136]

In many ways, Ford's personnel selections were affected by the political circumstances that prevailed for much of his administration. There were, in that sense, several important operational criteria at work in the selection process. As all Presidents do, Ford sought nominees who were politically and ideologically compatible with the policy objectives of his administration. The political compatibility test, however, was applied with less rigor than it had been under Nixon or in the final years under Johnson. As William Walker noted, "One seeks to find... those who are supportive of the President's initiatives and can contribute to his administration in a positive way. However, only a narrow political litmus test is applied."[137]

Two other factors enhanced the salience of political concerns in Ford's selection decisions. One of these was the growing boldness of the Congress in challenging presidential appointees. During the mid-1970s the Senate became far more vigorous in its scrutiny of the President's nominees than it had been for decades. This development will be discussed in detail later in this book, but its impact on Ford's personnel selections should be noted here. As Senate confirmation became more and more problematic, the PPO was required to pay increasing attention to the acceptability of its nominees to the Senate. Douglas Bennett found this the most frustrating aspect of his job.[138]

During the last year of his administration, Ford's election campaign also became a significant factor in the selection process. Though Bennett denies that selection decisions were governed by this concern,[139] they often appeared to be. During the primary campaign in New Hampshire, Ford announced the nomination of that state's attorney general as chairman of the ICC. The nomination of Jerry Thomas, a Florida businessman, as Under Secretary of the Treasury leaked to the press just before the Florida primary. Ford announced during the North Carolina primary campaign that he would nominate a resident of that state to serve as director of the Federal Mediation and Conciliation Service. There were other examples as well.[140] If, in fact, these nominations were not the product of electoral considerations, the timing of their announcement most certainly was.

Gerald Ford had a great interest in personnel decisions.[141] He made it a practice to meet several times each week with the director of the PPO. They would discuss specific criteria at the beginning of the selection process and the merits of individual candidates at the end. Ford almost always made the final decisions himself, after examining the backgrounds of the candidates and the assessments and recommendations of the personnel staff and other administration officials who had interviewed them.

The personnel record of the Ford administration is difficult to evaluate. Few of his appointees were in their posts long enough to make much of a mark on the long-term direction of federal policies. The quality of appointees is hard to assess objectively even when an administration lasts a full four or eight years; the difficulty is compounded for one that lasted only twenty-nine months.

In terms of the ability of the White House to control the selection process and to relate personnel choices to its policy objectives, assessment is somewhat easier. The record of the Ford administration in this regard is mixed. By emphasizing the search for quality and integrity, and by bringing his own considerable political sensitivities to bear on selection decisions, Ford was able to staff a number of the top positions in his administration with eminent and highly regarded individuals. At positions below the top, however, Ford's freedom of choice was often circumscribed by the precarious political circumstances of his tenure in office. Ultimately, the need to escape the shadow of Watergate, to fend off an aggressive Senate, and to win a presidential election prevented President Ford from fully utilizing his appointment powers to control and direct more effectively the government he led.

Jimmy Carter: The Transition Period[142]

As a rule of thumb, the manner in which a President campaigns for and wins election directly affects the initial staffing of his administration. If his winning coalition was built with the strong support of certain large interest groups, those groups will expect him to place their sympathizers in some of the choice positions in his administration. If his victory was a narrow one, he is likely to feel constrained to fill the top positions in his Cabinet with "safe" choices, people whose well-known reputations strike no terror in the hearts of business leaders, minority groups, or other concerned observers of the initial selection process. And if part of his appeal as a candidate was based on promises he made to the electorate to undertake drastic changes once in office, there will be considerable pressure on him to begin to redeem those promises in selecting the people to serve in his administration.

The early personnel decisions of the Carter administration are particularly interesting, because Carter's own perception of his obligations varied widely from those of other political actors. A number of groups, eyeing the closeness of the presidential election, felt that their contribution was the difference between a Carter victory and a Carter defeat. They believed, for that reason, that they had a right to be rewarded in the selection of people for Carter's Cabinet and other high-level positions in his administration. Big labor felt that way. So too did blacks, women, environmentalists, state and local Democratic party leaders, and, in some cases, congressional Democrats.

Carter, however, had quite a different perception. His feeling was that he had come from nowhere to win the election, that it was a personal victory accomplished through two years of very hard work, and that his debts to any particular groups or individuals—except perhaps to blacks—were minimal. As one of his personnel aides later said, "Quite frankly, Jimmy Carter didn't come to Washington with a lot of baggage."[143] The President himself noted at a press conference shortly after his election:

> I realize that a lot of different voting entities in our country have helped me become elected. But I completed my own election process, which lasted almost two years, without having made any commitment in private to anyone about an appointment to a Cabinet post or any other post in Government.
>
> And so I'm completely at liberty, absolutely completely at liberty, to make my decisions about the Cabinet membership on the basis of merit and who can do the best job in working with me harmoniously to lead our country. There are no other commitments.[144]

The political problems created by this difference in perceptions were further compounded by the tendency of Carter and his aides to make grandiose statements about the kinds of people who would serve in his administration. Carter had pledged to staff his administration with "a new generation of leadership,"[145] to make selections "strictly

on the basis of merit,"[146] and to have "a good geographical distribution of persons" and "a good representation of women and minority
groups as well."[147] Carter's close adviser Hamilton Jordan said, in a
statement that was often quoted,

> If, after the inauguration, you find a Cy Vance as Secretary of State and
> Zbigniew Brzezinski as head of national security, then I would say we
> failed. And I'd quit. But that's not going to happen. You're going to see
> new faces, new ideas. The government is going to be run by people you
> have never heard of.[148]

Ultimately, Carter set higher standards than he could meet.
This, combined with a series of political misjudgments in making and
announcing selection decisions, produced an unhappy chorus of complaints about the way these initial selection decisions were carried
out. Congressmen of his own party complained loudly about his failure to heed or acknowledge their suggestions.[149] Women and minority groups expressed persistent disappointment.[150] And the National
Democratic Committee, in a highly unusual move, unanimously
adopted a resolution rebuking the administration for failing to consult
with Democratic state officials in making federal appointments.[151]
Criticism of personnel selections is not uncommon, of course. But by
failing to recognize some legitimate political claims and by promising
a good deal more than it could deliver, the Carter administration
failed to capitalize fully on the political opportunities the selection
process provides, particularly in the initial stages of a new administration. Carter had sought to take firm control of the selection process.
He did so, but at no small cost to his political reputation.

In conducting the search for members of his administration, Carter employed a set of procedures that varied somewhat from those
used by his predecessors. In a clear divergence from precedent, for
instance, the Carter staff began to lay the groundwork for its personnel selections well before Election Day. A small group of people,
working in what was known as the Policy Planning Office, started the
process of gathering names of potential nominees in the summer of
1976. This was not an elaborate operation, merely the initial prepar-
arations for the large number of personnel choices that a newly elected
President is forced to make in setting up his administration. Jack
Watson, who headed the Policy Planning Office, gave this description
of the scope of this effort: "These are simply the names of talented
people—we haven't interviewed anybody—that Jimmy can use if he

chooses. They're organized by areas of interest, background, and experience. It's really just a catalogue, that's all."[152] No previous President had ever started so early to cope with the problems of staffing a new administration. Interestingly, however, these early preparations seem to have had little effect on the speed with which positions in the Carter administration were filled. Carter was the slowest of the postwar Presidents in naming his Cabinet, and a number of important subcabinet positions remained vacant several months after inauguration day. In part, this resulted from the deliberateness of his approach to the selection process, but it also reflected the determination of his administration to subject its nominees to a series of time-consuming security and conflict of interest clearances.[153]

In picking his Cabinet-level nominees, Carter made an effort to consider appointments in "clusters," to pick all the people in one policy area before moving on to another. This approach was a product of his concern with the compatibility among his top advisers in each area. He had said in an interview during the campaign that, in assembling his administration, "compatibility would be an important factor—not only with me but with other members of the Cabinet."[154] To ascertain the ability of potential nominees to work in harmony, he established the practice of holding meetings to which a number of candidates under consideration for positions in a particular policy area were invited. The meetings often lasted for several hours and covered a wide range of current issues in that particular area. In this fashion, the President-elect was able to assess not only the quality of advice each person seemed capable of providing but also the pattern of interaction that was likely to develop among them.

This procedure had an important side effect. Because it was impossible to hold these meetings in secret, the public quickly learned the names of the people being considered for important administration posts. As a result, the early selection process was far more open and visible than it had been under previous administrations.

Despite the pressures this put on the participants in these meetings and the potential embarrassment to those who received no offers of jobs, Carter thought this approach was a useful way to select people for the top positions in his administration.[155] It gave him a firsthand opportunity to see each individual in action, but it had other advantages as well. It provided the President-elect with an opportunity to evaluate the public reaction to the people he was considering before he made his final personnel decisions. When the names of people attending one of these meetings were published, interest groups, members of Congress, and others were quick to express their support or opposition. For Carter this was an effective—if not altogether tidy—way to get a sense of how certain nominations were likely to be received. Carter had employed this *modus operandi* in picking a Vice President. He was pleased with the results of that effort and happily applied the same set of procedures in picking his Cabinet.

Another innovation in the Carter selection process was the employment of advisory panels to aid in the search for nominees of high caliber. This was an important procedural part of Carter's attempt to ensure that merit would be the dominant factor in choosing candidates for certain types of positions. The most notable examples of this were the commissions established to screen and suggest nominees for ambassadorships, judges of the U.S. Circuit Courts of Appeals, and such other positions as Chairman of the National Endowment for the Humanities and the Director of the FBI.

The history of these advisory panels has not yet been written, and it is too early to make any conclusive judgments about their impact on the selection process. The early experience is not wholly encouraging, however. The FBI panel produced a list of five candidates so lacking in national reputation and prestige that the President felt compelled to reject all five. The individual ultimately selected to head the Humanities Endowment, though well qualified, was an early Carter supporter who had played a significant role in his campaign. Several of his initial ambassadorial appointments were old friends of the President from Georgia with no previous experience in foreign affairs.

During the early phase of the transition period, the Carter personnel operation was managed by two groups of advisers. One group of ten or twelve people reported directly to Hamilton Jordan, who had overall responsibility for the talent hunt. A larger group worked under the direction of Matthew B. Coffey, a former Johnson personnel aide. The division of labor between the two groups was never very clear, and there was much overlapping in their day-to-day operations. In broad terms, however, Coffey's group administered the so-called Talent Inventory Process (TIP), which was designed to identify candidates for administration jobs and evaluate their abilities, while Jordan's group was primarily responsible for handling the more sensitive political aspects of the selection process. The TIP was a direct outgrowth of the work done by Jack Watson's Policy Planning Office before the election. Its objectives were similar to those of personnel staffs under previous Presidents: to expand the search for administration nominees across the nation and across a broad range of professions and interest groups.[156]

In the selection of nominees for the Cabinet and a few other major positions, Carter himself played a very active part. He described his role this way:

> I spend, I would say, six or eight hours a day on the telephone calling different people around the nation in whom I have confidence, who have special knowledge about, for instance, foreign affairs, or defense capabilities, or finance, or international and domestic trade, or health, education and welfare or whatever the case might be, asking them for their advice on who ought to be considered for our Cabinet positions, or for lesser posts.
>
> Then, out of that series of recommendations that come to me from knowledgeable people, there almost inevitably develops a pattern which shows that many different people from many walks of life with different backgrounds recommend a certain group of persons.
>
> Then I turn that list over to my staff members, headed by Hamilton Jordan, and we do an in-depth analysis of that person, concentrating [on] questions about that person or group of persons . . . . And then out of that I form my own opinion, talk to the persons being considered either by telephone or in person and ultimately make a decision.[157]

Carter's direct participation in selection decisions was limited almost entirely to the handful of positions at the very top. From the outset of the selection process, Carter had made it clear that he intended to hold his Cabinet secretaries accountable for the way they managed their departments and that he, therefore, thought it necessary to delegate to each of them the authority to select their own subordinates. Not since Eisenhower's time had a President been so firm in his desire to decentralize appointment decisions.

This was not, however, a policy of absolute decentralization. In some departments, Carter did take a personal interest in the selection of the number two man. The Deputy Secretary of Defense, for instance, and the Under Secretary of Agriculture were selected by the White House with little direct participation by the newly designated secretaries of those departments. In a department like HUD, where the secretary had little appropriate substantive experience, the White House played a somewhat larger role in the search for subcabinet nominees. What the President desired was a system of "mutual veto," in which he reserved the right to reject an unsuitable subcabinet choice and granted to each Cabinet secretary the right to reject suggestions made by the White House. In practice, there is no evidence that Carter ever exercised his veto; the selection of subcabinet nominees in his administration was a highly decentralized operation.

After Carter took office, Matthew Coffey and a number of the people who had worked on personnel during the early phase of the transition went back to their jobs outside the administration. Leadership of the White House personnel office was then assigned to James B. King, who had no personnel experience but had been Carter's trip director during the campaign. King reported directly to Hamilton Jordan, who retained overall responsibility for personnel decisions. In the first year after the inauguration, the policy of decentralization remained in effect. That meant that the task of the White House personnel staff was primarily supportive. It continued to develop lists of qualified candidates to aid the departments in their own personnel searches, and it administered the variety of clearances to which all Carter appointments were subjected. But, in most cases, it did not play an initiating role in the selection process, as its counterparts had done in the four previous administrations.

Jimmy Carter's approach to the task of staffing his administration does not readily fit any of the patterns followed by other postwar Presidents. Carter became President by capturing his party, not by winning its heart. He campaigned against the symbolic bugaboos of cronyism and politics-as-usual. He strongly believed in Cabinet government. It is no surprise, then, that his initial selection procedures reflected nothing quite so much as an effort to pull away from traditional ways of doing things. With few exceptions, the developing trend since Kennedy's time had been toward a centralization of personnel decision-making in the White House. Carter reversed the trend. Personnel staffs in earlier administrations sought to ensure that selection decisions were made and announced in ways that minimized political costs and maximized political benefits. Carter, however, seemed more concerned with avoiding political embarrassment than with optimizing political opportunities. The use of advisory panels to screen nominees, the delegation of personnel selection authority to Cabinet officers, and the constant search for people with little Washington experience and no ties to prominent interest groups had the effect, in practice if not in design, of depoliticizing the selection process.

In his initial selection decisions, Carter accomplished many of the objectives he had set for himself. He conducted a more open and visible selection process than any of his predecessors. He imposed very tough conflict of interest standards on his nominees. He brought a great many new faces into the executive branch. And he placed far more women and minority group members in positions of significant responsibility than had any of his predecessors. These accomplishments, particularly the last, were substantial.

What the initial selection procedures of the Carter administration seemed to lack was a clear sense of the relationship between a President's appointment powers and his political and administrative leadership responsibilities. As the Carter administration entered its second year in office, it was increasingly criticized for its failure to establish any substantial measure of control over the executive branch and for its persistent inability to build political support, in the Congress and in the country, for its policy initiatives. It would, of course, be a ludicrous oversimplification to say that more effective and more carefully considerd use of his appointment powers could have solved all of these problems, since personnel selection is only one part of the political and administrative processes. The fact remains, however, that personnel decisions in the first year of the Carter administration were often made without any conscious effort to relate them to the President's political and administrative needs.

Taken individually, many of Carter's appointments were well received. But the problem is that most of these appointments were taken individually. Personnel decisions were made in so many places and for so many separate and unrelated reasons that there was little opportunity for the development of an administration personnel "plan." As a result, a President who needed to strengthen his ties to the Congress, who needed to broaden the base of his political support, and who needed to attract the loyalty of the disparate elements of the executive branch quickly and firmly lacked a personnel policy designed to help him do any of these things.

Notes

1. For a discussion of these early Cabinet replacements, see Richard Tanner Johnson, *Managing the White House* (Harper & Row, 1974), pp. 65–69.
2. Harry S. Truman, *1945, Year of Decisions* (Signet, 1955), p. 361.
3. *Ibid.*, p. 364.
4. Dean E. Mann, "The Selection of Federal Political Executives," *American Political Science Review*, 58, (1964): 89.

5. *Ibid.*
6. *Ibid.*, p. 97.
7. *Ibid.*, p. 84.
8. *Ibid.*, p. 83.
9. See, for instance, the differences between the Truman administration's stated civil rights objectives and its practices with regard to minority appointments in Donald R. McCoy and Robert T. Ruetten, *Quest and Response: Minority Rights and the Truman Administration* (University Press of Kansas, 1973).
10. See, for example, the factors affecting the selection of Lowell B. Mason to serve on the Federal Trade Commission in James M. Graham and Victor H. Kramer, *Appointments to the Regulatory Agencies: The Federal Communications Commission and the Federal Trade Commission, 1949–1974*, printed for the use of the Senate Committee on Commerce (GPO, 1976), pp. 5–7.
11. Dwight D. Eisenhower, *Mandate for Change* (Signet, 1963), p. 124.
12. Senator Everett Dirksen reflected the prevailing view among Republicans when he said, "I am not timid about the patronage matter. The Republicans are in control, and I have been serving in Congress for 20 years and never before this year have I had the opportunity to recommend the appointment of a postmaster. I am now doing my best to get a few offices now and then, and I am going to work harder at it." *Congressional Record*, 100 (January 25, 1954): 696.

    Sherman Adams noted in his memoirs that "no matter how hard we struggled during that first year . . . there was a steady rumble of criticism from the politicians of our own party. We weren't cleaning out the Democrats fast enough." Sherman Adams, *First Hand Report: The Story of the Eisenhower Administration* (Harper & Brothers, 1961), p. 77.
13. McKinsey and Company, "Restaffing the Executive Branch of the Federal Government at the Policy Level" (mimeograph, October 1952).
14. This roster of names provided little information about the candidates for appointment, and there was little follow-up from the state organizations. As a result, the list was never of much importance in the Eisenhower selection operation.
15. Laurin L. Henry, *Presidential Transitions* (Brookings, 1960), p. 645.
16. *New York Times*, November 25, 1952.
17. Adams, *First Hand Report*, p. 58.
18. This was referred to at the time as the "Morningside Heights Agreement" because it was agreed to at a meeting between the two men at Eisenhower's home at Columbia University.
19. See David Lawrence, "Clumsiness Seen in Choosing of Cabinet by Eisenhower," *New York Herald Tribune*, December 3, 1952, and *Washington Post*, December 16, 1952.
20. Henry, *Presidential Transitions*, pp. 523–524.
21. Eisenhower, *Mandate for Change*, pp. 282–287, and Adams, *First Hand Report*, p. 58. As employed here the term "patronage" is used to

describe appointive positions at the lower administrative levels that have little policymaking influence and are normally filled by people who are recommended to the President by his party, his allies in Congress, or other individuals and groups whose support he seeks. The concept of patronage has a variety of pejorative connotations, but no such implication is made or intended here. Patronage appointments have been made regularly since Washington's time. They are not a major focus of this study, but they are mentioned, where appropriate, as one aspect of the presidential use of the appointing power. For a fuller discussion of patronage at the federal and local level, see Martin Tolchin and Susan Tolchin, *To The Victor. . . Political Patronage from the Clubhouse to the White House* (Random House, 1971).

22. Eisenhower, *Mandate for Change*, p. 137.
23. Adams, *First Hand Report*, p. 57.
24. Henry, *Presidential Transitions*, p. 646.
25. Robert J. Donovan, *Eisenhower: The Inside Story* (Harper & Brothers, 1956), p. 98.
26. Adams, *First Hand Report*, p. 54.
27. Willis's attempts to systematize the process of filling vacancies in subordinate positions became a source of controversy in 1954. As the clamor for a more rapid and efficient distribution of patronage positions grew louder in the period before the 1954 midterm elections, Willis's attention was turned increasingly toward that problem and away from the task of filling executive positions. He sought to organize the dispensation of patronage more rigorously by centralizing the process in the White House and setting up patronage contact points in each of the agencies. The plan that he produced was titled "Operation People's Mandate," but became known more familiarly as the "Willis Plan." The primary objective of the Willis Plan was to improve the efficiency of the administration in selecting Republican Party loyalists to fill key positions, not only under Schedule C and other exempt statuses, but also in pay grades GS-14 to GS-18. Dissatisfaction among senior civil servants led to the disclosure of the Willis Plan, and it became an embarrassment to the administration. It was subsequently investigated by the Senate Post Office and Civil Service Committee, which called it "a serious affront to basic career service."

The Willis Plan, though it was never successfully implemented, was the first full-scale attempt by any presidential administration to create a centralized system for managing the President's personnel responsibilities. It is noteworthy for that reason, in spite of its failure. It indicated a belief that personnel selection procedures could be most effectively used for patronage purposes if they were carefully and pointedly organized to meet the President's needs. The source of the failure of the Willis Plan was in its attempt to extend the circle of presidential control too broadly and too rapidly. In its clumsiness it aroused the sensitivity of the Congress and of the President himself in regard to the sanctity of the merit system.

On the Willis Plan, see, Henry, *Presidential Transitions*, pp. 676

ff., and U.S. Senate, 85th Congress, 1st Sesstion (1957), Committee on Post Office and Civil Service, *Administration of the Civil Service System* (Committee Print No. 2), especially pp. 27–40.

28. Adams, *First Hand Report*, p. 76.
29. Eisenhower, *Mandate for Change*, p. 376.
30. Key party contacts varied from state to state and no set pattern governed this aspect of the clearance process. See Adams, *First Hand Report*, pp. 58–59.
31. Eisenhower, *Mandate for Change*, p. 159.
32. Adams, *First Hand Report*, p. 76.
33. Eisenhower, *Mandate for Change*, p. 127.
34. *Ibid.*, p. 123.
35. *Ibid.*
36. *Ibid.*, p. 283.
37. The decision to add previous judicial experience as a criterion was made after the appointment of Earl Warren as Chief Justice. See *Ibid.*, p. 287.
   38. *Ibid.*, p. 123.
39. *Ibid.*
40. *Ibid.*, p. 137.
41. Adams notes, for instance, that "Eisenhower never bothered to find out whether a prospective employee had supported him at the 1952 Republican Convention." Adams, *First Hand Report*, p. 77.
42. Of the Eisenhower executive selection decisions that Mann examined in depth, he found that in only 23 percent had the White House staff been a principal participant. This was slightly more than in the Truman administration (22 percent), but far fewer than in the first year under Kennedy (55 percent). See Mann, "Selection of Federal Political Executives" (note 4 above), p. 82.
43. Quoted from "Eisenhower on the Presidency," CBS Television News, November 23, 1961.
44. Leonard Hall, the Republican National Chairman, reported at a Cabinet meeting on July 17, 1953, that he could find not even six members of Congress who were indebted to the administration for appointments made at their behest. On a previous day, he noted, he had been asked by department heads to clear five candidates with local political leaders. All five, it turned out, were Democrats. Reported by Donovan, *Eisenhower*, pp. 99–100.
   Sherman Adams noted that at a meeting of legislative leaders shortly after Eisenhower took office, Senator Leverett Saltonstall (R.-Mass.) asked Speaker of the House Joe Martin (R.-Mass.) if he had had any success in getting federal appointments for any of his constituents. "New jobs?" replied Martin, "I lost the two that I got when Truman was in office." Adams, *First Hand Report*, p. 61.
45. Theodore C. Sorensen, *Kennedy* (Bantam, 1965), p. 284.
46. *Ibid.*
47. Arthur M. Schlesinger, Jr., *A Thousand Days* (Fawcett Crest, 1965), p. 625.

48. The following discussion of the Talent Hunt draws on several sources: Adam Yarmolinsky, "The Kennedy Talent Hunt," *The Reporter*, Vol. 24, (1961); Sorensen, *Kennedy*, pp. 280–288; Schlesinger, *A Thousand Days*, pp. 140–148; David T. Stanley, *Changing Administrations: The 1961 and 1964 Transitions in Six Departments* (Brookings, 1965); Dean E. Mann and Jameson W. Doig, *The Assistant Secretaries: Problems and Processes of Appointment* (Brookings, 1965), pp. 71–76; Graham and Kramer, *Appointments to Regulatory Agencies* (note 10 above), pp. 153–160; U.S. Senate, 95th Congress, 1st Session (1977), Committee on Government Operations, *Study on Federal Regulation, Volume I: The Regulatory Appointments Process* (committee print), pp. 95–160; *New York Times*; and *Washington Post*.

49. Yarmolinsky, "Kennedy Talent Hunt," p. 23.

50. This document is entitled *U.S. Government Policy and Supporting Positions* and is now published every time a new President is elected. It is commonly called the "Plum Book" both for what was once the color of its cover and because the positions listed therein are often regarded as political plums.

51. Interview with Dan H. Fenn, Jr., Waltham, Massachusetts, March 26, 1976 (hereafter cited as Fenn interview).

52. Letter from Fenn to the author, December 5, 1978.

53. Dan H. Fenn, Jr., "Dilemmas for the Regulator," *California Management Review*, 16 (Spring 1974): 88.

54. Letter from Fenn to the author, December 5, 1978.

55. Fenn interview.

56. U.S. Senate, Committee on Government Operations, *The Regulatory Appointments Process*, p. 123.

57. For a discussion of the remarkable extent of some of these self-initiated appointment campaigns, see Graham and Kramer, *Appointments to Regulatory Agencies*.

58. Letter from Fenn to the author, December 5, 1978.

59. Fenn interview.

60. *Ibid.*

61. Sorensen, *Kennedy*, p. 287.

62. Fenn, telephone conversation, May 24, 1976.

63. Dan H. Fenn, Jr., Letter to the Editor, *Public Administration Review*, 35, (March/April 1975): 213–214.

64. In his study of a sample of 108 appointees from three administrations, Mann found that 55 percent of the Kennedy selections came from a search in which the White House staff was a "primary participant." In the Truman administration the White House was a principal participant for only 22 percent of Mann's sample, and for Eisenhower the figure was 23 percent. See Mann, "Selection of Federal Political Executives" (note 4 above), p. 82.

65. Interview of John W. Macy, Jr., conducted by Emmette S. Redford and Richard L. Schott, Washington, D.C., September 11, 1976 (hereafter cited as Macy interview).

66. This discussion of executive selection procedures in the Johnson ad-

ministration is based on information drawn from the following sources: John W. Macy, Jr., *Public Service* (Harper & Row, 1971); "How Johnson Fills Jobs at the Top," *Business Week*, July 31, 1965, pp. 20–22; John W. Macy, Jr., and Matthew B. Coffey, "Executive Recruiting and Management Information in the White House," *Society for the Advancement of Management Journal*, 35, (January 1970): 5–13; Matthew B. Coffey, "A Death at the White House: The Short Life of the New Patronage," *Public Administration Review*, 34 (September/October 1974): 440–444; Joseph Kraft, "Johnson's Talent Hunt," *Harper's Magazine*, 230 (March 1965): 40 ff.; Jerry Kluttz, "The Federal Diary," *Washington Post*, May 11, 1965; *New York Times*; interview and personal communications with John W. Macy, Jr.; and the files of the Lyndon Baines Johnson Library (hereafter LBJL).

67. Macy interview.
68. Macy, *Public Service*, p. 226.
69. *Ibid.*, p. 228.
70. This number was cited by Macy in his interview with Redford and Schott. It is apparently an estimate. In *Public Service*, Macy says the files contained sixteen thousand names. An unsigned memorandum to the President, dated April 20, 1967, set the figure at forty-two thousand.
71. Macy interview.
72. Memorandum to the President from John W. Macy, Jr., "Statistical Highlights of the President's Appointments, 1963–1968," September 18, 1968, contained in LBJL.
73. Occasionally the memorandum to the President contained only one name. This was often the case when the personnel staff recommended the reappointment of an incumbent official. In a few other cases as well, when the one candidate was clearly best qualified, only that candidate would be suggested to the President. For example, a memorandum to the President from Macy, dated April 19, 1967, included only the name of William B. Sherrill as a candidate for a vacancy on the Federal Reserve Board of Governors (LBJL).
74. Johnson often claimed he followed the recommendation of his personnel staff 90 percent of the time. Macy is not sure the figure was quite that high, but he is certain that a majority of his staff's recommendations were accepted by the President. Macy interview.
75. *Ibid.*
76. Richard L. Schott and Dagmar Hamilton, "The Politics of Presidential Appointments in the Johnson Administration: Notes on Work in Progress," paper prepared for delivery at the annual meeting of the Southern Political Science Association, November 4, 1977, p. 7.
77. Graham and Kramer suggest this may have been a factor in the unusual delay prior to the announcement of the nomination of Mary Gardiner Jones to serve on the Federal Trade Commission in 1964. See Graham and Kramer, *Appointments to Regulatory Agencies* (note 10 above), p. 237.
78. Macy interview.
79. Schott and Hamilton, "Politics of Presidential Appointments," p. 6.

80. Macy interview.
81. White House press release, November 19, 1964.
82. "How LBJ Picks His Men," *Nation's Business*, 53 (July 1965): 37.
83. *Ibid.*, pp. 37, 78.
84. See Lyndon B. Johnson, *The Vantage Point* (Popular Library, 1971), p. 179.
85. Memorandum from Bob Faiss to Jim Jones, December 10, 1968 (LBJL). Kennedy, of course, had a much shorter term of office.
86. Eric Goldman, *The Tragedy of Lyndon Johnson* (Knopf, 1969), p. 370.
87. Macy interview.
88. Macy, *Public Service*, p. 227.
89. Quoted by David Halberstam, *The Best and the Brightest* (Fawcett Crest, 1969), p. 526.
90. Macy interview and Schott and Hamilton, "Politics of Presidential Appointments," p. 8.
91. Dom Bonafede, "Nixon's first-year appointments reveal pattern of his administration," *National Journal*, 2 (January 24, 1970): 189.
92. Laurin L. Henry, "Presidential Transitions: The 1968–1969 Experience in Perspective," *Public Administration Review*, 29 (1969): 474.
93. Bonafede, "Nixon's first-year appointments," p. 189.
94. *Ibid.* Also interview with Harry S. Flemming, Alexandria, Virginia, June 19, 1974 (hereafter cited as Flemming interview).
95. *New York Times*, November 23, 1968.
96. *New York Times*, December 14, 1968.
97. *New York Times*, January 5, 1969.
98. There was very little carryover of personnel material from the Johnson to the Nixon administration. John Macy gave Flemming duplicates of his job files and he turned over the entire computerized skill bank. Flemming found these to be of little use, however, and soon disregarded them. Flemming interview.
99. Richard M. Nixon, radio speech to the nation, September 19, 1968.
100. Flemming interview.
101. See U.S. House of Representatives, 94th Congress, 2d Session (1976), Committee on Post Office and Civil Service, Subcommittee on Manpower and Civil Service, *Final Report on Violations and Abuses of Merit Principles in Federal Employment* (Committee Print No. 94-28), especially pp. 139–170 (hereafter cited as "Violations and Abuses of Merit Principles").
102. "Management of Non-Career Personnel: Summary of Recommendations" (mimeograph, January 6, 1971), p. 15.
103. *Ibid.*, p. 10.
104. U.S. Senate, Committee on Government Operations, *The Regulatory Appointments Process* (note 48 above), p. 150.
105. Flemming interview. See also Rowland Evans, Jr., and Robert W. Novak, *Nixon in the White House* (Random House, 1971), p. 66.
106. Despite the problems created by Nixon's unplanned delegation of personnel responsibilities to department secretaries, Flemming had some sympathy for the concept of decentralization. He believed that

Cabinet members should be held responsible for the work of their departments and should thus have some freedom to choose the people who would manage that work. Flemming interview.

107. Quoted in John Pierson, "Nixon Talent Hunt: Off to a Good Finish," *The Wall Street Journal*, May 9, 1969.

108. "Management of Non-Career Personnel: Recommendations for Improvement," (mimeograph, December 18, 1970), p. 1. A shorter, revised summary of this report was submitted to the President in January 1971.

109. *Ibid.*, p. 5.

110. *Ibid.*, p. 7.

111. *Ibid.*

112. *Ibid.*, p. 12.

113. Dom Bonafede, "Nixon personnel staff works to restructure federal policies," *National Journal*, 3 (November 12, 1971): 2446.

114. *Ibid.*

115. "Management of Non-Career Personnel: Recommendations for Improvement," (mimeograph, December 18, 1970), pp. 30–31. In a letter to the author, October 23, 1978, Malek pointed out: "In reality the so called 'musts' did not have to be placed, but given every opportunity with consistent follow-up." He estimated that "we rated less than 1% in this category and placed about half of those."

116. "Violations and Abuses of Merit Principles," pp. 166–167.

117. "Federal Political Personnel Manual," original version (mimeograph, 1972), p. 6. This has been widely referred to as the "Malek Manual," though it was not written by Malek and he had no direct responsibility for its use or distribution. The genesis and employment of the manual are discussed in "Violations and Abuses of Merit Principles," pp. 158–170.

118. "Violations and Abuses of Merit Principles," p. 164.

119. Interview with Frederic V. Malek, Washington, D.C., June 19, 1974.

120. See, for example, "Impeachment Politics May Cost Nitze Pentagon Post," *New York Times*, March 22, 1974.

121. "Violations and Abuses of Merit Principles," p. 168. Also Dom Bonafede and Andrew J. Glass, "Haig revamping staff, shifts in patronage policy likely," *National Journal Reports*, 6 (April 6, 1974): 497.

122. "Management of Non-Career Personnel: Summary of Recommendations" (mimeograph, January 6, 1971), p. 1.

123. "Violations and Abuses of Merit Principles," p. 156.

124. Dan H. Fenn, Jr., "A View of the Practical Problems," *Public Administration Review*, 27 (1967): 382.

125. John Hersey, who spent a full week in 1975 observing President Ford, reported a number of meetings with Walker on personnel matters. See John Hersey, *The President* (Knopf, 1975).

126. Dom Bonafede, "Ford begins moves to reshape his administration," *National Journal*, 6 (December 14, 1974): 1879.

127. Richard L. Madden, "Ford Now Moves Slowly on Major Federal Jobs," *New York Times*, January 20, 1975.

128. "Ford Nominees: Tough Going in the Senate," *Congressional Quarter- ly Weekly Report*, 32 (December 7, 1974): 3254–3256.

129. Interview with Douglas P. Bennett, Washington, D.C., January 10, 1977 (hereafter cited as Bennett interview).

130. *Ibid.*

131. *Ibid.*

132. For a discussion of the problems recent presidential administrations have incurred in using personnel talent banks, see U.S. Senate, Com- mittee on Government Operations, *The Regulatory Appointments Process* (note 48 above), pp. 122–125.

133. Bennett interview.

134. *Ibid.*

135. Philip Shabecoff, "Ford Appointees Checked by Watergate Prose- cutor," *New York Times*, September 27, 1974.

136. Bennett interview.

137. Bonafede, "Ford begins moves" (note 126 above), p. 1879.

138. Bennett interview.

139. *Ibid.*

140. See Dom Bonafede, "Ford and His Staff are Singing the Appointments Blues," *National Journal*, 8 (April 17, 1976): 513.

141. Bennett interview.

142. This book was completed during the second year of the Carter admin- istration. Presidential administrations characteristically alter their selection procedures over time, and the Carter administration may ultimately do so as well. For that reason, the observations in this section should be deemed relevant only through the end of Carter's first year in office.

143. "Delay on Top Jobs: Good or Bad?", *Congressional Quarterly Weekly Report*, 35 (March 5, 1977): 398.

144. Jimmy Carter press conference, December 14, 1976.

145. Quoted in Neal R. Peirce, "Carter's Appointments: Holding Him to Promises," *Washington Post*, November 7, 1976.

146. Jimmy Carter press conference, November 15, 1976.

147. Jimmy Carter press conference, December 3, 1976.

148. Quoted in Dom Bonafede, "Cabinet Comment," *National Journal*, 8 (December 11, 1976): 1784.

149. See, for example, Rowland Evans and Robert Novak, "Vance's Men," *Washington Post*, January 7, 1977; Hedrick Smith, "Congress and Carter: An Uneasy Adjustment," *New York Times*, February 18, 1977; and Martin Tolchin, "Carter's Congress Lobbyist Battles Problems of Office," *New York Times*, February 25, 1977.

150. See "Interest Group Doubts Rise on Top Jobs," *Congressional Quar- terly Weekly Report*, 35 (April 30, 1977): 805–809.

151. Warren Weaver, Jr., "National Committee Scolds Carter for Bypassing State Party Chiefs," *New York Times*, April 2, 1977.

152. James T. Wooten, "Aides to Carter Prepare for Day He May Set Policy and Fill Posts," *New York Times*, October 12, 1976.

153. For a description of these clearances, see "Delay on Top Jobs" (note 143 above), p. 397.
154. Quoted in David S. Broder, "No 'New Generation of Leaders'," *Washington Post*, December 24, 1976.
155. See David E. Rosenbaum, "Public Controversy Helps Carter in Selecting Cabinet, Aide Says," *New York Times*, December 18, 1976.
156. The Talent Inventory Process is described in Joel Havemann, "The TIP Talent Hunt: Carter's Original Amateur Hour," *National Journal*, 9 (February 19, 1977): 268–273.
157. Jimmy Carter press conference, December 3, 1976.

3 Developments in the Selection Process: An Overview

Directions and Characteristics

Most presidential scholars regard the administration of Franklin Roosevelt as the turning point between the premodern and the modern presidency. In the years after 1933 the words "President" and "presidency" began to take on separate meanings. The presidency became a formal and increasingly structured set of offices and functions; the President the determiner of the purposes to which those offices and functions would be harnessed. Modern presidential leadership thus has two significant components: the institutional presidency and the personality of the President. Both have played a large part in the selection of presidential appointees in the years since World War II.

Woven through the postwar changes in the selection process are both themes and variations on themes. At a distance, the development of the personnel selection function in the White House seems almost unilinear. Up close, however, it is clear that the personal preferences and needs of each President are important in shaping the substantive, and in some cases even the technical, aspects of selection decisions.

As we have seen, several developments have contributed to the establishment of a modernized personnel operation in the White House. Most prominent among these is the creation and maintenance of a permanent personnel staff. While Truman and Eisenhower did assign personnel responsibilities to specific presidential aides, the Kennedy administration was the first clearly to distinguish this function by setting up a full-time staff to improve the manner in which selection decisions were made. No President after Kennedy sought, or even considered, a return to the days when selection decisions were made without the assistance of an organized personnel support operation. The development of such an operation was thus quickly and firmly institutionalized within the White House. It has become part of the formal machinery of presidential leadership.

It is important to put this in perspective. Institutionalization of presidential functions has become a common thread in the modernization of the presidency. The institutionalization of a White House personnel office is part of a pattern that includes such other developments as the central clearance of the President's legislative program and the formulation of an executive budget. These have all been attempts to match the President's capacity for leadership with his responsibility for leadership. They have been undertaken not only to strengthen the President's hand in dealing with the executive branch but also to enlarge his political advantages in dealing with the Congress and the host of other political actors involved in making and implementing public policy. As Stanley Kelley, Jr., has perceptively pointed out,

> A President can enhance his chances to control legislative output by centralizing the direction of trading operations carried on in his name. The fewer the number of voices speaking for him, and the less ad hoc trading operations are, the more likely it is that patronage will be spent in a manner that will maximize support for the presidential program as a whole and do so in accordance with the priorities the President has set for particular parts of it.[1]

While is is clear that every President since Kennedy has seen some value in maintaining a White House personnel office and in employing a reasonably consistent set of selection procedures, it should also be clear that each administration has had its own reasons for doing this. In fact, no two administrations in the period examined here have handled the personnel selection function in the same way or adapted it to the same purpose. There have been substantial variations in several of the chief characteristics of the selection process.

Administrations have varied, for instance, in the substantive objectives to which they have sought to harness their selection procedures. Substantive objectives, beyond the unanimously declared desire to find "the best person for the job," are largely a reflection of the predispositions and goals of each individual President. This is an important factor accounting for the differences among administrations in the backgrounds of the people each nominates to high office. John Kennedy put a premium on individuals with an action orientation, on people who fitted his own mold as part of "a new generation of leaders." Lyndon Johnson wanted his nominees to include a number of people with prior federal service, including those in career positions.

Richard Nixon became increasingly concerned about the unresponsiveness of the bureaucracy and wanted his nominees to be able to resist "capture" by the career civil servants and the clients of the agencies in which they served. Each President imposes his own set of criteria upon the selection process. That personnel staffs in each administration tend to find and recommend a preponderance of people who fit these criteria should not be surprising. It only reflects the degree to which the parameters of their search procedures are adjusted to indications of presidential preferences.

But Presidents also vary in the consistency of their preferences and in the clarity with which they communicate them to their personnel staffs and to their nominees. The primary source of variation here is in the personal role that each President plays in the selection decisions of his own administration. Some Presidents, like Lyndon Johnson, played a large and direct role in selection decisions. Others, like Richard Nixon, did not. It is, of course, hard to measure with any precision the impact of presidential involvement on the outcome of selection decisions. It does appear to be generally true, however, that close working relations and frequent communication between the President and the head of his personnel staff increase the likelihood that the attitudes and abilities of an administration's nominees will coincide with the preferences of its leader. The experience of the postwar Presidents can only lead one to conclude that a President who is concerned about the loyalty and professional competence of his nominees is well advised to take a personal and consistent part in their selection.

There is another dimension to the relationship between a President and his personnel staff, one that also varies from one administration to the next. That is the willingness of the President to use and protect his personnel office. Central coordination of the selection process has been a primary reason for the institutionalization of the personnel function in a separate White House office. But the temptations to circumvent the structured selection process are constant and often imposing. A President may be in a hurry to replace an important official and not want to submit to the routine delays that clearances require. Members of the White House staff sometimes have their own candidates for administration jobs, whom they recommend directly to the President without going through the personnel office. And, not uncommonly, intense political pressures may require the President to agree to nominate candidates proposed by congressmen or interest groups without first referring them to his personnel staff.

The frequency with which the personnel office is circumvented will depend almost entirely on the President's commitment to a consistent set of selection procedures. Where that commitment is high, as it was under Lyndon Johnson, there will be relatively few nominations that are not first subjected to comprehensive scrutiny by the personnel staff. Where that commitment is inconsistent, however, as it was under John Kennedy, selection decisions will sometimes be less carefully considered and candidates less carefully examined. The sensitive political antennae of the people around the President will soon determine the extent of his commitment to a structured selection process. His firm commitment will have a deterrent effect on their "end runs"; a weak commitment will invite them.

One other primary source of variation in the selection process is what might be called uncontrollable factors, or what Richard Fenno has referred to as "the conditions of the time."[2] No two Presidents face the same set of opportunities or constraints in selecting the personnel for their administration. Indeed, the opportunities and constraints will change, often dramatically, over the course of a single administration. An important variable in this regard is the manner in which a President comes to office. If his accession follows an electoral victory, particularly a substantial one and particularly if it means a change in the party controlling the White House, he has abundant advantages in staffing his administration. If, however, his accession follows the death or resignation of his predecessor, many of those advantages are absent.

Other external conditions also affect a President's selection decisions. The mood of the Congress is one of these. From the early 1970s on, the Congress took a much more interested and assertive attitude toward presidential appointments than it had in the preceding twenty-five years. Personnel staffs under Nixon, Ford, and Carter thus had to be much more conscious of congressional concerns in examining the qualifications of candidates for nomination than did their predecessors.

The conditions of the time also affect the salience of particular positions and thus the constellation of political forces that gather around individual selection decisions. The appointment of regulatory commissioners, for instance, rarely aroused much interest or controversy before 1970. But the growing political prominence of a number of self-declared public interest groups sharply increased the conflict engendered by these appointments in the decade that followed. Any number of things—a recent scandal, the special concerns of certain interest groups, contemporary policy controversies, etc.—can heighten the salience of a particular nomination. The likely effect when that happens is that the President's freedom of choice will be circumscribed.

All of these factors shape the pattern of selection decisions in each presidential administration. As a result, the selection process is still subject to considerable variation and still a long way from being systematic. The standardization and the technical improvements that characterize the postwar modernization of the selection process have occurred as a procedural overlay to its individualized substantive aspects, not as a substitute for them.

Explanations

In accounting for these recent changes in the way Presidents staff their administrations, it is useful to begin by noting that a system often acts like a system. A change in one of its parts usually leads to changes in others. But systematic change is rarely simple, since several essential elements must be present before it occurs. Incentive is one of these, opportunity another, a catalyst a third. Changes in presidential personnel selection resulted from the juxtaposition of all three of these elements in the period after World War II.

There were several incentives for the postwar developments in the selection process. One of these was an expansion in the number of important positions filled by presidential appointment. One residue of the New Deal and the war was a substantial broadening in the scope of the federal role in American society and a vast increase in the number of government agencies and officers required to carry out that role. It had also become the pattern during the New Deal and afterward to extend the requirement for presidential appointment down into an agency to include positions other than just the agency head. The result of this vertical and horizontal expansion in appointive positions was a strain on the capacity of any President to find and recruit nominees who were known quantities. Presidents after World War II consistently found that they had to reach out beyond their own acquaintances in finding competent people for major positions in their administrations. John Kennedy, for instance, was reported to have said after his election, "I thought I knew everybody and it turned out I only knew a few politicians."[3]

But the problem was more than simply quantitative; it was qualitative as well. Postwar Presidents found that they needed people who were not just generally competent, not just good politicians. They needed people who had specific kinds of professional background and technical training. Seasoned and respected generalists might be okay for Cabinet positions where responsibilities were broad and diffuse, but professional competence was a necessary qualification for many lower-level positions where responsibilities were often highly technical. It took more than a political hack to provide adequate service as Assistant Secretary of the Air Force for Research and Development, as an Atomic Energy Commissioner, or as head of the Antitrust Division in the Department of Justice. Presidents and their aides often did not know people with the right qualifications for these positions, and they found themselves in need of a support system to provide help in finding them.

The need to find more and better-qualified nominees was a strong incentive to improve the process by which administrations selected their personnel. Development of the selection process was helped along, however, by several other propitious conditions. One of the most important of these was the well-documented decline of American political parties.[4] For most of the life of this country, parties had been a prominent factor in selection decisions. They served as both a primary source of candidates for federal positions and as the largest and most compelling constraint on the President's latitude in choosing members of his own administration. Appointments (read: patronage) were widely regarded as a kind of political currency, useful for paying off debts and for purchasing support. "Parties," as George Washington Plunkitt was wont to say, "can't hold together if their workers don't get the offices when they win."[5]

In the late 1950s, however, political parties began to lose their grip on the electorate and on the avenues to political office. The number of presidential primaries increased; elections became more expensive; candidates were forced to raise their own funds; television replaced party organizations as the communications link between candidates and voters; and candidates ran their own campaigns or hired political consultants instead of relying on the expertise of party professionals. The shift to public financing of presidential elections in the mid-1970s further exacerbated this trend.

The result of all of this was a growing detachment of successful presidential candidates from the parties whose labels they bore. Newly elected Presidents came to office without much sense of indebtedness to their party and with no overwhelming concern for the state of the party's health during their administrations. The state and national party organizations continued to press their claims for the appointment of loyal party workers, as they always had. But after 1960 those claims were just one more competing presence in the political whirlpool surrounding the selection process. When parties lost their stranglehold on the gateways to the White House, they also lost their proprietary right to dominate selection decisions.

The resources available to postwar Presidents also enhanced their opportunities for improving the manner in which personnel decisions were handled. As White House staffs grew in size, greater specialization and division of labor were made possible. An effective personnel operation began to develop in the White House only after the President's staff grew large enough to permit the full-time deployment of several of its members to handle personnel responsibilities. The availability of computers further improved the capacity of the personnel staff for coping with large volumes of information. And new techniques of personnel recruitment and personnel administration were brought to the White House and adapted to its needs by people like Dan Fenn, John Macy, and Frederic Malek, all of whom had professional training and experience in the science of management. These resources and skills contributed abundantly to the search for new ways to deal with the changing character of the personnel selection process.

The catalyst in the development of the White House personnel function was Dan Fenn. Brought to the White House specifically to establish a system for better management of presidential personnel responsibilities, he oversaw the creation of the first full-time White House personnel staff and the first comprehensive and consistent set of selection procedures. Many of the innovations initiated by Fenn and his staff have persisted through several subsequent administrations: the use of a contact network, the maintenance of a talent bank, the creation of job profiles, the establishment of a recruitment capability, and the routinization of political and security clearances. Later administrations have occasionally modified these procedures to fit their own needs, but none have retreated in any significant way from the precedents established during the Kennedy administration. Fenn's imprint on the selection process was significant and lasting.

Impacts

Two fundamental objectives lie at the root of these developments in the personnel selection process. One has been the desire of the

White House to strengthen its capacity for personnel management; the other is the desire to strengthen its capacity for political leadership. The first involves the pre-eminent task of personnel administrators in any context: to fit the right individual to the job. The second involves the equally important task of Presidents in a political context: to accommodate personnel choices to prevailing political realities. A successful President can disregard neither.

Sound and thoughtful personnel management is essential to the achievement of a President's policy goals. Getting laws enacted is only one step in the policy-making process; implementation is quite another. If the people responsible for the implementation of laws are out of tune or out of touch with those who sponsor them, a high probability exists that the actual effect of the law will differ from the intended effect. The need for intelligent personnel management has become increasingly important to modern Presidents. They sit at the head of massive bureaucracies. Their claim on the loyalty of their "subordinates" is under constant challenge from congressional sub-committees, clientele groups, public employee unions, and professional organizations. Failure to pay scrupulous attention to the attitudes and abilities of the people nominated to lead the departments, agencies, and bureaus of the government is an invitation to future administrative frustrations.

Effective political leadership is equally essential to the achievement of presidential policy objectives. The policy-making process never ends. New problems constantly arise; new solutions must be found. To shape policy into forms they prefer, Presidents need help. They need the support of party leaders, committee chairman, and rank-and-file members of Congress. They need the support of large national interest groups. They need the support of the bureaucratic legions in the executive branch. And they need the support of the people. None of this is automatic; none of it can be had for free. Winning support for policy objectives usually requires the expenditure of some of the President's political capital. The President's formal control of the selection process is only one of his several forms of political capital, but an important one. Wisely spent, it can contribute significantly to the accomplishment of presidential policy goals.

Personnel management and political leadership are closely related concerns. But they are also competing concerns, and, in making personnel decisions, they must be balanced off against each other. Attention only to personnel management is bad politics; attention only to politics is bad management. Presidents rarely have the full freedom to make personnel decisions that are solely responsive either to their management needs or to their political interests. This is the most important complicating factor in the selection process.

The creation of the White House personnel staffs and the development of regular selection procedures should be viewed fundamentally as a response to this constant dilemma. Each administration, from Kennedy's through Carter's, has maintained a formal White House personnel apparatus to improve its capacity to strike the delicate balance between political and managerial concerns. Each has held to the view that the establishment of a central point of coordination in the selection process permits a President's management needs to be identified and addressed systematically. At the same time, it allows an administration to perceive broadly the full range of political pressures in the selection process, to set some priorities among them, and to deal directly with those that are most salient to the administration's objectives.

To say, however, that each administration has fully succeeded in this would be a misinterpretation of the evidence. Personnel structures and procedures are just one factor in the equation that leads to selection decisions. These changes in structure and procedure have had and will continue to have a number of potentially important effects on the way selection decisions are made and on the kind of presidential appointees they produce. Presidents, for instance, are now better able to search out and recruit talented individuals; they can more clearly identify the scope and nature of the political concerns that pervade the selection process; they are less likely to be embarrassed by the surprise disclosure of derogatory information about their nominees; they are able to be more consistent in the application of general and specific criteria to their selection decisions; and, most important, they have an improved capacity for knowing and assessing the people they nominate before they nominate them.

But these are all only potential improvements in the way selection decisions are made. The degree to which their potential benefits are reaped has depended and will continue to depend on the intelligence and determination with which these new personnel structures and selection procedures are employed. "Procedure," as Richard Neustadt has noted, "is no substitute for judgment."[6] The postwar developments in the selection process improve the opportunities available to presidential administrations to develop and carry out their own personnel policies, to relate selection decisions more closely to their perceived political and administrative needs. But the effective employment of these opportunities will vary with the skills of each administration and the nature of the political circumstances that prevail during its tenure.

Presidential control of the selection process, while potentially firmer now than it has ever been, is still far from absolute. The effect of the postwar developments on the ability of the White House to dominate selection decisions has been significant but not revolutionary. Presidential control of selection decisions will always be tenuous, just as presidential control of any set of political decisions is tenuous. As long as political actors think selection decisions are important, they will marshal their resources in order to influence them. And as long as Presidents need the support of these political actors, there will be times when they feel compelled to respond favorably to that influence. Great progress has been made toward more effective management of presidential personnel responsibilities, but total presidential control of the selection process is still a mirage.

Notes

1. Stanley Kelley, Jr., "Patronage and Presidential Legislative Leadership," in Aaron Wildavsky (ed.), *The President* (Little, Brown, 1969), p. 276.
2. Richard F. Fenno, Jr., *The President's Cabinet* (Vintage Books, 1958), p. 62.
3. Adam Yarmolinsky, quoted in Leslie H. Gelb, "Carter Finding Few Outsiders," *New York Times*, December 16, 1976.
4. On this, see Walter Dean Burnham, "The End of American Politics," *Trans-action*, December 1969, pp. 12 ff; David S. Broder, *The Party's Over* (Harper & Row, 1971); and Everett C. Ladd, Jr., and Charles D. Hadley, *Transformations of the American Party System* (W. W. Norton, 1975).
5. Quoted in "6500 Patronage Jobs Open to Nixon Administration," *Congressional Quarterly Weekly Report*, 27 (January 3, 1969): p. 15.
6. Quoted in Dom Bonafede, "The Collapse of Cabinet Government," *National Journal*, 10 (April 22, 1978): 641.

II

The Confirmation Process

4   Background

Like so many of the important decisions of the Constitutional Convention of 1787, the design of the appointment process was the result of a compromise. No consensus existed on the way federal offices ought to be filled, and little guidance was available from the variety of practices employed in the states and under the Articles of Confederation. For the Founding Fathers, the construction of the appointment process was an original enterprise.

Two competing views prevailed at the Constitutional Convention. One group of delegates wanted to give sole power to make appointments to the executive. Sharing Alexander Hamilton's view that "energy in the executive is the leading character in the definition of good government,"[1] they saw two principal advantages in the creation of an independent appointment power. First, because the executive alone would be held accountable for his appointments, there would be a high incentive for him to act responsibly in making them. Second, a single decision-maker was far less likely to become involved in the cabals and intractable bargaining that had been the practice in those states where the legislators played a dominant part in the appointment process. As James Wilson, a proponent of this view, noted at the Convention, "Experience shewed the impropriety of such appointments by numerous bodies. Intrigue, partiality, and concealment were the necessary consequences. A principal reason for unity in the Executive was the officers might be appointed by a single responsible person."[2]

But others disagreed. John Rutledge declared that he was "by no means disposed to grant so great a power to any single person. The people will think that we are leaning too much toward Monarchy."[3] Other delegates concurred. Better, they thought, to lodge the appointment power in a legislative body to prevent undesirable concentrations of power and to ensure broader consideration of possible candidates for office. Most attention focused on the Senate as the proper body to discharge this function. Luther Martin favored appointments by the Senate because "being from all states it would be best informed of characters and most capable of making a fit choice."[4]

Roger Sherman shared this view. The Senate, he said, "would be composed of men nearly equal to the Executive, and would of course have more wisdom. They would bring into their deliberations a more diffusive knowledge of characters. It would be less easy for candidates to intrigue with them, than with the Executive Magistrate."[5]

The Convention debated the question of appointments on a number of occasions between early June and mid-September. But consensus came slowly, only after many proposals had been defeated and discarded. As the Convention entered its final weeks, the Special Committee on Postponed Matters recommended this language:

> The President shall nominate, and by and with the advice and consent of the Senate, shall appoint Ambassadors, and other public Ministers, Judges of the Supreme Court, and all other officers of the U.S., whose appointments are not otherwise herein provided for.

A similar sharing of the appointment power between the President and the Senate had twice previously been considered and rejected, but on September 7 this version was adopted. In the following and final week of the Convention, provisions were added dealing with recess appointments and the appointment of inferior officers. With their strong differences thus compromised in vague language, the delegates approved Section 2 of Article II of the Constitution.

The most noteworthy characteristic of the appointment process shaped by the Founding Fathers is the legacy of ambiguity it left to subsequent generations of political practitioners. The prevailing view among the participants at the Convention was that the Senate's role in the appointment process would be largely reactive and, for the most part, passive. In a defense of this provision in the *Federalist Papers*, Hamilton wrote that

> ... every advantage to be expected from such an arrangement would in substance be derived from the power of nomination which is proposed to be conferred upon [the President]. In the act of nomination his judgment alone would be exercised; and as it would be his sole duty to point out the man, who with the approbation of the Senate would fill an office, his responsibility would be as complete as if he were to make the final appointment. There can in this view be no difference between nominating and appointing. The same motives which would influence a proper discharge of his duty in one case would exist in the other. And as no man could be appointed, but upon his previous nomination, every man who might be appointed would be in fact his choice.[6]

Hamilton (and most of his contemporaries) did not think it probable that the Senate would often object to the candidates proposed by the President. "It is not likely," he wrote, "that their sanction would often be refused, where there were not special and strong reasons for the refusal."[7]

The creation of Article II, Section 2 was only a starting point in the development of the appointment process. Little in the constitutional design or the Convention debates foresaw or suggested the direction that development would take. The delegates could not, or did not, envision the impact that political partisanship would have on the appointment process, nor could they imagine the scope to which that process would grow as the government expanded. Their compromise left many practical questions unanswered. And ultimately those answers would come only when the new government began to exercise the appointment powers that the Founding Fathers established.

Hamilton's expectations were quickly dashed by the first Senate, meeting in 1789. The nomination of Benjamin Fishbourn to be naval officer for the port of Savannah, Georgia was rejected for the simple reason that the two Senators from that state had their own candidate for the position, and it did not happen to be Fishbourn. It is unlikely that this is what Hamilton had in mind when he spoke of special and strong reasons for refusal. The precedent soon developed of senatorial dominance of appointment decisions for positions with jurisdiction wholly within one state.

Other important precedents were established in those first few years as well.[8] George Washington, for instance, decided not to present his nominations in person but to send them to the Senate in writing. All subsequent Presidents have done the same. The Senate initiated the practice, followed with only occasional exceptions since, of making the final determination on appointments by viva voce vote. All nominations were considered in executive session of the Senate until 1929, and only since that time has the tally of votes been made public.

From the very beginning, members of Congress sought to play a role in the nomination as well as the confirmation process. Often this was done informally, with members proposing candidates to the President. Occasionally, however, the more formal practice was followed of designating a committee to advise the President on a particular appointment. In 1794, for instance, a delegation representing members from both houses met with President Washington to recommend the appointment of Aaron Burr as Ambassador to France. Also, from the earliest days the Senate refused to limit its consideration of nominees only to simple questions of character and experience. Political and policy concerns became a prominent factor in appointment decisions during the first decade under the new Constitution and have remained so ever since. The nomination of John Rutledge as Chief Justice of the United States, for example, was rejected by the Senate in 1795 because of Rutledge's outspoken criticism of the Jay Treaty with England.

Characterizing the development of the appointment process over the years since 1789 is no simple matter. Development has not been unilinear; it has occurred in phases. Neither the President nor the Senate has been consistently dominant in determining the outcomes or in setting the standards for appointment decisions. All Presidents have had the bulk of their nominations confirmed, to be sure, but more than a few have found the Senate to be anything but an acquiescent partner in the appointment process. Abraham Lincoln, William McKinley, and John Kennedy, to name a few, had little difficulty in getting their nominees confirmed by the Senate. Others, however, were not so successful. James Madison found that even his freedom to nominate was often circumscribed by a determined clique of Senators. Ulysses S. Grant was in constant, and rarely successful, combat with the Senate over his appointments. Perhaps most unfortunate of all was John Tyler, whose nominees, including four to the Cabinet and four to the Supreme Court, were regularly rejected by the Senate. In fact, on a single day in 1843, Tyler's nomination of Caleb Cushing as Secretary of the Treasury was rejected three times.

The lesson of this historical experience is that any description of the relationship between the President and the Senate in the exercise of the appointment power must always be regarded as time-bound. Patterns of interaction or influence are rarely stable for long. Only the variables in this relationship are constant. The ambiguity of the constitutional language and the wide range of historical practice impose few limits on the behavior of modern participants in the appointment process. Essentially it is theirs to define as they wish, and as they can.

What is consistent throughout the history of the appointment process is the compelling impact of considerations peripheral to the character and credentials of specific nominees. On those occasions when Presidents have failed to have their nominees confirmed or have had to fight for those who were, opposition and contention were more often rooted in political or policy disagreements than in questions about the personal qualities of the candidates themselves. This has been a source of dismay to Presidents, to their supporters in Congress, to their nominees, and to most commentators on the appointment process. But, given the absence of a more constraining mandate from the Founding Fathers, it should come as no surprise that politics has been as pervasive an element in the confirmation of presidential appointments as it has in every other important aspect of the governing process in America.

For Senators and Senate committees, the confirmation process is both a responsibility and an opportunity. Confirmation activities compose a significant portion of the Senate's actual work load.[9] To handle its confirmation burden without crippling its capacity to cope with other demands, the Senate has routinized much of the process by which it considers the vast majority of the sixty thousand or seventy thousand nominations it receives from the President each year. To only a few hundred does it pay any substantial attention.

In reviewing these few hundred most important nominations, however, the Senate cuts a wide swath. Its investigations recognize few parameters. In the period after 1960, for instance, confirmation hearings (which are the centerpiece of the confirmation process) covered topics ranging across every conceivable aspect of government activity. The credentials and qualifications of individual nominees are usually a subject of inquiry during confirmation hearings, but they are rarely the sole topic—in many cases not even the most important. Senators use confirmation hearings to question and evaluate nominees, to be sure, but they also use the opportunities that confirmation hearings provide to carry out a full complement of other Senate functions: the representation of constituency and group interests, the creation and oversight of public policy, the protection of congressional prerogatives, and the search for essential information.

Hence the confirmation process involves more than the mere sharing of the appointment power. In a larger sense, it affords the Senate an opportunity to carry on in another context its persistent struggle with the executive branch to shape the contours of public policy. The confirmation process provides not only another forum for this struggle but other avenues of influence and other levels of control as well.

Notes

1. Jacob E. Cooke (ed.), *The Federalist* (Meridian Books, 1961), No. 70, p. 471.

2. Gaillard Hunt and James Scott Brown (eds.), *The Debates of the Federal Convention of 1787* (Oxford University Press, 1920), p. 56.
3. *Ibid.*, p. 57.
4. *Ibid.*, p. 275.
5. *Ibid.*, p. 276.
6. Cooke, *Federalist*, No. 76, p. 512.
7. *Ibid.*, p. 513.
8. The following three paragraphs draw heavily on the excellent history of the appointment process contained in Joseph P. Harris, *The Advice and Consent of the Senate* (University of California Press, 1953), chapters II–VI.
9. The Commission on the Operation of the Senate found, for instance, that 9 percent of all committee and subcommittee meetings in 1975 were for the purpose of considering nominations. On some committees, like Commerce and Armed Services, the percentage was in excess of 15 percent. See U.S. Senate, 94th Congress, 2d Session, Commission on the Operation of the Senate, *Legislative Activity Source Book*, pp. 14–15.

5   Senate Concerns: The Personal Qualities of Nominees

The most elementary of the purposes for which the confirmation process is used is that of examining and passing judgment on the character and competence of the President's nominees. Evaluating nominees is not, however, a simple matter. For one thing, most of the individuals nominated by the President are intelligent and accomplished members of the political, economic, or academic communities.[1] In recent times, at least, most nominees would satisfy even the most stringent minimum qualifications for public service. And yet the question that must be asked by the Senate is not whether these are "good" men or "good" women, but whether a particular individual possesses the necessary and appropriate qualifications to serve in a particular position. The question of "fitness" thus has both a general and a specific component. Nominees are expected to be persons of high integrity and proven ability, but they are also expected to have acquired the appropriate training, insight, and sensitivity for service in a specific government office.

The task of nominee evaluation is further complicated by the fact that there is not now, nor has there ever been, any universally accepted qualifying standard for public service, any consistent set of criteria for judging fitness. There are a few specific criteria that apply to particular positions, some statutory and some traditional. But the President is as aware of these as the members of the Senate and rarely fails to nominate someone who satisfies these well-recognized standards. The difficulty occurs in those hazy areas where the standards are not set in the concrete of tradition or law. When judgment must be passed on an individual's past performance, his personel and financial integrity, the level of his competence, and his political acumen, then Senators have to make decisions for which there are few exact precedents and even fewer useful guidelines.

There is, therefore, much inconsistency in the manner in which Senate committees evaluate the personal qualifications of the nominees who come before them. The level of concern with a particular nomination and the criteria by which it is judged are very often affected by the mood of the moment. A criterion stringently applied one year may be all but forgotten the next. For those who like consistency and tidiness in governmental processes, there is nothing quite so dismaying as this ad hoc quality of confirmation decisions. In spite of this persistent inconsistency, however, the task of evaluating nominees is marked by several recurring themes. Most of the expressed concerns about the personal qualifications of nominees fall into three broad areas: conflict of interest, character and integrity, and professional competence or experience.

Conflict of Interest

There are two types of conflict of interest with which the Senate concerns itself in passing judgment on presidential nominees. One is financial. The other, though frequently alluded to in confirmation proceedings, has no common name and will be referred to here as predispositional conflict of interest. In both cases the Senate must decide whether the nominee is capable of making governmental decisions objectively, whether he can submerge his personal interests and, in some cases, his personal beliefs in order to perform his assigned duties as far as possible in the national interest.

On the surface, at least, it would appear that financial conflict of interest would be the easier type to deal with, since it is the easier to detect. It is, after all, not very difficult to determine whether a nominee is likely to derive personal financial gains from his actions in the public service. It is clear enough that when an individual is employed by or holds stock in a corporation that is subject to the jurisdiction of an agency to which he is nominated, the potential for conflict of interest then exists. What is not so clear, however, and what makes this a far more difficult question for the Senate than it appears to be on the surface, is that cases of potential conflict of interest are rarely simple enough to be easily resolved.

With the scope of government involvement in the national economy having grown so broad in recent decades, there are few financial interests that do not fall within the jurisdiction of some government agency or, indeed, of a number of government agencies. And a great many of those who are prime candidates for government service are persons who are likely to have achieved a measure of financial success in their private careers and to have accumulated the positions and assets that come with success: stocks, bonds, property, corporate directorships, partnerships, and so forth. Indeed, the problem is usually made still more difficult by the fact that individuals who are prime candidates for appointments in a particular area of government activity are usually those most likely to have achieved their successes and acquired their financial interests in that area.

There are no simple solutions for the Senate in coping with the problem of financial conflict of interest. It would be irresponsible for the Senate to disregard the problem and leave it to some other agency or court to deal with post hoc when evidence of actual conflicts occurs. And it would be counterproductive to apply a standard of conflict of interest so rigorous that anyone would be forbidden from serving in any government post that exercised any authority whatsoever, directly or indirectly, over any area in which he had a personal financial interest. In evaluating nominees, therefore, the Senate must operate in the gray area between these two parameters, where the footing is uncertain.

There are, of course, some statutes that address the problem of financial conflict of interest and help to shape the way the Senate deals with it in confirmation proceedings.[2] But the existence of statutory guidelines does not resolve the Senate's dilemma. The problem comes in applying these statutes to individual cases, in making specific determinations on the basis of some rather general laws.

There is a further problem as well. The Senate has rarely been willing to limit its conflict of interest concerns solely to statutory requirements. Most Senators are politicians first and lawyers second. Their primary desire is to ensure the *appearance* of financial integrity, even if that necessitates making demands upon a nominee that surpass the requirements of the law. Hence the codified law is only a guideline in this process, or perhaps only a starting point. The Senate's decision to advise and consent must pay heed to the law, but it must also satisfy public appearances and the concerns of those parties who will be affected by an appointee's actions once he is confirmed. A full-scale study of the conflict of interest problem undertaken by a committee of the Association of the Bar of the City of New York emphasized the relatively minor importance of the statutes during Senate confirmation proceedings. "The statutes on conflict of interest have received little mention in confirmation hearings," the study committee reported. "The confirmation hearings repeatedly emphasized the significance of appearances and the need for maintaining public confidence."[3]

The process by which potential financial conflicts of interest are identified and resolved varies among Senate committees. There is no uniform set of criteria for determining the existence of such potential conflicts, nor is there any regular or required set of procedures for dealing with them.[4] Some committees require nominees to file a full financial disclosure statement, others do not. Some committees make these statements public, others do not. Some committees have established certain threshold criteria for determining the existence of a financial conflict of interest, but again others have not.[5]

Even where committees have attempted to routinize their procedures or to set some identifying standards, they often find it necessary to adapt those procedures and standards to the demands of particular positions or the financial status of particular nominees. Hence, when a genuine potential for financial conflict of interest exists, resolution nearly always results not from the straightforward application of some consistent decision rule but from a process of negotiation between the nominee and members of the committee. The consequence of this, not surprisingly, is a pattern of outcomes with little overall conformity.

In the confirmation process, most concern over financial conflict of interest focuses on stock holdings. Problems occur most frequently when a nominee has substantial holdings in a corporation whose financial condition may potentially be affected by the decisions he makes as a government official. Traditionally conflicts of this sort have been dealt with in two ways: by requiring the nominee to sell his stocks or by requiring him to put them in a "blind trust."[6] The clear preference of Senate committees is for divestiture, for a nominee to sell his stock and thus cut all ties between himself and the financial holdings that posed the conflict of interest.[7] When the president of General Motors was nominated to serve as Secretary of Defense in 1953, he was required by the Senate Armed Services Committee to sell all of his General Motors stock. The same demand was made in 1961 when the president of Ford Motor Company was nominated to the same position. By selling their stock as required, the nominees satisfied not only the law and appearances but also the Committee's rule that nominees to the Defense Department must divest themselves of any interests in corporations holding contracts with the Department totaling more than $10,000 in the last reporting period.

In 1969, however, when the nomination of David Packard to be Deputy Secretary of Defense was before the Committee, the problem of potential conflict of interest was not so easily or satisfactorily resolved. Packard was chief executive officer of the Hewlett-Packard Corporation, a large defense contractor, and owned Hewlett-Packard stock worth more than $300 million. Divestiture was not a reasonable option in this case. Packard's holdings represented about 30 percent of the outstanding stock of the corporation. Divestiture not only would impose a great financial loss on the nominee but would also significantly depress the market value of the stock and thus create a financial loss for all Hewlett-Packard stockholders. The committee deviated, therefore, from its normal requirements and agreed to allow Packard to put his holdings in a charitable trust for the period of his government service, provided that he refrain from participating in any Defense Department decisions that might in any way affect the Hewlett-Packard Corporation. The Commerce Committee, facing a similar problem with the 1965 nomination of John T. Connor as Secretary of Commerce, also permitted the nominee to establish a blind trust instead of requiring him to sell his substantial holdings of stock in the pharmaceutical company of which he was president.

Negotiations between nominees and Senate committees do not always succeed in finding a satisfactory resolution for touchy conflict of interest problems. Sometimes nominations are withdrawn when it becomes apparent that the potential source of conflict cannot be negotiated away. This was the case, for instance, with the sizable severance contract held by Andrew Gibson, President Ford's first nominee to head the Federal Energy Administration.[8] At other times, negotiations between the committee and the nominee simply break down when neither side is willing to budge from a position that is unacceptable to the other. In 1976, for example, J. Ralph Stone was nominated to head the Federal Home Loan Bank Board. Stone had personal holdings of $2.5 million in savings bank stock. Stone proposed that he be allowed to place his stock in the hands of independent trustees during his term of office, with any increase in its value going to charity. But members of the Senate Banking Committee, noting that the Federal Home Loan Bank Board regulates savings banks, did not find Stone's proposal satisfactory and demanded instead that he divest himself of his savings bank stock. Stone refused to do this, and the Committee took no further action on his nomination.

The inconsistency that characterizes the resolution of financial conflict of interest questions in the confirmation process has several sources. In large part, of course, it results from the enormous variety in the offices and agencies that make up the federal government and from the broad range of backgrounds of the people each administration recruits to fill them. The breadth of people and offices confounds the effort to apply consistent standards and procedures in guarding against financial conflicts of interest.

But there is another problem as well, and that is that Senators · have traditionally had contradictory attitudes about financial conflicts of interest. There is, of course, an overwhelming consensus that the Senate has a responsibility to examine the financial holdings of the President's nominees and to take whatever precautions are necessary to mitigate potential conflicts of interest. Few confirmation hearings are devoid of some concern with this issue.

But other feelings about financial conflict of interest also exist in the Senate. There is a firm strain of opinion, for instance, that the Senate should be careful about confirmation practices that will deter qualified individuals from accepting positions with the federal government. Senators are cognizant of the impact of establishing conflict of interest standards that are too stringent and of applying them too aggressively. Senator Norris Cotton once said that

> . . . we want people who are successful in private life.
>
> If they haven't been successful in private life, they aren't going to be very effective in public service and anyone who had been successful in private life is likely to have accumulated a little of this world's goods.[9]

Senator Jacob Javits expressed a similar view when he noted that he did not believe in "prying into the personal affairs of a nominee. We are glad to get good men. We do not want to make it so tough for them they will say they do not like the idea of serving in government."[10]

Another notion that appears often in Senators' statements at confirmation hearings is the reluctance many of them feel to impose a set of ethical standards on nominees that members of the Senate have traditionally been unwilling to impose on themselves—the problem of the dual standard. Senator Mark Hatfield made just this point at the confirmation hearing for a former oil company executive who had been nominated to serve in the Federal Energy Administration:

> [W]hat troubles me most of all is that conflict of interest seems to exist only in the executive branch of government. We sit here as judges on whether or not an individual whose name has been submitted to us for confirmation by his background represents any possible conflict of interest that would disqualify him from representing the best of the public interest.

> I have used the example many times before, and I shall use it again, that one of the Members of our own body, owning 90 percent of an oil company stock and president of the oil company, serving as U.S. Senator helped lobby through the extension of the oil depletion allowance, as a Member of the United States Senate, and there was no particular conflict of interest.
>
> . . . I think if we are going to get hyper-pious about the possibility of conflict of interest in the administration of public policy, we had better be just as concerned about the possibility of conflict of interest in the enactment of public policy through the legislative process.[11]

These three objectives—to prevent conflicts of interest, to avoid the creation of disincentives to public service, and to minimize hypocrisy—weave persistently through Senate confirmation proceedings. The latter two concerns have a tempering effect on the first. And guided as it is by several competing objectives, the Senate finds it difficult to define and adhere to any single comprehensive decision rule. Instead, it has generally assumed the role of "adjuster" in these confirmation controversies over financial conflict of interest. Its committees have tended to deal with individual cases on an ad hoc basis and to search for resolutions that satisfy legal requirements and public appearances without raising barriers to the recruitment of successful individuals into government service.

Variety continues to exist in the way the Senate treats the problem of financial conflict of interest, because each of its committees has different responsibilities, different memberships, and different perspectives. Potential conflicts of interest take a multiplicity of forms, and the ethical environment in which they must be considered is anything but static. Hence Senate committees have continually placed a higher value on flexibility in making confirmation decisions than on consistency in their outcomes. They have shown little disposition to surrender their discretion to a rule book.

Of the two forms of conflict of interest mentioned earlier, financial conflicts are the less troublesome for the Senate. Presidents are as anxious to avoid the appearance of financial conflict of interest as Senate committees and thus rarely nominate individuals whose potential conflicts cannot be satisfactorily resolved. As a result, there have been few sizable controversies over financial conflict of interest in the confirmation process in the years since World War II.

The same cannot be said for predispositional conflicts of interest, which appear far more frequently and pose much more difficult problems. Since the sources of predispositional conflict of interest are numerous, there are few nominees who are totally immune to it. The possibility that an appointee's government decisions will be colored by his preappointment experiences is usually high. Over the course of their lives, all nominees have established certain associations and developed certain biases. They often do not have totally open minds when they take on a new government position, nor are they without some preformed opinions. Whatever its source—geographical, philosophical, occupational, or political—the potential for predispositional conflict of interest is inherent in the way individuals are recruited to serve in major federal positions.

Predispositional conflicts are not specifically financial, although indirect financial considerations may be involved. The problem is not that appointees may be inclined to make governmental decisions that have a salutary effect on their net worth. Instead, the problem is that appointees may be unable, because of their personal preferences and prejudices, to make objective or impartial decisions. It is not a financial conflict, but one of attitudes or emotions. It is not the national treasury that is imperiled, but the national interest. Senator Hubert Humphrey seemed to capture the difference between financial and predispositional conflicts of interest in a statement he made at a confirmation hearing in 1971:

> [W]hat I am worried about is your economic philosophy. I believe that you can put all your bonds and stocks—and I don't hold that against you—I mean that is to your credit that you have been able to do well, or reasonably well. I think that you earned everything that you have. You can put all that in escrow, but I don't think you can put your philosophy in escrow.[12]

Predispositional conflicts of interest appear in a variety of shapes and forms. The most common, however, are those that occur when a nominee (1) has spent the bulk of his working life in an industry that falls within the jurisdiction of the agency to which he has been nominated; (2) has publicly expressed or advocated specific positions on issues that will fall within his area of governmental responsibility; (3) has been required, during his previous government experience, to work for the special interests of a particular city, state, or public agency; (4) has spent his whole life in one geographical region of the country; or (5) has consistently supported and vigorously worked for a major political party.

A potential predispositional conflict of interest occurs when an individual who has been identified with one set of interests is nominated to a position that has responsibility for government actions that affect those interests. The question the Senate must ask is whether the biases that such a person brings to government service are of sufficient consequence to prevent him from acting impartially or, more important, whether those biases create an appearance of conflict of interest that cannot be removed.

On few aspects of its confirmation practices has the Senate been more criticized than on the way it copes—or, in the view of its critics, fails to cope—with predispositional conflicts of interest. It is a problem that will not go away, and it is a problem that lends itself to no simple solutions. The Senate has been unable to find mechanical or procedural ways to identify significant predispositional conflicts, and it has found no panaceas for eliminating them or curbing their impacts. It has been even less consistent in dealing with predispositional than with financial conflicts of interests. But, of course, the problems are much greater.

From World War II through 1970, with a few exceptions, the Senate had a high tolerance for predispositional conflicts of interest. Its members rarely opposed nominees whose backgrounds raised the specter of predispositional conflict of interest; even more rarely did it defeat their nominations. As long as a nominee had the full support of the President and met minimal standards of competence and integrity, significant Senate opposition was not likely.

In the early 1970s, however, the Senate began to intensify its scrutiny of presidential nominations. The reasons for this will be examined later, but one of the areas in which Senate sensitivity was particularly heightened was the question of predispositional conflicts of interest. The Senate began to inquire into the scope and strength of nominees' predispositions and to formulate some operational procedures for handling this sort of conflict of interest. It began to act assertively to minimize both the extent and the appearance of predispositional conflicts.

Its effects have taken three forms primarily. Recognizing that it is both impractical and unwise to reject every nominee whose experience poses a potential conflict, the Senate's first response has been to use the confirmation process to sensitize nominees to the problem, to make them cognizant of the aspects of their own backgrounds that may well conflict with their government responsibilities, to emphasize the importance of objectivity, and, in some cases, to ask nominees to state their commitment to impartiality for the public record. For instance:

Senator Jackson: Under present law, as Secretary of the Interior you would be in a position to make administrative decisions. . . . The American people, of course, have a right to expect your decisions as Secretary to reflect your best judgment of the interests of the Nation as a whole in these matters.

. . . Do you believe that you will be able to take an unbiased view of your duties as Secretary even when Alaska interests are involved? Governor Hickel: Thank you, Senator Jackson. I believe sincerely that interests that Alaska might be involved in, whatever they may be, as Secretary of the Interior I will take the broad national interest. . . . I see no conflict in my mind and philosophy and I would without a doubt, Mr. Chairman, take the broad national interest.[13]

Senator Javits: So you are ready to assure us then that both intellectually and administratively those with whom you may disagree intellectually will get a fair break and that you feel in conscience and as an educator fully capable to undertake that degree of objectivity in asking for our confirmation?
Mr. Berman: I certainly hope so, Senator.
Senator Javits: Not you hope so, but you do.
Mr. Berman: Yes.
Senator Javits: You are a man of conscience and your answer is very important to me.
Mr. Berman: It is an emphatic "Yes, sir."[14]

A second way in which the Senate has sought to reduce the incidence of predispositional conflicts of interest is by imploring the White House to be sensitive to the problem in making personnel selections. In part, this has been done through direct communications between Senate committees and the President or his personnel staff. The Chairman of the Senate Commerce Committee, for instance, wrote a letter to President Ford shortly after his assumption of office, seeking to continue the practice whereby the

. . . White House personnel office [has] worked with us, mindful of our responsibility to consider the qualifications of such appointments, in seeking nominees who bring to these roles a record of public service which gives evidence of independence of mind from industries to be regulated, a demonstrated commitment to pursuit of the public interest, unquestioned integrity, and the highest levels of demonstrated competence.[15]

In a political environment, communication need not always be direct or explicit. And the Senate has been able to communicate its attitudes about predispositional conflict of interest by the actions it has taken (and not taken) in the confirmation process. By the intensity of its scrutiny and by its reluctance to approve nominations when serious conflict of interest questions had been raised, the Senate made it clear to the White House after 1970 that its standards were changing and its tolerance narrowing.

The third and most dramatic of the Senate responses has been a greater willingness to defeat nominations where the potential for conflict of interest was particularly ominous, or at least particularly visible. In 1973 the Senate rejected the nomination of Robert E. Morris for a seat on the Federal Power Commission. It was the first time a regulatory appointment had been rejected in twenty-three years, and it indicated the seriousness of the Senate's new commitment to address the problem of predispositional conflict of interest. Senator Philip Hart, a leading opponent of the Morris nomination, spoke of the attitudes that led to its rejection:

> Surely we have learned that one item that government, public business, is short on is credibility. I am suggesting that the nominee could be the wisest, most resourceful public utility lawyer in America. And when he goes on the Power Commission he might be the most objective and discerning pro-public voice. But that Commission is going to have to come up with decisions that will displease enormous segments of the community in this country, and we hope that the public will believe that such decisions are compelled because of overriding public necessity. We are going to have an extremely tough job selling it if the voice we put on now has been the voice of Standard of California for the last 10 or 15 years.[16]

In the years subsequent to 1973, the Senate rejected or forced the withdrawal of a number of appointments for reasons similar to those underlying its action in the Morris case.

Senators often discuss predispositional conflict of interest in terms of what they call "the problem of balance." Most Senators recognize the need to be realistic about predispositional conflicts and to accept the fact that the federal government's need for expertise and relevant experience sometimes requires that federal officers be recruited from the interests and corporations they will have to oversee. The prevailing view in the Senate has been that this practice is acceptable as long as no single agency is dominated by appointees of the same political or philosophical stripe. The important objective, in this view, is to ensure a wide representation of backgrounds and predispositions at the top levels of government agencies, to balance one interest against another: producer with consumer, regional with national, liberal with conservative, general with particular. The goal, as one Senator pointed out, is "to maintain a balance where the public interest comes out in the end and not put a lot of rabbits in the cabbage patch or foxes in the chicken house."[17]

From the Senate's point of view, this strategy of balance has several advantages. It permits the government to recruit talented people from a wide range of sources without applying overly stringent predispositional conflict of interest criteria. It relieves the Senate of the distasteful responsibility of rejecting the nominations of highly competent people because their backgrounds pose such a conflict. And it both permits and encourages a degree of functional representation in government agencies. In general, therefore, the Senate has found it preferable to deal with the problem of predispositional conflict of interest in the aggregate rather than case by case.

The Senate has not been consistent, however, in its treatment of predispositional conflicts of interest. The same year it rejected the nomination of Robert Morris to the Federal Power Commission, it confirmed the nomination of William Springer, who had been a consistent supporter of the interests of the power industry while serving as a member of the House. It rejected the nomination of Joseph Coors to the Board of Directors of the Corporation for Public Broadcasting because of his personal interest in a corporation that produced television news stories, yet it confirmed to the board a number of others who also had direct interests in the broadcasting industry. Other examples abound, but the point is that there are no firm standards by which the Senate governs its treatment of predispositional conflicts of interest. They appear in different guises, and it treats them in different ways.

The Congress and the President explored some mechanical ways of dealing with the predispositional conflict of interest problem in the 1970s, but with no significant success. The Senate did begin to demand that nominees sever all formal connections with the industries or associations from which they were recruited. And both branches, with varying degrees of effectiveness, have attempted to get nominees to promise not to take a job immediately after leaving the government with any organization over which they had jurisdiction.[18] But even when nominees do sever their formal ties, and even when they agree not to go to work for an industry they have regulated, no guarantee exists that predispositional conflict of interest has been eliminated. The problem remains one of attitudes, not formal associations, and there is simply no fully effective way to force nominees to leave their old attitudes on the doorstep when they enter government service.

Predispositional conflicts of interest are a natural, if undesirable, facet of the American administrative system. Despite their recurrence, however, few have suggested that we remove them by creating a career ministry or by applying rigid and narrow standards of conflict of interest. Instead our choice has always been to maintain the "inner and outer" system for its positive aspects and to trust our political institutions to perform the maintenance necessary to keep that system in working order.

There are no real mechanical solutions to this problem, short of an outright ban on the appointment of people with previous experience or a previous public record in the field in which they would serve. But that medicine is too strong for the malady. Protection of the national interest from predispositional conflicts of interest must thus rely in large part on the vigilance exercised by the White House and the Senate in the appointment process. But this is imperfect protection, for these are political institutions. They are subject to the waxing and waning of political forces. They make political judgments. And, as a result, the conflict of interest problems remain with us, the relentless legacy of the political process by which we choose our administrative and judicial officers.

Character and Integrity

In its evaluations of the personal qualifications of nominees, Senate decisions are governed by several broad sets of expectations. The first, as already indicated, is that nominees will be relatively free of financial or predispositional conflicts of interest. The second is that they will satisfy certain implicit standards of character and integrity. In determining whether nominees measure up to the latter expectation, Senate inquiries tend to focus on two questions: Is the nominee a person of apparent good character? Is there anything in his public or private record that raises questions about his integrity?

The Senate spends very little time examining the character and integrity of presidential nominees. But this should not be taken to mean that it doesn't care about them. In fact, whenever legitimate questions are raised about a nominee's character and integrity, they are scrupulously investigated. But such questions are seldom raised. And the reason for that is quite straightforward. Because the character of nominees is an important criterion in the confirmation process, it is an important criterion in the selection process as well. Presidents and their personnel staffs are aware of Senate expectations in this regard, and they do everything possible to ensure that their nominees satisfy those expectations. The multitude of checks and clearances that compose the selection process are most effective at weeding out potential nominees with flawed characters. Thus the Senate rarely has to decide whether to confirm nominees whose personal integrity is questionable, because the President rarely nominates such people.

Only occasionally, therefore, is any significant amount of time devoted to these concerns at confirmation hearings. Usually this happens when information is brought to the attention of a Senate committee requiring that committee to raise questions about a nominee's integrity. This is a discomforting responsibility for Senators who are generally reluctant to spotlight these usually trivial or groundless bits of information. And it is embarrassing for nominees who may legitimately feel that such information has no bearing whatsoever on their fitness to serve in the position for which they have been nominated. Elliot L. Richardson, for instance, who has been nominated to serve in many high-level positions, has had to answer questions on several occasions about the poor driving record he compiled as a young man.[19] He has on each occasion fully and openly explained his record and responded to all questions concerning it. The committees holding hearings on his nomination have never thought this a matter of great importance in determining whether ot not to confirm him. And yet its constant reintroduction into public view is a recurring personal embarrassment from which Richardson has been unable to escape.

While Senators are generally reluctant to bring up questions of individual character and integrity, they do not hesitate to do so when such matters are already part of the public record or when they generally reflect upon the nominee's fitness to serve. When Romana Acosta Banuelos was nominated by President Nixon to be Treasurer of the United States in 1971, her confirmation hearings became little more than an investigation of charges that as president of a food company in California she had employed illegal aliens. The main question was not her competence to perform the largely honorific duties of the Treasurer, but rather whether her record as an employer was sufficiently unethical to disqualify her from public service of any kind. Press investigations of this issue became, in effect, a demand upon the Finance Committee to examine Banuelos's business background thoroughly.

A similar process evolved during the confirmation hearings on the nominations of William J. Casey to be chairman of the SEC in 1971 and of Robert F. Collins to be a federal district court judge in 1978. In both cases, information produced by sources outside the government reflected on the ethical standards of the nominee. Casey was accused of being involved in the sale of a fraudulent manuscript for a book and of signing a newspaper advertisement that provided misleading information during the debate on the antiballistic missile system. Collins was charged with improper conduct while serving as a New Orleans magistrate. In both cases the committees held lengthy hearings over several days to investigate the charges, to get them on the public record, and to allow the nominees to respond directly. The outcome in these two cases, as in the Banuelos case, was that the committees were satisfied that the air had been cleared and that the past behavior in question was not important enough to require that confirmation be withheld. All three nominations were eventually confirmed.[20]

The standards of character and integrity set by the Senate are high, but they are not so unreachably high that any indiscretion is a cause for disqualification. The Senate has tended not to deal in absolute standards, but rather to investigate nominees carefully when there is pressure to do so, to weigh the nature of their alleged indiscretions, and—in the absence of flagrant or illegal misbehavior—to give the nominee the benefit of the doubt. The important point here, however, is that Senate committees seldom have to get into the matter of individual integrity at all. After preliminary screening, political clearance, and an FBI investigation, there is little likelihood that individuals with serious character deficiencies will ever have their names submitted to the Senate as presidential nominees. The cases mentioned here are illustrative, but they are also isolated. This is simply not a matter that looms large in the confirmation process.

There is one issue that, though not conventionally regarded as a question of personal integrity, is examined under that rubric in the confirmation process. That is the matter of racial bias. Racial bias is not viewed merely as a predispositional conflict of interest. Nor is its apparent existence weighted differently in confirmation decisions for different positions. Without exception, Senate committees treat evidence of racial prejudice in a nominee as a serious and troublesome reflection on the nominee's character and on his fitness for public service.

Senate committees, however, do not lightly make or accept accusations that nominees are racially biased. Indeed, they have a history of demanding a high level of proof that such charges are not spurious. The notion that a man or woman is a racist is subjective at best. Agreement on what constitutes racist behavior or what constitutes sufficient evidence of racial prejudice is rare, particularly in a body as diverse as the United States Senate. Hence, when such an accusation is made, the relevant committees normally undertake extensive investigations before giving it credence. When, for instance, the nomination of William L. Martin to be U.S. Marshal for the Middle District of Georgia was before the Senate Judiciary Committee in 1969, the accusation was made that the nominee was a confirmed segregationist. The chief counsel of the committee was dispatched to Georgia to investigate the charges thoroughly. Upon returning he told the committee that he could find little substantiation, and the nomination was subsequently approved. What is perhaps most noteworthy in this is the willingness of the Judiciary Committee to hold public hearing and to carry out so extensive an investigation on a nomination to so minor a position.

A nominee's views on racial matters are always regarded as appropriate subjects for examination in confirmation hearings and for discussion in confirmation debates on the Senate floor. But few nominations are ever defeated or even seriously endangered by charges of racial prejudice or insensitivity. There were two cases in the early 1970s in which accusations of racial bias were a significant factor in confirmation decisions. One involved the nomination of G. Harrold Carswell to be an Associate Justice of the Supreme Court, the other the nomination of Ben B. Blackburn to be Chairman of the Federal Home Loan Bank Board. Both nominations were rejected, but each was also encumbered by other serious problems. There is little reason to believe that either would have been rejected had the nominee's views on racial issues been the only source of contention.

There are several reasons why the Senate rarely makes a collective confirmation decision on the sole basis of charges of racial bias. For one thing, these charges are exceedingly hard to substantiate. Out-and-out racists simply do not get through the presidential screening process. When the Senate has to deal with this matter, the evidence of racial discrimination is usually peripheral or flimsy. Even when the evidence is more substantial—and it rarely is—there is no clear collective sense in the Senate of what in fact constitutes racial bias. Senators, like nominees, represent a broad variety of cultural backgrounds. Their views on racial questions reflect this breadth and hence eliminate the possibility that any single standard will be applied in all cases.

Competence

In assessing the personal qualifications of nominees, the Senate normally pays more attention to questions of competence than to questions of character. As in most of the matters the Senate considers in carrying out its confirmation responsibilities, there are few specific or consistent criteria that apply here. Nominees come from a wide variety of backgrounds, and Senators are not especially well equipped to evaluate the meaning of a nominee's employment history. They lack the resources or inclination to undertake extensive reference checks on each nomination they consider, and they find it unendingly difficult in any case to evaluate the relationship between private sector experience and public sector responsibilities. While the belief is widespread that competent executives in the private sector are likely to be competent executives in the public sector, the correlation is not perfect. There are substantial differences in the requirements for success in the private and public sectors. An individual's performance in the former, even when it can be properly evaluated, is not necessarily a true indicator of his likely performance in the latter. Frederick Malek once noted, for instance:

> It is obvious that success in the private sector is not automatically transferable to the public sector. In fact, to succeed in government the businessman must develop some qualities that are almost the opposite of those he needed to succeed in business. Where he was persistent, he must now also be resilient; where he was guarded, he must be open; where he was arbitrary, he must be sensitive; where he viewed problems with a narrow focus, he must deal comprehensively with them; and where he was informed, he must be at least a little intuitive.[21]

Not knowing quite how to evaluate or interpret experience in the private sector, Senate committees usually treat the matter rather perfunctorily. Questions such as "What are your qualifications for this position?" or "Do you think you are qualified to handle this job?" are commonly asked at confirmation hearings but rarely pursued. Once in a while, a nominee's competence is seriously questioned. In 1977, for example, the nomination of Kent F. Hansen to the Nuclear Regulatory Commission was rejected by the Senate Environment and Public Works Committee, in part because of the committee's reservations about Hansen's lack of experience in dealing with the kinds of questions that came before the commission. But normally, as long as a nominee from the private sector satisfies the statutory and technical qualifications for a position, and as long as no significant criticism of his past performance is raised by witnesses or private sources, Senate committees spend little time inquiring into his background.

Not all nominees come from the private sector, however. Many have previous government experience. When that is the case, Senate committees are often a good deal more inquisitive. Senators generally feel more confident in their ability to evaluate a nominee's government service and tend to believe that it is a useful indicator of his likely future performance. As one Senator once noted in a confirmation hearing, "When an appointee has served in the government and has made a record for himself in the government, I think this is an important criterion to be considered."[22]

In nearly every case in which the President nominates an individual with previous experience in the federal government, the nomination itself is an indication of the President's satisfaction with the nominee's demonstrated ability.[23] Since the President has probably cleared any such nomination with important Senators prior to announcing it, the Senate is not likely to disagree with the President's assessment. It is not uncommon for such a nominee to skate through his confirmation hearing with few questions and much praise.

On occasion, however, a President may reappoint or promote an individual whose performance record is not viewed as sanguinely by all members of the Senate as by the President. Sometimes Presidents make such a nomination because of pressure from important political supporters. Sometimes they are simply unaware of any measurable level of dissatisfaction with the nominee. And sometimes Presidents will make nominations they know will be controversial because they honestly believe one candidate is far better equipped than any others to carry out presidential wishes.

In 1975 the Senate Commerce Committee rejected the nomination of Isabel A. Burgess for reappointment to a seat on the National Transportation Safety Board. Its investigations indicated that during her first term Burgess has been absent from 27.5 percent of the board's meetings, had incurred travel expenses more than twice as large as the average board member, had accepted free travel and lodging from corporations subject to the board's jurisdiction, and had even purchased stock in one of those corporations. Her reappointment was not endorsed by any of the incumbent members of the board. In the view of the majority of the committee, the record of her first term did not justify confirmation for another.

In 1966, President Johnson nominated Rutherford M. Poats as Deputy Director of the Agency for International Development. A number of Senators—Senator Bayh in particular—used this opportunity to criticize the American AID program in Southeast Asia and to blame the nominee for his role as Far East Regional Director of AID:

> Senator Bayh. The Senate . . . is being asked to approve this appointment on the basis of the nominee's past experience.
>
> Mr. Chairman, it is precisely on this point, namely the nominee's past performance, that my objection and opposition to this appointment are based. . . .
>
> If our aid program to Vietnam has been badly run—and I believe the evidence bears this out beyond reasonable doubt—then the man in charge of administering that program must assume the burden of the responsibility.[24]

Bayh and those who shared his point of view were able to block the Poats nomination in the 89th Congress, but President Johnson resubmitted it in the 90th, and, after a motion to recommit was defeated 42–43, the Senate confirmed Poats on a vote of 61–24. The opposition to this nomination is illustrative of the occasional willingness of members of the Senate to challenge a nominee because of his involvement in the administration of an unsatisfactory program. But the failure of the opposition movement in this case is illustrative as well of the difficulties inherent in trying to fix responsibility on a single administrator for the inadequacies of an entire program.

The Senate will frequently use confirmation hearings to explore the past administrative activities of a nominee. It will often, in fact, take this opportunity to castigate a nominee for those activities and to advise him sternly to avoid repeating them in the future. But it will seldom go so far as to disapprove a nominee for diligently executing the instructions of his superiors, however much it may disagree with those instructions. One of the rare exceptions was the unwillingness of the Foreign Relations Committee to approve the nomination of C.

McMurtrie Godley as Assistant Secretary of State for East Asian and Pacific Affairs in 1973. Godley had been Ambassador to Laos for the previous four years and had been, in the committee's view, an enthusiastic activist in support of U.S. policies in Vietnam. The committee felt that his intimate association with those policies would make it impossible for him to act objectively in making future decisions in this area. Hence it voted 9–7 to kill the nomination.

These cases are exceptions to the pattern normally followed by the Senate in evaluating the personal qualifications of nominees. Most nominees do not have a prior record of service in a federal position the same as or similar to the one to which they have been nominated. And most do not have such lively skeletons in their closets.

On the question of the experience and preparation that it expects of presidential nominees, the Senate is curiously of two minds. It has never arrived at any collective stand on whether it regards extensive and directly relevant experience as essential for confirmation or not. The record of Senate confirmation proceedings is speckled with hearings in which some Senators criticize a nominee for his lack of relevant experience while others praise the nomination for precisely the same reason. A number of confirmation hearings in the mid-1970s were the forum for just this kind of debate.[25] The shape of the conflict in viewpoints is illustrated by the controversy over the nomination of Carla Hills for Secretary of Housing and Urban Development in the Ford administration.

At the time of her nomination, Carla Hills was serving as head of the Criminal Division in the Department of Justice. She had compiled a distinguished record as a lawyer in both private practice and government service, but she had no substantial experience in the field of housing or urban affairs. When her nomination came before the Senate Banking, Housing, and Urban Affairs Committee it was criticized by the chairman:

> At a time when housing starts in the country have dropped below 900,000 and when the administration has frozen virtually all assisted housing starts, this is no time for on-the-job training for a new secretary of H.U.D.
>
> We have just been through a two-year disaster period because Mr. [James T.] Lynn, like Mrs. Hills, is an able and intelligent lawyer who had no background or qualifications for the job. The result: No housing.[26]

But the chairman's view did not prevail. Other committee members regarded Mrs. Hills's lack of experience as an affirmative qualification, one that would free her of any ties to the mistakes of the past. Senator John Tower said, "It'll be good to have some fresh thinking in HUD." And Senator Alan Cranston said, "I question whether there are any such experts. No previous secretary of HUD has brought to the job your qualifications. In fact, I think the major qualification of Mrs. Hills is that she is not a housing 'expert'."[27]

Expressions of concern over the absence of substantial or relevant professional qualifications are a recurring feature of the confirmation process. Such expressions, however, are often politically motivated. As a general rule, a Senator is not very likely to show much concern about the professional qualifications of a nominee if that individual is nominated by a President of the Senator's party, if he is on the same philosophical wave length as the Senator, or if he is from the Senator's home state. Few Senators, as a result, are very consistent in either the strength or the direction of their attitudes about this particular criterion.[28]

Indeed, this same point applies in substantial measure to each of the criteria by which Senate committees evaluate the character and qualifications of individual nominees. The Senate views the issues of conflict of interest, personal integrity, and professional qualifications through a political lens. Wherever there is an absence of legal or objective criteria—and, as we have seen, that is almost everywhere—the Senate has considerable latitude to expand or narrow its parameters of acceptability. And it does so constantly, fitting its expectations and requirements to the changing political climate and to the shifting alignment of participants in the confirmation process.

Notes

1. See David T. Stanley, *Men Who Govern: A Biographical Profile of Federal Political Executives* (Brookings, 1967).
2. There is a substantial discussion of these statutes in Bayless Manning, *Federal Conflict of Interest Law* (Harvard University Press, 1964).
3. Association of the Bar of the City of New York, *Conflict of Interest and Federal Service* (Harvard University Press, 1960), p. 116.
4. The following paragraphs were written early in 1978, at a time when a bill was pending before the Senate (S. Res. 258) that would establish an Office of Nominations to centralize and standardize Senate investigations of nominations.
5. For a description of the procedures employed by individual committees, see Common Cause, *The Senate Rubberstamp Machine* (Common Cause, 1977); Judith H. Parris, "Nominations and the Senate Commit-

tee System," in U.S. Senate, 95th Congress, 1st Session, Temporary
Select Committee to Study the Senate Committee System, *Appendix to
the Second Report with Recommendations* and G. Calvin Mackenzie,
"Senate Confirmation Procedures,"in U.S. Senate, 94th Congress, 2d
Session, Commission on the Operation of the Senate, *Committees and
Senate Procedures.*

6. A "blind trust" generally involves the following conditions: (1) It is ir-
revocable for the period of the nominee's government service. (2) The
trustee has total control over the investment and reinvestment of the
trust funds. (3) The trustee may not consult with the nominee or any
member of the family on matters regarding the trust funds during the
time of the nominee's government service.

     In some cases, e.g., David Packard's nomination to serve as Deputy
Secretary of the Defense Department in 1969, an agreement may be
reached between a committee and a nominee to the effect that all profits
or earnings from a nominee's financial holdings will be donated to charity
during the period of the nominee's government service. A charitable
trust makes greater demands upon a nominee than does a blind trust and
is usually required only when a nominee's holdings are in an area that is
likely to fall within his jurisdiction as a government official.

7. NOTE: To conserve space, Senate confirmation hearings are hereafter
identified by the year in which they were held, the name of the committee, and the name of the nominee and the position to which nominated.

     See, for instance, 1972—Armed Services—Robert P. Nesen: Assis-
tant Secretary of the Navy (Financial Management), and 1965—Interior
and Insular Affairs—Harry R. Anderson: Assistant Secretary of the
Interior (Public Land Management). In both cases, the nominees owned
stock that posed a potential conflict of interest. Both willingly agreed to
dispose of that stock when the relevant committee requested that they
do so.

8. See p. 58 in Chapter 2.

9. 1965—Commerce—Mary Gardiner Jones: member, Federal Trade
Commission, p. 15.

10. 1964—Banking and Currency—Joseph W. Barr: member, Board of Directors, Federal Deposit Insurance Corporation, p. 2.

11. 1974—Interior and Insular Affairs—Melvin A. Conant: Assistant Administrator, Federal Energy Administration, pp. 92–93.

12. 1971—Argiculture and Forestry—Earl Butz: Secretary of Agriculture,
p. 57.

13. 1969—Interior and Insular Affairs—Walter J. Hickel: Secretary of the
Interior, pp. 10–11.

14. 1971—Labor and Public Welfare—Ronald S. Berman: Chairman, National Endowment for the Humanities, p. 7.

15. Letter from Senator Warren G. Magnuson to President Gerald R. Ford,
September 24, 1974 (from the files of the Senate Committee on Commerce).

16. *Congressional Record,* 119 (June 13, 1973; daily edition): S11099.

17. *Congressional Quarterly Weekly Report,* 31 (December 29, 1973): 3449.

The Senate's concern with the issue of predispositional balance has not been limited solely to multimember boards and commissions. In some single-headed agencies, it has also sought to ensure the existence of a balance of philosophies and backgrounds among the top appointees. See for example, 1966—Commerce—Werner A. Baum: Deputy Administrator, Environmental Science Services Administration, p. 2, and 1966—Interior and Insular Affairs—Walter R. Hibbard: Director, Bureau of Mines, p. 9.

18. A statutory requirement exists—18 *U.S.C.* 207 (a) and (b)—which prohibits a regular officer or employee of the government from "representing anyone other than the United States in connection with a matter to which the United States is a party or has an interest and in which he participated personally and substantially for the government." This statute is difficult to administer, however, and is rarely enforced. In the period from 1966 to 1976, for instance, only six individuals were prosecuted for violating it.

Jimmy Carter required his Cabinet and other high-level appointees to sign an agreement that included the following language: "In addition to complying with the restrictions which may be imposed on me by Federal law after termination of my Government service, including those contained in 18 *U.S.C.* Section 207, I will not for two years following such termination, engage in any activity from which Section 207 (b) will bar me during the first year after such termination."

19. See, for example, 1969—Foreign Relations—Elliot L. Richardson: Under Secretary of State.

20. A similar case in 1977 produced a different outcome. Robert H. Mendelsohn, nominated by Jimmy Carter as an Assistant Secretary of the Interior, was accused of improprieties in the financing of his campaign for a state office in California. The Senate Energy and Natural Resources Committee withheld final action on the nomination pending a state investigation of Mendelsohn's campaign finances. When the California Fair Political Practices Commission filed a civil suit against Mendelsohn, his nomination was withdrawn.

21. Frederick V. Malek, "Mr. Executive Goes to Washington," *Harvard Business Review*, 50 (September 1972): 67. For a more detailed description of the special characteristics of executive positions in the public sector, see Marver Bernstein, *The Job of the Federal Executive* (Brookings, 1958), pp. 26–37.

22. Statement by Senator Strom Thurmond in 1966—Banking and Currency—Robert C. Weaver: Secretary of Housing and Urban Development, p. 11.

23. This is not always the case, of course. Occasionally perceived political necessity induces Presidents to renominate, promote, or transfer individuals for reasons other than the high quality of their prior government service. The successive renominations of Ashton Barrett to a seat on the Federal Maritime Commission are a case in point. For an excellent discussion of the political factors involved in these renominations, see U.S. Senate, 95th Congress, 1st Session (1977), Committee on Govern-

ment Operations, *Study on Federal Regulation, Vol. I: The Regulatory Appointments Process*, pp. 95–99.

24. 1967—Foreign Relations—Rutherford M. Poats: Deputy Administrator, AID, pp. 31, 38.

25. See, for example, 1975—Finance—William N. Walker: Deputy Special Representative for Trade Negotiations; 1977—Banking, Housing, and Urban Affairs—Patricia R. Harris: Secretary of Housing and Urban Development; and 1978—Commerce, Science and Transportation—Frank Neel: member, Board of Directors, Amtrak.

26. Statement by Senator William Proxmire, quoted in *New York Times*, March 14, 1975.

27. Quoted in *Boston Globe*, February 25, 1975.

28. Senator William Proxmire of Wisconsin is a notable exception to this. He has consistently held that a nominee's background should reveal experience and training in the specific areas with which he will have to deal as a government official. Proxmire has often voted against nominees lacking such qualifications.

6   Senate Concerns: Constituency Representation

The representative function knows few bounds. It appears as regularly in the confirmation process as it does in other areas of Senate activity. Because confirmation decisions may have an important bearing on the relationship between federal agencies and certain parts of the country, Senators often use the opportunities that the confirmation process provides to pursue the specific interests of the states and regions they represent. They do so primarily in two ways: first, by playing what is often the dominant role in the appointment of federal officials whose jurisdiction is wholly within a single state, and second, by making an effort at confirmation hearings to sensitize nominees to the problems of individual states and regions and to explore with them possible solutions to those problems. The first tactic derives from the practice of "senatorial courtesy."

Senatorial Courtesy

When the first Senate rejected George Washington's nomination of Benjamin Fishbourn to be naval officer of the port of Savannah, it did so because of the objections of the two Senators from Georgia. No reason was stated for their objection to the Fishbourn nomination; they simply preferred another candidate. The full Senate deferred to the sentiments of the Senators from the state in which the nominee would serve. Thus was established a precedent that has survived in one form or another for the life of the Republic.

Senatorial courtesy turns the constitutional description of the appointment process on its head. Instead of the President's selection of a nominee and submission of him for the approval of the Senate, the Senators from the state in question select the nominee who is then (usually) nominated by the President and confirmed by the Senate. In practice, there are some routine constraints on this process. Normally, senatorial courtesy is a privilege granted only to Senators of the President's party. They consult with the President when a vacancy occurs in a federal position in their state and, in most cases, recommend a candidate. If the President nominates that candidate, confirmation normally comes as a matter of course. Should the President select some candidate other than the one suggested by a Senator of his party from that state, the unhappy Senator may then go to the floor of the Senate and claim that the President's nominee is "personally obnoxious" to him and therefore should not be confirmed. His Senate colleagues will usually grant him the courtesy of rejecting the President's nomination.

This is not a theme without variations, however. Senatorial courtesy is a custom, not a rule. Its actual operation is heavily dependent on the political climate and substantive circumstances that surround individual cases. Senators, for instance, sometimes claim the privilege of senatorial courtesy when a resident of their own state is nominated to a position with a regional or national jurisdiction. A Senator who is strategically located in the Senate power structure may claim the privilege of approving nominees for positions in his state even if he is not of the President's party.[1] And if both of a state's Senators are not of the President's party, they may be able to negotiate an agreement with him whereby they will have some role in the selection of a percentage of the appointees to positions in that state.[2]

Presidents do not always accept the recommendations of Senators of their own party for a nomination in the Senators' states. But, with very few exceptions,[3] the Senate has rejected presidential nominees when the President refused to exercise senatorial courtesy and the slighted Senator then pressed his claim on the Senate floor. It has become the case in recent years, however, that the Senate expects its members to state sufficient reason to reject nominees for positions in their states. No longer is the unsubstantiated claim of "personal obnoxiousness" always regarded as reason enough to support a colleague. Substantiation need not be terribly compelling, however. In 1976, for instance, the Senate refused to act on the nomination of William B. Poff for a district court judgeship in Virginia. Its rejection resulted from the opposition of Senator William Lloyd Scott of Virginia. Scott did not criticize Poff in any way. He only claimed that he had his own candidate for the nomination and that his candidate's philosophy was a little closer to his own than was Poff's.[4]

The Senate normally examines senatorial courtesy nominations only superficially. There is a norm of reciprocity that seems to apply within the Senate on matters pertaining to appointments within a particular state. Rarely do Senators interfere in what they regard as another Senator's business. But here too there are occasional exceptions. In 1965, for instance, the Senate considered the nomination of Francis X. Morrissey to a district court judgeship in Massachusetts. Morrissey was an old friend and retainer of the Kennedy family, and his nomination was the result of a recommendation made to President Johnson by Senator Edward Kennedy of Massachusetts and Senator Robert Kennedy of New York. Morrissey, however, was so poorly qualified to be a federal judge that the criticisms of the legal community forced the Senate to hold extensive hearings on the nomination. The absence of any significant qualifications quickly became apparent during these hearings; to avoid prolonged embarrassment to the President, the nominee, and the two Senators, the nomination was withdrawn before it came to a final vote.

The postwar years have been marked by a decline in the importance that Senators once attached to the practice of senatorial courtesy. Though most Senators still involve themselves in local federal appointments, many of them have been willing to limit the range of positions to which senatorial courtesy applies and to delegate much of their personal control over appointments in their states. They have done this, collectively, by supporting legislation that transferred into the career service a number of positions once subject to Senate confirmation.[5] And a number of them have done this, individually, by establishing advisory panels within their states to assist them in finding well-qualified candidates to serve as judges and U.S. attorneys,[6] or by permitting the Justice Department to make these suggestions subject only to senatorial veto.[7]

Several things account for these changes. As the political fortunes of modern Senators have come to rely less and less on their relationships with their state political parties, the patronage importance of federal appointments has declined. Many Senators began to feel that the frequent and difficult choices that these appointment decisions imposed were no longer justified by the political benefits they produced. Few tears were shed, therefore, over the reduction in the number of positions to which the practice of senatorial courtesy applied.

There continues to be substantial interest in the Senate in appointments that have a direct bearing on the implementation of federal policies within the states. But interviews with Senate and White

House staff personnel indicate that the focus of attention has shifted in recent years away from those positions which had patronage value but little real impact on policy outcomes. Senate interest often centers now on the selection of federal regional administrators who play a significant role in determining the federal reaction to local needs, in processing federal grants, and in the interpretation of federal statutes. Appointments to most of these positions do not require the advice and consent of the Senate. That, however, has not stopped Senators from recommending candidates for important administrative positions in their states and regions or from reacting strongly when their candidates are not appointed. They continue to push their constituency interests in the appointment process, but they have begun to do so in different places.

Advocating Constituency Interests

The more important evidence that Senators use the confirmation process for representative purposes is found in confirmation hearings. There Senators make abundant efforts to communicate the concerns of their constituents to the President's nominees and to explore the extent to which nominees are likely to be responsive to those concerns.

In dealing with these regional or constituency interests, Senate committees rarely act as a unit. Instead, individual Senators or small groups of Senators use the public hearing as a forum for expressing their own concerns. Not uncommonly, a committee will contain members whose constituency interests are diametrically opposed. A Senator from New England seeking to bring about an increase in oil import quotas, for instance, will be regularly at loggerheads with a Senator from an oil-producing state who favors lower quotas. The likelihood that an individual Senator will completely succeed in getting the responses he seeks is, therefore, not very great. Senators persist in this kind of activity, however, hoping in whatever way possible to keep their concerns in the public eye and in the nominee's purview.

This kind of direct representation takes several forms. The most common is the use of confirmation hearings to inform the nominee of the needs or wants of individual states. Frequently a Senator will be satisfied simply to indicate his own interest in a particular issue by asking a question or two to probe the nominee's opinion or knowledge. On numerous occasions, for instance, Senator J. William Fulbright expressed his view that something needed to be done about Common Market programs to tax soybean imports.[8] Fulbright's home state, Arkansas, is a major producer of soybeans. Senator Henry Jackson, the chairman of the Interior Committee, asked Louis B. Bruce, a Nixon nominee for Commissioner of Indian Affairs, what he intended to do in regard to the problems of particular Indian tribes in Jackson's state, Washington.[9] Senator John Tunney expressed grave concern to Secretary-designate of Commerce Elliot Richardson about California'a failure to receive its "fair share" of Economic Development Administration funds to combat unemployment.[10]

This kind of constituency-oriented questioning occurs with great frequency in confirmation hearings. For the most part, the Senator who initiates such a discussion is not looking for a particular commitment on the part of the nominee but rather is attempting to inform the nominee of his personal interest in the matter and to elicit the nominee's pledge to "look into it." Such discussions frequently focus on specific projects that affect key industries in the Senator's home state, as the following statements indicate. The first is a part of an effort by Senator Leverett Saltonstall to inform Graeme C. Bannerman, an Assistant Secretary-designate of the Navy, of the needs of the Boston Navy Yard; the second an attempt by Senator John Sherman Cooper to inform a nominee to the Board of Directors of the TVA of the criticisms that some of his constituents were making of certain TVA policies:

> Senator Saltonstall. Another question, a local question. The Boston Navy Yard—we have heard a lot about Navy Yards in recent months. The Navy Yard is getting some additional procurement in the utilities that make it possible to repair ships and so on, but we are desperately in need of drydocks, additional drydocks, and perhaps some further installation in the Boston Navy Yard. Have you had an opportunity to get into that question at all?
> Mr. Bannerman. No, sir, I have not.
> Senator Saltonstall. Would you do so?
> Mr. Bannerman. I would be glad to.
> Senator Saltonstall. I think we feel that quite strongly in our area.[11]
>
> Senator Cooper. I want to ask you a question as a representative of the State of Kentucky which TVA serves, in part. I may say that I have

always been a supporter of TVA, but on the other hand I have not failed to question some of their operations when I did not think they were wholly good or successful. . . .

[T]he allegation is made from time to time, and I am not going to say whether or not this is correct, that TVA's coal purchasing policy tends to drive the price of coal down, to the detriment of the mining industry.

I assume the TVA wants to buy coal as cheap as it can and that may be the motivation behind this policy. But I want to tell you that their coal policy is under great criticism in Kentucky.[12]

If a particular Senator is especially concerned about the impact of a program on his constituents, or if he doubts seriously that the nominee shares his concern, there are other steps that may be undertaken to raise the nominee's consciousness. First, written statements on specific projects or plans may be requested. Senator Hugh Scott, for instance, gave Dean Burch a memorandum "expressing the concern some of my constituents feel over FCC policy in the area of channel and spectrum allocations" and requested that Burch provide written answers to Scott's questions about this matter to include in the hearing record on his nomination as Chairman of the FCC.[13]

Second, the Senator may try to get the nominee to reveal the likely shape of future projects that are still in the planning stage. How will the new Secretary of Agriculture deal with the price policy for wheat?[14] Will the new Secretary of Commerce reintroduce the export limit on black walnut logs?[15] What is likely to happen to the Portsmouth-Kittery Naval Shipyard when a new team takes over at the Defense Department?[16] Questions of this sort serve to indicate the Senator's and the state's concern to the nominee; they also give the Senator an opportunity to get some advance warning of program changes that are likely to affect his constituency directly. If he discovers that such changes are in the works, he can then begin to muster his own influence and that of like-minded colleagues to redirect or support the thinking of the relevant officials in the executive branch.

A third way in which this representative function is exercised is somewhat more affirmative than the two already discussed. Given the opportunity that a confirmation hearing provides, Senators will occasionally try to persuade the nominee to give them direct assistance in resolving a particular problem in their states or regions. Often this problem will involve only an individual constituent, a small group of constituents, or a relatively minor federal project. Senator Richard Russell once said to Under Secretary of the Navy-designate Paul B.

Fay, "Mr. Secretary-to-be, Georgia does not have any naval yard, but we are one of the original states and we are on the Atlantic Ocean. Please see if you can find anything for us."[17] Senator Russell was speaking in jest, of course, but other Senators at other times have made similar remarks in total seriousness. Senator Edward Kennedy used the hearing on the nomination of Jesse L. Steinfeld as Surgeon General as an opportunity to reexamine with him the administration's decision to close the Framingham Heart Study in his state.[18] Senator Charles Percy used the hearing on Carlos C. Villareal's nomination to be Urban Mass Transportation Administrator as an opportunity to explain to him the funding and developmental needs of the South Suburban Transit Authority in the Chicago area.[19] In other confirmation hearings, Senator Strom Thurmond of South Carolina instructed a nominee to investigate the possibility of getting an ROTC unit placed at Newberry College in his state,[20] Senator Hiram Fong was able to get an Assistant Postmaster General–designate to pledge to see what could be done about modernizing some dilapidated post offices in Hawaii,[21] and Senator George Aiken tried to determine what the Environmental Protection Agency intended to do about a paper mill on the New York side of Lake Champlain that was polluting the water on the Vermont side.[22]

Senators will also use the confirmation hearings to perform a kind of ombudsman function for their constituents by bringing problems and complaints directly to the attention of a nominee in whose jurisdiction those problems will fall. Senator Everett Dirksen asked a man nominated to be Chief Counsel of the IRS about a tax ruling that related specifically to an individual constituent.[23] Similarly, Senator John Williams asked Sheldon S. Cohen, a nominee to be Commissioner of Internal Revenue, about the impact of certain IRS rulings on farmers in the state of Delaware.[24] Senator John Sparkman asked Sherman Unger, a Nixon nominee for General Counsel of HUD, to investigate and try to clear up a case in Alabama where an interpretation by the previous General Counsel had held up funds for a project that had already been approved.[25] And Senator Claiborne Pell used the confirmation process to express to William H. Stewart, a Johnson nominee as Surgeon General, the complaints of his constituents about the quality of the Public Health Service in Rhode Island. "When you do become Surgeon General," he said, "I wish you would perhaps look into the Public Health Service doctor under contract with you in Newport, Rhode Island, who doesn't have much to do but who needs to be jacked up in his willingness to do it."[26]

In all of these cases, the individual Senators were attempting to communicate specific concerns and problems to the nominees, to get an agency or individual to take some action affecting their states, or to get some decision that had already been made, or had been rumored to have been made, reexamined or reversed. The confirmation process is not the only forum in which this kind of constituency representation or lobbying takes place. It does provide, however, an institutionalized mechanism through which Senators can openly and routinely attempt to educate and persuade administrative officials regarding the needs and wants of their separate constituencies.

One intriguing aspect of this is that Senators will sometimes try to use their influence in the confirmation process to get from executive branch officials certain things that they have been unable to get from their own colleagues in the Congress. Probably no case demonstrates this more clearly than the efforts of the Senators from northern New England to improve their region's deficiency in air transportation. Senators Norris Cotton of New Hampshire and Winston Prouty of Vermont were the leaders in this effort. For much of the period between 1964 and 1974, both served on the Commerce Committee, which had jurisdiction over all nominations in the field of civilian air transportation. In virtually every confirmation hearing for a nomination in the field of aviation or transportation, Senator Prouty or Senator Cotton would initiate a discussion of the primitiveness of air travel in their region. The special problems of aviation in northern New England do not lend themselves readily to government solutions, but the Senators from that region persisted in trying to impress their needs on those nominees who would be dealing with this issue. Senator Cotton became more and more unhappy about this over the course of the decade, finally declaring in 1972 that until some satisfactory action was undertaken in regard to the problems of air service in his region he would "neither support nor oppose any appointment to the CAB."[27] When President Nixon made a nomination to the ICC that continued to leave the Northeast without a representative on the commission, Senator Cotton became even more assertive:

> After all the years I have put in on this committee and we have two representatives on this committee from New England, and I am sure that Senator Prouty feels as I do—if my own administration isn't willing to show the section we represent just consideration, the next time that there is a vacancy, I can promise them that there will be opposition to it even if they nominate St. Peter!

I have said so before. I have said so in this hearing. I have said so in private conversations with representatives from the White House. Yet it has been completely ignored. . . .

[I]f, as it appears, the administration has written off the Northeast entirely in nominating persons to the ICC I am not going to submit to it without a loud long protest from now on. . . .

[F]or reasons I have stated, I am most unhappy and I am going to get more unhappy as time goes on. Somebody is going to come up here from the White House some day and want me to do something. I may find it necessary to do just the opposite to get my point across.[28]

Another matter of great concern to the regional constituency of the New England Senators was the abnormally high cost of home heating fuel in their area. In hearing after hearing in which the nominee had some jurisdiction in this area, the Senators from New England pressed this question. Senator Edmund Muskie of Maine expressed the depth of their concern during the hearings on Walter Hickel's nomination to be Secretary of the Interior:

I think you ought to consider the fact that there is no way for you, as I understand it, to divorce yourself of your responsibilities with respect to the oil import program as there appears to be for the White House. Since you cannot divorce yourself of these responsibilities, we are most sensitive in my area to the question whether when the crunch comes, you are going to be influenced by the points of view you have developed up to this point or by your desire to be objective.

Now in your statement you said that you recognize that there might have to be some increase in imports with respect to some areas of the country. That statement does not reflect the sense of urgency we in New England feel about this problem.[29]

The New England region was only one of several in which the Senators shared a particular regional concern, which they articulated frequently in confirmation hearings. The Senators from the upper Midwest sought on numerous occasions to persuade federal maritime officials that the Great Lakes were part of the national seacoast and ought to be given the consideration to which that status entitled them. Senators Robert Griffin and Philip Hart of Michigan expressed this view in every relevant hearing in which they participated. Senators from the Southwest and California shared a similar mutual interest in federal policies relating to the Colorado River basin.

With occasional exceptions, like Senator Cotton's frustration and Senator Muskie's strong words, this kind of regional representation is not characteristically based on threats, but rather on persistent publicity and persuasion. The Senators involved have normally sought to serve their regions' interests, not through dramatic action like defeating a nominee or holding one hostage to a policy pledge that he and the administration were unlikely to honor, but rather by using the hearing process to communicate firmly and effectively the concerns of the people of their region to every nominee who will be in a position to respond to those concerns.

This, of course, is not a strategy that guarantees success. This kind of persuasion does not always bring immediate or effective results. Because there are rarely more than one or two Senators from each region on a committee, and because the weight of their influence is often counterbalanced by Senators from other regions who oppose the policy goals they seek, the ability to force any particular course of action on a nominee is greatly diminished. Given the normal existence of those conditions, persuasion and supplication must replace force as the means of exercising influence over the relations between the federal government and individual states and regions.

Notes

1. While he served as Chairman of the Senate Judiciary Committee, Senator James Eastland (D–Mississippi) was a major influence in appointments to the Fifth Circuit Court of Appeals during both Republican and Democratic administrations.
2. During the Nixon administration, for instance, Senators Alan Cranston and John Tunney, both Democrats from California, made an arrangement whereby every third federal judicial appointee in that state would be a Democrat. See Nina Totenberg, "Will Judges Be Chosen Rationally?" *Judicature*, 60(1976): 93–95.
3. There have been occasions historically when the Senate has disregarded the objections of certain Senators regarding nominations in their states. In nearly all cases, this has occurred after a Senator has broken with the leadership of his party or failed to show the expected courtesy to his colleagues. Among those who had problems exercising the privilege of senatorial courtesy were Senators Huey Long (Louisiana), Theodore Bilbo (Mississippi), Rush Holt (West Virginia), and Robert LaFollette, Sr. (Wisconsin).
4. Senator William Lloyd Scott, press conference, Richmond, Virginia, January 23, 1976.
5. These include such local officials as customs agents, internal revenue collectors, and postmasters.
6. As of the beginning of the 95th Congress, Senators from six states— Florida, Kentucky, California, Iowa, Massachusetts, and Georgia—had

established advisory panels to guide their recommendations for district court judgeships. Senators from other states have subsequently begun to follow suit.

7. Professor Harold W. Chase pointed out in his excellent study of judicial selections that the role of the Justice Department in the appointment of district court judges is substantial. "The time has come," he noted, "to set aside the simplistic explanation that senators alone determine the appointments to the Federal bench. For better or worse, the process is much more complicated and, indeed, much more interesting." Harold W. Chase, *Federal Judges: The Appointing Process* (Minnesota University Press, 1972), p. 47.

8. See 1969—Foreign Relations—Carl J. Gilbert: Special Representative for Trade Negotiations, and 1969—Finance—David M. Kennedy: Secretary of the Treasury.

9. 1969—Interior and Insular Affairs—Louis B. Bruce: Commissioner of Indian Affairs.

10. 1975—Commerce—Elliot Richardson: Secretary of Commerce, p. 97.

11. 1965—Armed Services—Graeme C. Bannerman: Assistant Secretary of the Navy (Installations and Logistics), p. 9.

12. 1966—Public Works—Dan McBride: member, Board of Directors, TVA, pp. 14–15.

13. 1969—Commerce—Dean Burch: Chairman, FCC. For other examples of requests by individual Senators for written reports relative to some constituency interest, see 1967—Public Works—Lowell K. Bridwell: Administrator, Federal Highway Administration, and 1970—Commerce—Kenneth M. Smith: Deputy Administrator, FAA.

14. 1971—Agriculture and Forestry—Earl L. Butz: Secretary of Agriculture.

15. 1965—Commerce—John T. Connor: Secretary of Commerce.

16. 1969—Armed Services—Melvin R. Laird: Secretary of Defense, and 1969—Armed Services—John H. Chaffee: Secretary of the Navy.

17. 1961—Armed Services—Paul B. Fay: Under Secretary of the Navy, p. 4.

18. 1969—Labor and Public Welfare—Jesse L. Steinfeld: Surgeon General.

19. 1969—Banking and Currency—Carlos C. Villareal: Urban Mass Transportation Administrator.

20. 1970—Armed Services—Richard J. Borda: Assistant Secretary of the Air Force (Manpower and Reserve Affairs).

21. 1964—Post Office and Civil Service—Tyler Abell: Assistant Postmaster General (Facilities).

22. 1970—Public Works—William D. Ruckelshaus: Administrator, Environmental Protection Agency.

23. 1965—Finance—Mitchell Rogovin: Chief Counsel, Internal Revenue Service.

24. 1965—Finance—Sheldon S. Cohen: Commissioner of Internal Revenue.

25. 1969—Banking and Currency—Sherman Unger: General Counsel, Department of Housing and Urban Development.

26. 1965—Labor and Public Welfare—William H. Stewart: Surgeon General, p. 11.
27. 1972—Commerce—Whitney Gilliland: member, CAB, p. 63.
28. 1970—Commerce—Donald W. Brewer: member, ICC, pp. 13-14.
29. 1969—Interior and Insular Affairs—Walter J. Hickel: Secretary of the Interior, pp. 41-42.

7 Senate Concerns: The Impact on Public Policy

Public policy issues dominate the confirmation process. No topic is discussed more widely in confirmation hearings; no factor looms larger in shaping confirmation decisions. Above all else, the confirmation process is a forum in which the preferences and concerns of the Congress are brought to bear on the development and implementation of American public policy.

Public policy concerns pervade the confirmation process in several ways. At one level, confirmation hearings provide a mutually useful opportunity to Senators and nominees to get to know one another, to express their own policy views, and to listen to each other's. The confirmation process is a time for getting acquainted, for clarifying individual opinions, for discussing plans and objectives, and for initiating working relationships between Senate committees and the presidential appointees with whom they will work.

The confirmation process also provides an opportunity for Senate committees to acquire information from nominees or from other sources in the executive branch, information that is often difficult to obtain through normal channels. The confirmation process not only gives committees access to people who possess this kind of desired information, it also enables them to overcome the reluctance of executive officials to provide certain types of information by making such provision a precondition to confirmation.

At a third level, the confirmation process provides a convenient and effective opportunity for Senators to explore and question the operations of particular government programs. Confirmation hearings often put Senators across the table from people who have extensive experience in the management of federal programs. Given this kind of opportunity, Senate committees tend to focus their questions on the programs themselves rather than on the specific qualifications of the nominees or even on their involvement in those programs. Confirmation hearings, as a result, are often little more than oversight hearings carried out under an assumed name.

At yet another level, the Senate uses its confirmation power as part of its arsenal of weapons for influencing the shape and direction of public policy. The Senate has the power to make final decisions on who will or will not serve in important government offices. It uses that final power to exert some leverage on policy decisions. If it is unhappy with the personal policy views of presidential nominees or with the current thrust of the administration policies for which certain nominees will have responsibility, it may use its confirmation power in one of several ways to influence policy decisions. It can, of course, reject a nominee and indicate to the President that it did so because it found his policy views unacceptable. But it does not often do that. More commonly, the Senate uses its power of rejection as a threat. It may withhold final action on a nomination until a nominee or the White House agrees to pursue certain courses of action about which the members of a Senate committee feel strongly. It may require the nominee, as a condition of his confirmation, to make policy-related promises to the committee during his confirmation hearing. Or it may use its power to delay or reject a nominee as a bargaining chip to force the administration into some policy action unrelated to the nomination in question. The confirmation power is thus a versatile tool for the Senate in its efforts to enlarge its influence on public policy decisions.

The injection of public policy concerns into the confirmation process flies in the face of many of the most common prescriptions for the exercise of the advise and consent power. Joseph R. Harris, for instance, argued in his study of the confirmation process:

> The Senate is justified in considering a nominee's philosophy in regard to policies which he will be called upon to carry out if confirmed. But it should confine its jurisdiction to subjects relevant to the duties of the office and should not inquire into general opinions or attitudes of nominees.[1]

Senators themselves often state similar views:

> Senator Patrick McNamara. We cannot demand total purity or conformity of views among those whom we place in high office.[2]

> Senator Edward Kennedy. I think all of us would pretty much agree that we certainly do not want just to subscribe to a political test or a simplistic philosophical test in trying to reach a decision about the approval or disapproval of a candidate.[3]

Senator Roman Hruska. Whether the nominee is liberal or conservative should not concern this Committee. Whether we agree or disagree with him is not the issue. Political questions should play no part in our decision.[4]

Senator Everett Dirksen. I vouch for him without reservation.
Senator J. William Fulbright. That does not mean you necessarily agree with everything he thinks about foreign relations.
Senator Dirksen. Oh no. I disagree violently with him and I have had occasion to do that only recently as the history books will indicate.[5]

So there is a curious paradox here. On the one hand, Senators state their support for the abstract ideal of allowing the President to choose whomever he pleases to serve with him as long as his nominees meet minimum standards of competence and integrity. Yet, on the other hand, they persistently demonstrate a keen interest in the philosophies and policy views of the President's nominees.

Two things help to explain this apparent schizophrenia. First, it is not uncommon for abstract congressional ideals to run aground on the rocky shoals of specific issues and programs. Members of Congress often preach one course of action and practice another. They call for reduced federal spending but fight to the death against cuts in their favorite programs. They collectively praise the goal of congressional reform, but vote individually against reorganization proposals that diminish their own power. The confirmation process is no exception. Members will support the traditional ideals that govern that process only as long as those ideals do not interfere with their desire to use the confirmation process for more specific—usually policy-oriented—purposes.

There is also the matter of salience. There is no evidence to indicate that Senators are anything but sincere in their statements supporting traditional notions of the Senate's role in the confirmation process. There are times, however, when a particular nomination is of such salience to some Senators that they feel compelled to violate these traditional norms. This may be caused by strong feelings about the nominee as an individual, but it is far more likely to be the product of concern with the office to which he is nominated and the programs over which he will have jurisdiction. To put it more bluntly, the general view among Senators seems to be: I'll usually go along with whomever the President wants as long as the nomination doesn't threaten my own policy priorities or those of my constituents and supporters.

Confirmation hearings are thus dominated by public policy concerns because Senators—as George Washington Plunkitt of Tammany Hall might have put it—"sees their opportunities and they takes 'em." The principles to which they pay lip service do not prevent them from taking advantage of the leverage the confirmation power provides or from using that leverage to affect the course and substance of public policy decisions.

Exchanging Views

Whatever else it may be, a confirmation hearing is fundamentally an opportunity for a committee and a nominee to communicate with one another. This is an obvious point but, in a system where the legislative and executive branches share political power, an important one. Effective coordination of the work of the two branches often depends on the facility of communication among individuals. Confirmation hearings are often the place at which relationships of this sort begin. They are likely to be the first of many contacts between the members and staff of a Senate committee, on the one hand, and an executive branch official on the other. The impressions formed at the confirmation hearing are the basis on which long-term working relationships are constructed. The fact is not lost on Senate committees or on nominees that their relationship will continue after the nomination is confirmed. Both sides thus have a stake in setting an appropriate tone for future interchanges and in improving the chances for legislative–executive cooperation.

The communication that occurs at confirmation hearings also gives nominees and committees an opportunity to familiarize themselves with each other's primary interests and goals. In the process by which the Senate seeks to gain influence over public policy, this is an important—if informal—first step. The confirmation hearing allows committees to learn the relevant policy views of the nominee and the administration, and it provides the Senators with a forum for making their own ideas and concerns apparent to the nominee. Senator Milton Young made this point at Earl Butz's confirmation hearing. "I think it is a healthy thing for the committee to be holding these hearings," he said. "It enables the committee and the farmers to find out the philosophy of the Secretary of Agriculture designate. It gives us an opportunity to find out what he might do when he becomes

Secretary. I think it is also helpful to the President to know what the farmers are thinking."[6] Indeed, this kind of discussion is a necessary precondition to the attempts at persuasion and negotiation that frequently follow.

Before a Senate committee can react to a nominee's policy views, it must discover those views. Its ability to exercise some influence in particular policy areas is aided as well by advance knowledge of the President's future plans. Hence considerable effort is expended in confirmation hearings on trying to get nominees to reveal some sense of their own and the White House's plans for specific agencies and programs. The difficulty of this task results from the normal unwillingness of nominees to respond directly to inquiries of this kind. Rarely are hairs so carefully split or phrases so delicately turned as in the attempts of presidential nominees to evade a direct answer to questions dealing with controversial public policies.[7] Reasons for this abound, but two predominate. The first is that executive branch officials, especially those close to the White House, do not want to let members of Congress into the policy development process until the initial choice of options has been made and refined. To do so is to reduce the policy-maker's latitude by allowing congressionally initiated political pressures to be brought to bear early in the decision-making process. Executive control over the shape of policies and programs is heavily dependent upon the ability to present Congress with initiatives that have been fully studied, well refined, and carefully argued. This is not facilitated by the interference of the Congress at the early stages of policy development.

The second and more immediate reason for evading controversial policy questions at confirmation hearings is the fear that they may blow up into a source of contention over the nomination itself. A nominee who wantonly stakes out a clearly defined position on an issue not only curtails his future latitude as a policy-maker but also runs the risk of angering those Senators who have strong reservations about his views and the firmness with which he holds them. It has not been uncommon for recent administrations to counsel their nominees to "go innocent" into confirmation hearings, to claim a reluctance to take a position on current policy issues because of a lack of familiarity with their details.[8] But this strategy must be practiced carefully. Senate committees expect nominees to be reasonably up to date on relevant issues and to be willing to discuss those issues at confirmation hearings. An overly reticent nominee may have as many problems with a committee as one with too firm a commitment to any single point of view. Committees often have as little patience with political neuters as with ideologues.

In the face of this reluctance on the part of nominees to reveal their positions on controversial policies, Senate committees have to be especially assiduous in ferreting these out. Of particular interest to most committees are the nominee's personal views, as distinct from those of the administration. "I think we have a right to know," Senator Javits told John Doar, "what you think as opposed to what your boss thinks."[9] Senator Clifford Case told a nominee that "your job, of course, is to answer questions for the government later. But your job now is to try and tell us and to tell the world where you stand. And I want only to get to the bottom of your views . . . for our guidance in our vote for your confirmation, and in our dealing with the broad problems that we all face."[10]

Senators often wish to know if the nominee disagrees with any of the stated intentions of the President. On occasion such disagreements do exist, as, for instance, between President Nixon and his Secretary of Labor-designate, Peter Brennan, over the issues of the minimum wage and compulsory arbitration. In such cases the committee will probe the depth of the disagreement to make sure that the nominee is not going to undermine established government policy, but also to get a sense of his ability to inject his own independent judgment into the policy-making process.

Senators are also interested in the kinds of policy changes they can expect when one official relinquishes his post to another. In a remark more suggestive than inquisitive, Senator Joseph Clark asked Lincoln Gordon, a Johnson nominee for Assistant Secretary of State, to "tell us whether your policy is going to be to continue the hard line of Mr. Mann [his predecessor] or to attempt to push the Alliance for Progress with a little more emphasis on reform, land reform, housing reform, fiscal reform, and little less emphasis on supporting political dictatorships."[11]

The questions that Senate committees ask in attempting to uncover a nominee's policy views are often directed less at determining his specific opinions than at getting a sense of his general approach to the problems he will face. Senator Leverett Saltonstall, for example, asked Daniel M. Luevano, who had been nominated to serve as Assistant Secretary of the Army for Installations and Logistics, to specify what "framework" he would use for making decisions on specific requests on military building projects.[12] Senator Vance Hartke put a similar question to a nominee for a seat on the FCC. "In general," he asked, "is your philosophy and approach to regulatory bodies that they should attempt to extend regulation, or do you think that they should attempt at any time possible to curtail all regulation to that which is a bare minimum?"[13] Here committee members are seeking to get some sense of the perspective through which a nominee is likely to view the problems that come before him.

The direct communication that takes place at confirmation hearings is useful to both sets of participants. It gives committee members the opportunity to examine the attitudes, philosophies, and thought processes of nominees. But is also gives nominees a chance to state their views directly without the interference of inaccurate reporting or misinterpretation. To the extent that they have the time and interest to use this opportunity, committee members are enabled by it to cast their confirmation votes with a clearer sense of the ideas and perspectives of the individuals they confirm or reject.

Information Gathering

One of the principal uses to which the Senate puts its confirmation power is the collection of information relating to its legislative and oversight responsibilities. Very often this occurs quite apart from the central task of confirmation hearings, which is, of course, to evaluate the qualifications of individual nominees. Instead of asking a nominee questions about himself, committees will use him as a resource, plying him with questions about issues and programs with which he is familiar. So great is the Senate's need for substantive information that the search for it pervades every aspect of Senate activity. The confirmation process is no exception.

The confirmation process lends itself to this search in several ways. Many nominees, though lacking in government experience, are experts in particular issue areas and have spent many years studying or dealing with topics that are of concern or interest to the Senate. Confirmation hearings give individual Senators a chance to "pick the brains" of these subject matter experts. Nominees who have been working in government, at whatever level, are also a prized source of information. Senators often ask for their firsthand observations or criticisms of existing or proposed programs and policies. What makes the confirmation process an especially useful tool for information gathering, however, is the leverage it affords the Senate in trying to pry hard-to-get information out of reluctant nominees or a reluctant President. The Senate has not hesitated to use its ultimate control over appointments to force the release of information it has been unable to obtain through other means.

Senators and committees often use the confirmation process for purposes that can best be described as general education. This is likely to be so when a nominee is a recognized expert in his field or when his previous experience has brought him into close contact with specific economic, social, or scientific problems. For instance, the confirmation hearing of Edward F. Zigler, a child development specialist from Yale, was spent almost entirely in a specific and technical discussion of such matters as individual character formation, the scientific validity of IQ tests, and the value of work. Another nominee, George H. Moore, an expert in quantitative economic research, was asked a number of questions about the procedures that are normally used to gather and interpret economic statistics. Robert M. White, a meteorologist, led the Commerce Committee through a long and detailed discussion of trends and developments in weather forecasting techniques. In each case the purpose of these discussions was not to establish the competence of the particular nominee—each of the nominees was highly praised by the committee before the questioning began. The hearings were used instead as a general educational forum, with little or no attempt to deal with specific problems of public policy.

The one committee that routinely uses its confirmation hearings for this purpose is Foreign Relations, although here the relevance of the information gathering to the committee's obligations is somewhat clearer. A majority of the nominees who appear before the Foreign Relations Committee are experienced professionals in the Foreign Service. Their nomination to one post normally follows directly upon their service in another. Not surprisingly, therefore, confirmation hearings tend to focus on the nominee's experience in the position he has just left. When U. Alexis Johnson was nominated to serve as Ambassador to Japan in 1966, his confirmation hearing dealt for the most part with his recent service as Ambassador to Thailand. Chairman Fulbright acknowledged that Johnson's years in Thailand made him an "expert in the area" and then proceeded to question him at length about matters on which the committee was inadequately informed. In virtually every case in which a nominee has immediate past experience in an overseas position, the committee will spend a good deal more time examining that experience than discussing the position for which he has been nominated most recently. Indeed it treats the nominations of foreign policy-makers and academic specialists in much the same way, probing their minds, trying to get their informed and expert views on foreign events and foreign policy needs.

But Senators tend to be practical men, and Senate committees tend to be mindful of their responsibilities. Hence they are far more likely to seek out information for purposes that are more instrumental than those just examined. Most of the time, Senate committees use the confirmation process to gather information that will enhance their ability to play a larger role in policy-making or to be more effective in carrying out legislative and administrative oversight. The bulk of the information that is sought in confirmation hearings has some direct relevance to issues and policies of current importance that fall within the jurisdiction of the committee.[14] When the Foreign Relations Committee held hearings on the nomination of William M. Roth as President Johnson's Special Representative for Trade Negotiations, it spent the entire hearing gathering information about the "Kennedy Round" international trade negotiations, in which Roth had been participating. On questions for which he could not give specific factual answers off the top of his head, he later submitted written information for the record. The transcript of this confirmation hearing is a very comprehensive review of the positions taken by the American negotiators at the Kennedy Round meetings. In similar fashion, the Finance Committee used the nomination of Frederick L. Deming for Under Secretary of the Treasury as an opportunity to obtain information on the operations of the regional Federal Reserve banks. Deming had been president of the Federal Reserve Bank of Minneapolis, and his entire hearing was spent discussing such matters as gold flow, interest rates, and the balance of payments as they related to the banks in the reserve system.

Not uncommonly in confirmation hearings, the nominee will be unable to provide all the information that the committee desires on a particular issue, not because of any reluctance on his part but simply because he doesn't have the information with him at the time and has not committed it to memory. It is not at all unusual in such circumstances for the committee to request, and for the nominee to provide, such information in writing for the hearing record. In most cases this involves statistics, charts, or a few paragraphs of explanatory prose. On occasion, however, a committee will require a nominee to submit a detailed informational report on some matter of interest. When

Robert L. Bartley appeared before the Commerce Committee in 1965 as a candidate for reappointment to the FCC, Senator John Pastore engaged him in a discussion of the application of the fairness doctrine to educational television. Pastore was not satisfied with the caliber of the discussion and asked the nominee to get the Chief Counsel of the FCC to submit a memorandum on the matter.[15] A long report was subsequently submitted and placed in the hearing record.

The picture painted thus far is somewhat rosy: Committees use confirmation hearings to seek information from nominees, and the nominees provide it, either verbally or in writing. It isn't always that easy. Because information is an important resource in establishing positions of political power, it is something of a valuable, indeed a hoardable, commodity. Recent experience reveals numerous instances in which incumbent and future officials of the executive branch have been highly reluctant to provide information to congressional committees. In many cases there are sound justifications for this reluctance, but the refusal to provide requested information rarely sits well with Senate committees. This is especially so in confirmation proceedings, where to the normal argument that Congress needs all the information it can get to carry out its legislative and oversight obligations can be added the further argument that without sufficient information the Senate cannot adequately fulfill its responsibility to advise and consent on a nomination. Senators are not unwilling to use the power the Constitution gives them in the appointment process to force nominees to provide desired information. Senator Alan Cranston expressed his willingness to do this during the hearings on the nomination of Frank Carlucci to head the Office of Economic Opportunity:

> I will oppose the motion to poll the committee on the nomination with all due deference to the chairman, with regard to Mr. Carlucci, because he has not been able to supply us with certain information we want, some of which he lacks.
>
> I feel that we are not equipped, in turn, to judge him and how he will perform in this position, until we see how he responds to the information, and with what dispatch he responds to the information that he does not have yet at his disposal.[16]

The difficulty with direct threats of this kind, as Senator Cranston discovered in the Carlucci hearings and as Senator Harold Hughes later discovered in the hearings on Carlucci's successor,

Phillip Sanchez, is that it is not easy even to get a majority of the members of a Senate committee to agree that a particular piece of information is crucial in determining whether or not a nominee should be confirmed. Only in a case where there is broad consensus within the committee that certain information is central to the confirmation decision or where there is a legitimate suspicion that the nominee has been disingenuous in not revealing the extent of the information he possesses is a committee likely to sustain a threat to hold up a nomination. This happens occasionally, as the L. Patrick Gray hearings of 1973 clearly indicate,[17] but it is not a normal occurrence. The simple fact is that within the immediate context of a confirmation hearing, nominees rarely fail to provide whatever information a committee requests. Committees do not normally make unreasonable demands, and Presidents are rarely prepared to withhold information if such an act is likely to mean the defeat of a nomination. Almost never is a nomination allowed to "twist slowly in the wind," as Patrick Gray's was by the Nixon administration.

In a direct sense, therefore, Senate committees are normally capable of getting the information they want from presidential nominees. But in the persistent struggle between the President and the Congress for access to information this is not the only, nor perhaps even the most important, purpose for which the confirmation process is employed. Many nominees are new to their jobs and do not possess the kind of information that committees would most like to obtain. The specific operational information, the unprocessed data, and the other kinds of information that Senate committees would most like to have—but have the greatest difficulty obtaining—is rarely in the hands of executive branch officials until after they have been confirmed. It would seem then that such information is beyond the reach of the confirmation process. That, however, is not entirely so.

The Senate has occasionally used the confirmation power as a vehicle for punishing those who, in their previous government service, have failed either to produce information or to testify at the behest of Congress. The most important historical example of this was the Senate's failure to confirm the nomination of Lewis Strauss to the position of Secretary of Commerce in 1959. While serving as chairman of the Atomic Energy Commission, Strauss had repeatedly failed to respond to the requests of the Joint Atomic Energy Committee for information. He had so infuriated the Senate in this and in his evasiveness at his confirmation hearing that it took the highly unusual step of refusing to confirm a nomination to the President's Cabinet.[18]

A similar case arose in 1973, when action was delayed on the nomination of William J. Casey to serve as president of the Export-Import Bank. While serving as Chairman of the Securities and Exchange Commission in 1972, Casey had sent the SEC files on an ITT antitrust suit to the Justice Department in response, he said, to a Justice Department request for information relevant to its investigation of that entire affair. The Chairman of the House Interstate and Foreign Commerce Committee, Harley O. Staggers, testified, however, that Casey was only trying to keep those files out of the hands of the House Committee, thus depriving a congressional committee of information it had requested. Staggers's testimony was supported by Deputy Attorney General Ralph Erickson, who reported that the Justice Department had never requested the files. Casey's nomination was not acted upon at all in the first session of the 93d Congress and was not confirmed until well into the second session.

The use of the confirmation power to effect this kind of retroactive punishment serves two purposes. First, it gives the Senate a means of dealing directly with those who have not been forthcoming with information or testimony in the past, assuming of course that these people are nominated to other positions that require the advice and consent of the Senate. But second, and far more important in the long run, such action serves as a warning to other executive branch officials, telling them, in effect, that their refusal to cooperate with the Congress is going to be a factor in Senate consideration should they ever be nominated to serve in another high government position.

The Senate's willingness to use its confirmation power as a means of prying information out of the executive branch does not always directly involve the particular nominee whose hearing provides the forum for such an effort. In some cases, in fact, a nomination will be used as a kind of hostage in a transaction between the legislative and executive branches. An individual Senator or Senate committee will threaten to withhold action on a nominee until it gets what it wants from some individual or agency in the executive branch.

For several weeks in mid-1974 the Joint Economic Committee had been trying to get President Nixon's chief economic adviser, Kenneth Rush, to testify in open session. Rush, citing executive privilege, had repeatedly demurred. When Nixon nominated Alan Greenspan to be Chairman of the Council of Economic Advisers, the members of the Joint Economic Committee sought to use the confirmation power as a means for putting pressure on Rush. The Greenspan nomination would be heard by the Senate Banking Committee, not the Joint Committee. But the chairman and the ranking member of the Banking Committee both sat on the Joint Committee as well, and they were able to use their membership in the former as a way of serving the purposes of the latter. No sooner had the Greenspan nomination been announced than Senator Proxmire told the press that he would attempt to delay action on the nomination until Rush agreed to testify before the Joint Economic Committee. Shortly thereafter, Rush changed his mind and appeared before the Joint Committee. The Greenspan nomination then proceeded to confirmation without great difficulty.

The Senate Finance Committee took similar action in 1978, when it used the nomination of Donald C. Lubick as Assistant Secretary of the Treasury as a bargaining chip in trying to get information from the Treasury Department. Senator Abraham Ribicoff, a member of the committee, was concerned that a law denying foreign tax breaks to American firms that participated in the Arab boycott against Jewish-owned companies was not being adequately enforced by the Treasury Department. Lubick himself was not an issue here, but Ribicoff threatened to hold up his confirmation until the committee received an adequate explanation of the guidelines the department was using to enforce the antiboycott law.

By far the most common way in which the Senate attempts to use its confirmation power to fulfill its information needs is in requiring nominees, as a condition of their confirmation, to promise to testify and to provide information freely during the period of their government service. This has become a primary concern of Senate committees in the years since the mid-1960s, especially for the Committees on Armed Services and Foreign Relations, which depend so heavily on the executive branch as a source of information. Both committees now routinely request those nominees who appear before them to pledge that they will testify whenever the committee asks and that, with the exception of a valid claim of executive privilege or national security, they will respond to the committee's requests for information. Time after time, committee members will reiterate their constant need for honest, accurate, and complete information. They will continually remind the nominee of his obligation to provide such information. The following colloquy between Senator John Stennis and W. Brewster Kopp, a Johnson nominee as Assistant Secretary of the Army for Financial Management, is characteristic of these exchanges:

> Senator Stennis. You recognize, of course, that you would be a member of the executive branch of government, but especially being

in the financial part, you recognize that it is the legislative branch of the Government, and the legislative only, that supplies the money.
Mr. Kopp. I recognize that.
Senator Stennis. We must have all the facts that we can get in order to make a decision with reference to how much money the executive will have, and you would recognize your responsibility to give us all the facts, those favorable to the Department of Defense and those that are unfavorable; is that right?
Mr. Kopp. I recognize that.
Senator Stennis. This is a very serious question. . . . We are talking about constitutional principles now. So you fully recognize that it is your duty and your responsibility?
Mr. Kopp. I recognize that responsibility; yes, sir.
Senator Stennis. And no one in the Department of Defense or in the Army, either, has any control over you as far as that responsibility goes; is that correct?
Mr. Kopp. Yes, sir.[19]

The practice of requiring nominees to promise to testify when called and to provide requested information to congressional committees was formalized in January 1973, when the Senate Democratic Conference approved the following resolution:

Whereas, the Constitution of the United States, Article II, Section 2, vests the President with the power of appointment "by and with the Advice and Consent of the Senate";
Whereas, on behalf of the Senate, Committees of the Senate are authorized to summon witnesses to appear and testify before duly constituted Committees of the Senate;
Whereas, appointed officials, subsequent to Senate confirmation, have refused on occasion to appear and testify before duly constituted Committees of the Senate;
Resolved by the Democratic Majority of the Senate:
(1) That a prerequisite to confirmation is the commitment of Presidential appointees to appear and testify before duly constituted Committees of the Senate in response to committee requests.
(2) That all Senate Committees bear a responsibility to determine, prior to confirmation, the commitment of Presidential appointees to comply with committee requests to appear and testify before Committees of the Senate;
(3) That Committee reports to the Senate on all cabinet designees and such other appointees as deemed appropriate should contain an evaluation of their commitment to respond to committee requests to appear and testify before duly constituted Senate Committees.[20]

The principal effect of this resolution has been to institutionalize and routinize a practice that a number of committees had already initiated independently. The conference resolution adds the weight of the Democratic majority to committee demands that nominees promise to provide information or testimony when asked to do so. And it forces nominees to make that promise for the public record, so that there can be no quibbling about their obligations when committees subsequently request them to testify.

Oversight

Senate committees have traditionally regarded confirmation hearings as an appropriate and useful forum for the conduct of inquiries relating to their oversight responsibilities. In the postwar years particularly, the dialogue between committees and nominees has abounded with discussions of the administrative policies, decision-making processes, and substantive actions of executive agencies. It is not uncommon, in fact, for a confirmation hearing to be dominated by oversight concerns when a nominee falls into one of these categories: (1) He is being promoted to a higher position within an agency where he has immediate past experience; (2) he is being reappointed to a position in which he currently serves; or (3) he is being transferred from one agency or department to another. In any of these circumstances, the committee has an opportunity to examine both the performance of an individual administrator and the activities of the agency in which he has worked.

Among the oversight topics that frequently arise at confirmation hearings are matters relating to the recruitment and deployment of agency personnel. Concern with this issue ranges from the very general to the very specific. It is not unusual for Senators to inquire about the number of people working in a particular agency or about the ratio of professionals to nonprofessionals.[21] Senators are often interested in determining which individuals are carrying out which functions— whether, for instance, it is civilians or soldiers who have control over the letting of Defense Department contracts.[22] Not uncommonly, questions are asked about the likelihood of future increases or decreases in the size of an agency staff. When particular issues take on enlarged importance in national affairs, members of the Senate will frequently ask about or suggest changes in personnel in the offices that deal with those issues.[23]

Individuals who are nominated to head agencies or bureaus are nearly always asked whether they have any plans to make personnel changes. It is quite commonplace for Senators to make suggestions to the nominee concerning possible improvements in personnel policies or even about the hiring or firing of specific individuals. When George Romney appeared before the Banking and Currency Committee in 1969, Senator Edward Brooke expressed the hope that Romney would "see the great benefit in finding qualified black men to serve with you in your Department and to integrate it at every level."[24] In the hearings held by the Labor and Public Welfare Committee on the nomination of Christopher M. Mould to be an Associate Director of ACTION, Senator Alan Cranston spent most of his time inquiring into the personnel actions the agency had undertaken in regard to a Mr. Chuck Crawford.[25] Similarly, the Senate used its control over the nomination of Walter Hickel to force the Nixon administration to pledge that it would nominate Russell Train, a noted conservationist, to be the number two man in the Interior Department. Conservation-minded Senators were highly dissatisfied with Hickel's views on the use of natural resources, and the Senate as a whole was being lobbied intensively by environmental groups opposed to the Hickel nomination. The demand that an individual of Train's stature and reputation be nominated was viewed as a way of balancing Hickel's tendencies and thus of saving his nomination.[26]

Senators sometimes use a confirmation hearing to question the adequacy or capacity of an administrative staff. Senator Javits, for instance, inquired of John Doar, a Johnson appointee to head the Civil Rights Division of the Department of Justice, whether his staff of lawyers was large enough to carry out the growing responsibilities of that division. Senator Proxmire complained to George Boldt, the Chairman-designate of President Nixon's Pay Board, that reports had been received of poor staff work in the early phase of the board's operations. And when vacancies occur in important staff positions in an agency, a committee will often use a confirmation hearing to try to determine why staff people are leaving and what steps are being taken to replace them.[27]

Senate committees are as interested in the process by which subordinates are chosen as they are in determining who the particular individuals will be. This is especially true in policy areas that are of high importance to the committee. The Labor and Public Welfare Committee, unhappy with the restrictions the Nixon administration had placed on its first Commissioner of Education, James Allen, attempted to ascertain the kind of freedom his successor would have in choosing his own subordinates:

> Senator Claiborne Pell. The Office of Education has a good many top-level jobs vacant now. One thing that concerns me about these jobs, many of which are of a technical nature, is how much political clearance is necessary for them.
>
> Dr. Sidney Marland. Senator Pell, when I was invited to accept this nomination, I took occasion to inquire into that subject, and I was assured that while there would be some political considerations, by and large I would be free to name the top staff that I would hope to discover for the Office of Education.
>
> Senator Pell. I don't mean to embarrass you in any way. There is nothing wrong with political patronage. I am a politician too. If a man is being considered for appointment to one of these top-level jobs, does he need clearance from the national committeeman in his state?
>
> Dr. Marland. Not that I know of, I do not think this is a condition of patronage as far as I can tell.[28]

Hearings on several of Jimmy Carter's high-level appointments to the Justice Department focused at length on candidates for other appointments within the Department. Members of the Senate Judiciary Committee were most concerned that several top positions in the department be filled by individuals with distinguished civil rights records to balance what they believed to be the absence of any demonstrated commitment to civil rights in the record of Griffin Bell, the Attorney General. Intensive questioning at his confirmation hearing forced Bell to reveal that Wade McCree, a black federal judge, would be the President's nominee for the position of Solicitor General. A year and a half later, confirmation hearings on the nomination of Benjamin Civiletti as Deputy Attorney General were dominated by long discussions of the process by which U.S. Attorneys were selected. This line of inquiry was an immediate response to the administration's firing of David Marston, the U.S. Attorney for the Eastern District of Pennsylvania.

Another recurring oversight interest at confirmation hearings is the process by which decisions are made within executive agencies and within an administration generally. The Senate's interest in how decisions get made in the executive branch is rooted in its sense of its own constitutional responsibility and in its collective self-interest. To ensure that accountability can be enforced, the Senate must know who is making important decisions and who is responsible for administrative actions. And to maintain or increase its own influence in those decisions, it must be able to identify and have access to those points in the system where influence can be most effectively exercised. This explains the constant Senate effort in confirmation hearings to learn who participates in a particular chain of command, who reports to whom, or what the coordination points are between agencies. These relationships are not constant. Each new appointment has within it the potential for rearranging the flow of authority within some portion of the executive branch. Hence the constant need for the Senate to seek to determine who is really running things "downtown."

Senators are persistent in attempting to identify the actual policy-makers. They will frequently ask nominees, "Will you be simply an administrator carrying out policies, or do you anticipate having an active role in making policy?"[29] Senators' questions are often phrased in a way that suggests that an individual nominee ought to have a larger or a lesser role in determining policy directions. Sometimes a Senator will express his view that the nominee's new post is essentially administrative or supportive and that the Senate will not look approvingly on any usurpation of policy-making prerogatives. This is especially true when the position under consideration is in the uniformed armed services or the civilian intelligence establishment.

Presidents sometimes use new appointments, rather than institutional reoganizations, to change the flow of administrative power within their administrations. Consecutive appointees with the same title may be given vastly different responsibilities, and the Senate is constantly on guard to detect these changes. Senator Stuart Symington posed the question directly to a Nixon nominee as Assistant Secretary of State for Administration when he asked if the nominee "could draw a functional chart as well as a structural chart as to what are the people supposed to do along with their titles."[30] Many of the posts that have been made subject to Senate confirmation in recent years are not directly subordinate to any Cabinet department. And because they are somewhat free-floating within the administrative structure of the executive branch, the power they exercise tends to vary with the holder. Hence it is common Senate practice to ask each nominee to one of these positions what his power and responsibilities will be relative to those of his predecessor. Carl J. Gilbert, President Nixon's first nominee to serve in the post of Special Representative for Trade Negotiations, was required to appear separately before both the Finance and the Foreign Relations committees. Both committees inquired at length about the amount of authority the nominee would have in this post and what his policy-making responsibilities would be relative to those of his predecessors. Similar questions are often asked of nominees after there has been an executive reorganization,[31] or when a nominee's area of jurisdiction aligns with that of a man of national stature like a Henry Kissinger or a Daniel Patrick Moynihan.[32]

By all appearances, the Senate is as interested in the power relationships between government agencies as in those within them. The nature and the mechanics of coordination between agencies, between federal and state governments,[33] and between the government and private industry[34] are recurring topics in Senate confirmation hearings. The problem of coordination, which is central to the problem of administration, is a prime concern of the Congress in carrying out administrative oversight. But most Senators view the problem of coordination not through the perspective of some normative notions about administrative science, but rather in terms of its impact on policy outcomes. Questions about interagency coordination usually become salient only when particular Senators or committees feel that a policy or program has been weakened by the failure of separate agencies to coordinate their roles in administering it.

In a long colloquy at the reappointment hearing of James L. Robertson, a member of the Federal Reserve Board of Governors, Senators Joseph Clark and Jacob Javits questioned the nominee in depth about the specific mechanisms through which national economic policy was coordinated. Their questions reflected their concern that the left hand of government was too often out of synch with the right hand, largely because of a failure of the several agencies with jurisdiction over economic policy to communicate with one another. Get "the views of persons making policy in allied fields," they told the nominee, "so the monetary policy can be integrated with others who have responsibility for the economy, hopefully so in the end the administration speaks with a unified voice."[35] In a confirmation hearing in 1970, Senator James Pearson stated his exasperation at State Department dominance of international issues in which other departments had a legitimate interest. He wanted to know why this seemed invariably to be the case. "What is the mechanism and consultation and so forth," he asked, "regarding international problems. . .? Who is your counterpart in State? What is the method of consultation? What is the decision machinery?"[36] A similar point was raised with Leroy Collins at the 1965 hearing on his nomination to be

Under Secretary of Commerce in questioning by Senator Warren
Magnuson:

> What I am suggesting is that the liaison between the Export-Import
> Bank and the Department of Commerce, which has the responsibility
> policywise to encourage exports, has not been, in my opinion, as good
> as it should be. Therefore it seems to me that you should give a great
> deal of consideration to working with the Export-Import Bank so that
> credit lines could be extended to a potential American exporter who
> may be in competition with other nations in the world even though it
> may not appear that this is a so-called first-class risk to a commercial
> banker.[37]

The Senate's interest in identifying power structures *within*
agencies is based on its desire to be able to affix responsibility and to
exercise influence. Its interest in power relationships *between* agencies is more closely related to its efforts to ensure the effectiveness of
public policy, to review government activity through the perspective
of government output. But in using the confirmation process to determine how decisions are made in the executive branch, it has a third
interest as well. The Senate constantly wants to know if the ability of
individual agencies to exercise their own independent judgment is
being subverted by the White House. While the Senate wants policy
to be coordinated, it doesn't want that coordination to come about at
the expense of the access and the relationships that have been nurtured so carefully over the years between congressional committees
and executive agencies. The "enemies" most frequently identified at
confirmation hearings by members of the Senate are those presidential assistants in the White House and the Office of Management and
Budget who regularly seek to undermine the independence of the
individual agencies and to cut the heart out of the policies they administer. That many of these presidential aides are not themselves
subject to Senate confirmation does not make them any more lovable
on Capitol Hill.

Members of the Senate often make a point of asking nominees to
important Cabinet and subcabinet positions how independent they
will be of presidential assistants working in the same policy area.
George Romney, for instance, was asked to give a detailed explanation of the plans that he had made for the coordination and division of
responsibility between Daniel Patrick Moynihan, a White House
aide, and himself. Gerard C. Smith, a Nixon nominee to head the
Arms Control and Disarmament Agency, was asked by the Senate

Foreign Relations Committee to outline his relationship with Henry Kissinger and the National Security Council and to assure the committee that his relationship with Kissinger and the NSC did not give him, ipso facto, the right to invoke executive privilege whenever he pleased. In each case, it appeared to be the goal of the Senate to keep policy direction in the hands of those to whom it has the greatest access, that is, out of the hands of White House subordinates.

Nominees are often warned to make every effort to protect their programs from the budget-cutters and the impounders of OMB. Nothing, it seems, is so well calculated to raise the ire of a Senator than to have someone in the White House Office refuse to spend money that has been duly appropriated for a favored project. This problem is difficult to solve directly through the confirmation process, although the possibility of withholding action on nominations as a short-term bargaining point for getting the President to spend impounded funds was discussed at meetings of the Senate Democratic Conference in January 1973. More often the confirmation process is used as a forum for exhorting nominees to fight for their budgets, to defend themselves against those at OMB and on the President's staff who have little stake in the outcome of particular programs or projects. Senator Alan Bible used the confirmation hearing of Rogers C. B. Morton to complain about the impoundment of some $132 million that had been appropriated for national parks:

> Senator Bible. Would you assure me, if you are confirmed as Secretary of the Interior, you would reach for the telephone and call the Bureau of the Budget and say "Now here is something that has already been authorized, which has been approved, for which the dollars have been appropriated: would you please, please, please [shake] loose $135 million?" . . . What we want is to get the money shaken loose. That doesn't take any complicated procedure, it just takes a phone call from you. With your massive personality and your tremendous influence that could be done with one phone call to one place.
> Senator Jackson. What he is saying is to go over there and sit on them. You are big enough to do that.
> Senator Bible. Because this has all been accomplished, the Congress has carried it out.
> Mr. Morton. I realize that and I will use a stronger weapon than the telephone.
> Senator Bible. Whichever one you want, that is fine. I wanted to be sure we could move forward. It is frustrating for us to work and read these messages of great hope of bringing parks to the people and get-

ting them in the big cities and we accomplish it and then somebody
takes the money away so we can't get it done.[38]

Sometimes the threat to an agency's independence comes not
from the White House but from one of the Cabinet departments or
regulatory commissions with an overlapping jurisdiction. Senate
committees grow comfortable in their dealings with individual
bureaus and agencies; they build relationships over time that provide
opportunities for the exchange of ideas and influence. Challenges to
the sanctity of the agency's domain are viewed by the committee as
threats to its own influence over that domain. Such challenges are not
taken lightly. The Small Business Administration, for instance, is an
independent agency whose jurisdiction overlaps that of the much
larger Commerce Department. This is a source of some paranoia to
the Senate subcommittee that oversees the SBA. Senator Thomas
McIntyre, the chairman of that subcommittee, expressed this fear to
Hilary Sandoval, whom President Nixon had chosen to head the SBA:

> I really do not need to say this, Mr. Sandoval, but in deference to your
> newness here in Washington and this matter we are talking about—the
> Commerce Department and the SBA—you seemed a little lukewarm,
> you know, on this. You want to get one message. If somebody starts
> pushing you around on this—I am talking about Commerce moving in
> on SBA—you have a lot of friends up here on the Hill, at least on this
> side of Congress. You get on the telephone or come running up here.
> That is the message we want to get to you this morning.[39]

Hearings may also be used, and in fact frequently are used, as a
forum for reviewing the past performance of an agency, office, or
commission. Discussions between the committee and the nominee
may center almost entirely on one or a few issue areas within the
latter's jurisdiction. Or they may focus solely on the recent activities
of an agency, even if the nominee himself was not directly responsible
for those activities. In this sense, a confirmation hearing may well
take on all the characteristics of an oversight investigation. Senator
Birch Bayh once stated this connection during intensive questioning
of a nominee about the programs he had administered:

> Very frankly, and I hope without sounding melodramatic because I do
> not feel that way about it, but just from a very practical standpoint, I
> finally asked myself, "Did the Founding Fathers really mean anything
> by giving the Senate the power to advise and consent to administration

appointees?" If there was wisdom in these actions—and history, I think, indicates great wisdom—then any member of this body has not only the right but the solemn obligation to actively oppose nominations believed not to be in the best interests of the country. . . .

[T]his issue does not concern [the nominee] alone. It concerns our broader responsibility as Senators to exercise our function of legislative oversight—our function to review the administration of programs that Congress has authorized and funded.[40]

Not infrequently nominees are taken to task by individual committee members for the failure of the agency with which they have been or will be affiliated to carry out a particular program as intended by the Congress. Confirmation hearings provide a unique opportunity for Senators to communicate their frustrations about this directly to those who administer the programs. The Chairman of the Labor and Public Welfare Committee did just that in his questioning of Roy E. Batchelor, whom President Nixon had nominated to be Assistant Director of OEO in 1971. "I wonder," the Chairman asked, "if I could get a picture of the community action program, and specifically why I receive so many complaints that there just doesn't seem to be a logical flow of funds, that there are stoppages along the way after programs have been approved.[41]

A good example of the use of the confirmation process to perform oversight functions involves not one but four hearings held during the summer and fall of 1972. All of these dealt almost exclusively with the allegation that unauthorized bombing had been carried out in Southeast Asia at the command of John D. Lavelle, an Air Force general. This activity came to light as a result of an exchange of correspondence between a member of Congress and an enlisted man in General Lavelle's command. The general was given the opportunity to retire "voluntarily" after his role became known; as is customary in such cases, his retirement would be in a permanent rank higher than the one he then held. Because such a promotion required confirmation by the Senate, it afforded the Armed Services Committee an opportunity to explore the bombing question in depth. The committee members and staff geared up for a comprehensive investigation of the entire matter, and the hearing rambled on for days until the investigation was completed to the committee's satisfaction. But that was not the whole of the Senate's exploration of the Lavelle affair. The Armed Services Committee also made a number of pointed inquiries about it at subsequent hearings it held on the nominations to higher rank of General Alexander M. Haig and General Creighton W. Abrams. It had done so earlier in the summer at hearings on the renomination of Admiral Thomas N. Moorer as Chairman of the Joint Chiefs of Staff. The coincidence of all these nominations at roughly the same time gave the Armed Services Committee a convenient vehicle for exploring the unauthorized bombing of North Vietnam with several of the leading participants in the chain of command.

It is the convenience of confirmation hearings that makes them so amenable to the pursuit of oversight concerns. Senators have crowded schedules that make it difficult for committees to hold special oversight hearings on a regular basis. But confirmation hearings, like appropriations hearings, are a routine part of the Senate work load and often become the best available forum for examining the daily operations of executive agencies.

But confirmation hearings have advantages beyond their mere convenience. They are often more visible and more widely reported than routine oversight hearings. The concerns expressed at confirmation hearings may thus have a larger audience and a wider impact than they would in some other forum. A Senate committee staff member noted, for instance:

> When you have a confirmation hearing, you have the attention of the national media, which focuses the general public and the newspapers on the issues that the senators are pursuing; so in a sense, the confirmation hearings are your best chance to perform oversight. [42]

Influencing Policy Decisions

Probing a nominee's policy views, gathering information, and pursuing oversight concerns are all ways in which the Senate injects policy considerations into the confirmation process. But the willingness of Senate committees to use the confirmation power for policy-related purposes hardly stops there. As already noted, substantial leverage results for the Senate from its final control over appointments through the confirmation power. Senate committees are not unwilling to apply that leverage in trying to shape future policy decisions.

In a very real sense, a nominee is a captive of a committee until his appointment is confirmed. And during his time in "captivity" committees have several procedures they employ to pressure the nominee into modifying his own intentions or even agreeing to follow a policy course suggested by the committee. It may be helpful to conceive of these procedures as graduated steps in the confrontation between committees and nominees. Each one is a slightly more potent tactical instrument, and each is likely, therefore, to be more effective than the preceding one in bringing the nominee's future actions into line with the committee's policy preferences.

The first and mildest procedure involves little more than providing guidance to a nominee with regard to the future performance of his responsibilities. Senators, often acting individually, mention certain problems the nominee is likely to face and suggest appropriate courses of action for him to follow. Sometimes these are suggestions expressed without any threat that reprisals will ensue if they are not heeded. Senator Howard Baker's remarks to a Johnson nominee to the Appalachian Regional Commission are an example:

> I agree that you can't develop every community on the side of the hill, but I often wonder if we don't tend to build roads where it is cheapest to build roads, and often spend our money in metropolitan areas where the local justifications for such commitments are more apparent than in less-populated and more depressed areas, and if we might not give extra and added emphasis to the matter of creating access to these remote areas and providing more stimulation for basic development of regions which are not as accessible and are not moving as fast as some of those otherwise characterized as "areas with future growth potential."
>
> I don't ask you to reply to that. I simply think this hearing is a good place for me to present that view for whatever it is worth to you, and have it in this record. [43]

Suggestions such as these appear throughout the confirmation process. They are not merely limited to the hearings. Senator Jacob Javits, for instance, used the floor debate on the nomination on Nicholas Katzenbach for Attorney General to admonish the new appointee to give the highest priority to the effort to ensure legal protection of the right of Negroes in Dallas County, Alabama, to register to vote. He urged Katzenbach to "take this action without a moment's delay" because it was "a subject of the highest priority and responsibility."[44]

If sufficiently displeased with government action in a particular policy area, Senators will sometimes couch a policy suggestion in strong language and couple it with the threat of further, more drastic, action if the suggestion is not heeded. The following portion of a long discussion between Senator Norris Cotton and Harold C. Passer, an Assistant Secretary–designate of Commerce, is illustrative of this technique:

> Senator Cotton. Now I can't conceive of a person of your background—and it is a very find background—going down there in this highly responsible position having to do with broad economic policies and not sitting in and being one of the advisers on this matter of foreign trade policy. There are a large number of us who have come to the end of our patience. We have seen what has happened to textiles. The cotton textile industry has sustained the full blow. Some protection has finally been given the industry—but it is too little and too late. . . .
>
> When Secretary Stans told us of his efforts to protect the remainder of the textile industry, I asked him about shoes. He said, "One thing at a time. We aren't going to do anything about shoes until we try to do something about textiles. One thing at a time."
>
> Well, the one thing at a time business is like opening the henhouse door and chasing one hen while the rest all escape.
>
> My point is this: Some of us mean business up here. For example, 32 Senators—30 Senators and 2 pairs—voted against the confirmation of Mr. Gilbert. Now, Mr. Gilbert is a very fine man. However, we opposed him because of his views against any unilateral action by the United States in the area of foreign trade to protect our domestic industries.
>
> Now, I am telling you frankly that I have reached a point where I am not going to vote to confirm another official in this Government who has any jurisdiction or advisory capacity on this matter if I am convinced that his attitude is that neither Congress nor the Executive should do anything to protect our dying industries. . . .
>
> I certainly hope you will consult the Secretary on this matter. I may even request the Chairman of the Committee to have another hearing on just that point. Understand that I do not direct this at you personally, for I have the highest regard for you. But this is a desperate matter and my colleagues and I are gravely concerned. . . .
>
> I hope that ultimately you will be confirmed, and if so, I shall be among the first to wish you great success in your position.
>
> However, the only way for some of us to get attention is to become difficult. And from now on, on this matter, I am going to be very, very difficult regardless of whose administration is in office.[45]

Senate committees are often particularly eager to offer guidance and instructions to nominees who will be serving in newly created governmental offices. One reason for this is that the burst of energy and interest that surrounds the creation of a new agency or office carries over into the process of selecting the first individual to lead the agency or fill the office. "In view of the great involvement of this committee in that legislation," said Senator Harrison Williams to the first nominee to fill a newly created office at the Equal Employment Opportunity Commission, "We are naturally most interested in the person who will be filling this key position."[46] A second reason for unusual interest in providing guidance to those who will be the first to serve in new positions is the desire on the part of a committee to have the nominee share its sense of the purpose of the authorizing legislation and the intent of the Congress in enacting it. Since past experience provides no clues as to what is expected of those who serve in such a position, the committee attempts to fill the vacuum with statements of its own views on the matter. "Although the Congress does not encumber the administration of one of its acts," said the Chairman of the Public Works Committee in 1965, "the members of the Senate and the Congress do have a responsibility to see that the intent of the Congress, the purpose written into the bill, be carried into effect."[47] Coming as it does right at the interstices of legislative enactment and administrative implementation, the confirmation process provides abundant opportunities for this kind of guidance.

There are several ways in which the intent of a committee and the Congress is communicated to the nominee. The most frequently employed is simple and direct instruction: A member of a committee walks the nominee through the statute, explaining the meaning and purpose of each section as he goes along. By and large, this "walk-through" is conducted by the Senator who had primary responsibility for authoring the legislation. When William D. Ruckelshaus appeared before the Public Works Committee as the first nominee to head the Environmental Protection Agency, he received just this sort of treatment from Senator Edmund Muskie. The following few sentences are indicative of the kinds of concern the Senator expressed:

> Senator Muskie. With respect to section 310 which I have just read, this makes you a self-starter, whenever you, unilaterally, see an environmental risk. You are given the responsibility to raise the red flag.
>
> What is involved here is not an input to somebody else's decision and somebody else's statement. This is an issue to be taken by you. The reason that we are making you independent is so that you will be independent. I think the Council and you have a responsibility for seeing to it that whenever an environmental evaluation is made,

whether pursuant to section 102 or this, that that evaluation enters the public domain as soon as you have made it.

To wait until it can be buried in some promotional or developmental agency's report or statement is to give it less than the emphasis we intended for it.

We want you to be the advocate that you described in response to Senator Gurney's question. We want you to be the gadfly. That is the whole purpose of it. I would like to make that clear.[48]

"The concern of the committee," Muskie said later in the hearing, "is that we achieve the objectives that we have laid down."[49]

Since Senators who author or who have a profound interest in certain pieces of legislation are not always themselves members of the committees that hold the relevant confirmation hearings, those committees will commonly invite or accommodate requests from other Senators to attend. On occasion the same privilege is granted to members of the House of Representatives who are also deeply interested in the administration of programs and policies for which they have worked. When Sidney Marland appeared before the Labor and Public Works Committee in 1972 as the first nominee to be Assistant Secretary of Education in the Department of HEW, one of his questioners was Representative John Brademas, whom the Senate committee had allowed to participate in the hearings. Brademas, who had been a leading proponent in the House of the legislation creating this new office, had requested the opportunity to question the nominee because of his desire to "review the intent of Congress with respect to the new position."[50] He spoke not only to the nominee but to the Committee as well:

> [T]he outlook and actions of the first Assistant Secretary for Education will give important shape to the future of that position in our government. Let us make sure that the die is cast in accord with Congressional intent. . . .
>
> I hope this great committee, if it decides to recommend confirmation on the nominee, will make clear the duties and the authority of the Assistant Secretary as well as the limits of those duties and authority.[51]
>
> I am here to say this seems the appropriate time for legislators to reflect on the intent of Congress and give voice to this intent. And I think if we do not give voice to apprehension before the horse is let out of the barn, we have only ourselves to blame.[52]

Few pieces of new legislation are so specific that they include guidelines for every activity a newly created office or agency will undertake. Because statutes always leave some measure of discretion to the new official, committees often use confirmation hearings to discern as clearly as possible how that discretionary authority is to be exercised. Committee members will often want to know what priorities the nominee has or, if the new position is subordinate, what duties are going to be assigned to him by his superiors.[53] Sometimes the committee will ask the nominee to draw a chart showing the relationships and lines of authority the new legislation will cause to occur within an existing agency.[54] If Senate interest in a new program or agency is keen enough, a committee may well require a nominee to submit a report within a given period of time detailing the way in which he is carrying out the duties of the new position.[55] Not only does this provide the Congress with a certain amount of immediate feedback on the operations of the new office, it also puts the nominee in the position of knowing that the Congress is watching closely to see that his activities adhere to the purposes for which the position was created.

When Senators or committees feel deeply about an issue or program, they are not always satisfied merely to communicate their concerns to a nominee. Often they want a surer way to get him to recognize, to respect, and—not uncommonly—to act upon those concerns. When this is so, other more authoritative techniques may be employed. The most frequently used technique is the elicitation of pledges from the nominee regarding his actions in office after his confirmation.

One of the purposes for holding public confirmation hearings is to "make a record." Not only do Senate committees wish to determine, in Senator Proxmire's words, "whether or not a proposed nominee would carry out the law and the will of the Congress,"[56] but they desire as well to get a full statement of the nominee's ideas and priorities on the public record so that in the future they and the American people will have some clear basis for judging his performance and his honesty. Also implicit is the belief that the nominee will feel a commitment to act in accord with the statements and promises he made publicly at his confirmation hearings. As a general rule, such statements are not lightly made; they may well come back to haunt the unfortunate nominee who is unwilling or unable to act upon them. One of the pledges most frequently demanded of nominees has already been discussed, namely, that they promise to provide testimony or information to a Senate committee in reponse to any reasonable request. Requests for pledges from nominees are quite often more specific than this, however. Such pledges may refer to future procedural operations or future policy decisions in which the nominee is likely to be personally involved.

William D. Eberle, nominated as President Nixon's Special Trade Representative, was forced to bear the brunt of the Finance Committee's unhappiness over the Congress's lack of influence in recent foreign trade agreements. The committee sought to rectify this by securing a promise from the nominee that he would do whatever he could to see that Congress would be involved in further agreements of this sort:

> Senator Wallace Bennett. This committee has had some difficulties with the executive agreements which have attempted to bind the hands of Congress. The GATT is one. The Anti-Dumping Code is another. Can we be assured that you will not be a party to any executive agreement in the development of which Congress has not been taken into your confidence and the confidence of the administration?
> Mr. Eberle. I can assure you, speaking as an individual, that this committee will be informed prior to any such agreement and your advice will certainly be taken.[57]

During the period when the Watergate scandal was very much on the minds of members of Congress, Senate committees found the confirmation power a useful instrument for advancing the investigation of the Nixon administration. In considering the nominations of Elliot Richardson and William Saxbe to the position of Attorney General, the Judiciary Committee used its confirmation power to help ensure a speedy and objective investigation of the entire Watergate affair. When President Nixon nominated Richardson to replace Richard Kleindienst, he suggested that a "special prosecutor" be appointed for the sole purpose of investigating the scandals. During confirmation hearings, the Judiciary Committee made a point of requiring Richardson to select and announce the name of the special prosecutor and to pledge to the committee that the prosecutor would have complete independence from the White House and the Justice Department in carrying out its investigation. Richardson, after a period of initial reluctance, acceded to the committee's demand (it had refused to act on his nomination until he did). He named Archibald Cox as the special prosecutor and pledged to support his independence. When William Saxbe was nominated to succeed Richardson as Attorney General, the Judiciary Committee was no less assiduous in demanding that he too promise his support for the independence of the new special prosecutor.

Occasionally a nominee's confirmation is conditioned on a pledge made not by him but by the President. In late 1975, for instance, some members of the Senate Armed Services Committee expressed their reluctance to support the nomination of George Bush as director of the CIA. They regarded Bush as an active political partisan and a potential Republican vice-presidential nominee in 1976. This contradicted, as Senator Frank Church noted, "the very purpose of political objectivity for which the agency was created."[58] At his confirmation hearing, Bush refused to rule himself out as a future vice-presidential candidate, and the committee reacted by delaying a decision on his confirmation. The impasse was not overcome until the committee received a letter from President Ford declaring that he "would not consider" Bush as his running mate in 1976. The Bush nomination was subsequently approved by the committee and confirmed by a 64–27 vote in the Senate.

Senate committees sometimes elicit pledges from nominees as a way of assuaging their doubts about a nominee's personal policy views. The more "controversial" those views or the more they run counter to sizable bodies of opinion in the Senate, the more likely it is that they will be examined in depth and that the nominee will be required to pledge to take or not to take certain actions after he has been confirmed. This is a kind of escape mechanism for the Senate. While it may not be attractive to individual nominees or to the President to have such commitments required of them, it does provide the Senate with a means of satisfying those who are unhappy with the nominee's views or past actions without having to take the ultimate step of defeating the nomination. To get the man he wants, the President may have to pay the price of accepting some restrictions on that man's freedom of action.

The nomination of James R. Smith for Assistant Secretary of the Interior for Water and Power Development fits into this category. Smith had recently served as an employee and director of the Mississippi Valley Association. The association had consistently opposed federal statutes giving preference to consumer-owned electric systems in the sale of power produced and marketed by U.S. government agencies. Because Smith admitted that he had "tacitly concurred" with the position of the MVA on this issue, the Interior Committee demanded that he pledge to "support the preference clause wherever it is written into the laws of the land."[59]

A better-known example, and one that more fully elaborates the potential extent of the Senate's influence over a nominee's future policy decisions, was the treatment of Walter Hickel's nomination as Nixon's first Secretary of the Interior. When Hickel's nomination was announced in December 1968, little was known about him outside the State of Alaska, where he was a first-term Governor. In the month that followed, however, he quickly became the most controversial of the original Nixon nominees—in many ways the most controversial Cabinet selection since Lewis Strauss in 1959. Two things happened in that month to fan the flames that nearly consumed the Hickel nomination. First, a searching examination of Hickel's past performance as a Governor and as a businessman was undertaken. Alsaka in 1968 was still very much a frontier state, inching along at the edge of economic development. As Governor, Hickel was concerned with industrial growth and impatient with environmental restrictions that might well inhibit such growth. He had not hesitated to take that position publicly.

After the announcement of his nomination, he was subjected to searching inquiries about his policy views from members of the press. Unfamiliar with the jackal instincts of national journalists and not sufficiently cognizant of the caution that is necessary in dealing with them, Hickel make several unfortunate statements about his policy views, which began almost immediately to haunt him and to endanger his nomination. Most troubling to the members of the Interior Committee were his attacks on water quality standards and his statement that he did not believe in "conservation for conservation's sake." It is something of a tradition in the Senate to grant the President wide latitude in the selection of Cabinet officers. In order to follow that tradition without falling down in its own obligation to ensure that government officials will uphold the law and carry out the will of Congress, the Interior Committee elicited several firm policy commitments from Hickel before it voted to support the nomination.

It required him to promise that he would uphold the Interior Department's rule of "no degradation" with respect to water quality, that he would refrain from opening up more wildlife refuges to commercial oil drilling, and that he would not—as he had suggested publicly he would—reverse the freeze that Interior Secretary Stewart Udall had placed on public lands in Alaska until after the Congress could deal with the complex question of native land claims. Hickel's administrative discretion was limited as well by the strong pressure that the committee put on him and on the White House to nominate as under secretary an individual with a sterling record on conservation issues. In an apparent attempt to save the Hickel nomination, the White House announced its intent to nominate Russell Train, president of the Conservation Foundation, to fill that post. Hickel, though he had never met Train and undoubtedly would have preferred someone of his own choosing, wholeheartedly endorsed the Train nomination. Again in this case, as in the others previously discussed, the Senate was able to confirm the President's nominee and at the same time gain some assurance that the nominee would not act in violation of prevailing Senate attitudes on certain important public policy issues.[60]

There is a difference, of course, between making a pledge and keeping it. Once pledges have been made and a nomination is formally confirmed, it cannot subsequently be unconfirmed should the nominee renege on his promises to a committee.[61] Senate committees, therefore, have had to develop techniques for following up on the pledges made by presidential appointees. The techniques employed most frequently for this purpose are reporting requirements and direct intervention.

Senate committees occasionally require written reports from appointees as a means of examining their activities in the period immediately following their confirmation. Secretary Hickel, for instance, was asked to submit a report setting forth "the objectives of the Department and the issues it will face in the years ahead."[62] Senator Jackson, the Interior Committee chairman, told the nominee of his plans to hold hearings on the substance of this report within the following six to eight weeks. In another instance, General William McKee was required to report to the Commerce Committee on the status of the medical department of the Federal Aviation Administration after he took over as its administrator and also to report in writing to the committee whenever a civilian employee was replaced by someone in uniform.[63]

There is perhaps no better example of the use of this technique than the Senate's treatment of the nomination of Robert L. Bennett to head the Bureau of Indian Affairs. The frustation that the Interior Committee had frequently expressed over the inability of the government effectively to resolve the problems of American Indians was the central focus of this hearing. The committee had few complaints about the nominee personally; indeed, he appeared to be held in rather high esteem by some members. That he was the first native American to be nominated for this position was a factor convincingly in his favor. But the committee used the opportunity that this nomination provided to express scathing criticisms of the past performance of the Bureau and to communicate to the nominee a whole series of instructions regarding needed changes in its structure, goals, and operations.

To emphasize its concern and to "elaborate on the numerous subjects discussed at the hearing which reflect the committee's dissatisfaction with the pace of progress in elevating the American Indian to a level of parity with other citizens of the country," the committee took the unusual step of issuing a formal report on the nomination.[64] The committee not only detailed its own views on the policies and programs of the bureau, it also instructed the nominee to "formally advise the Committee, in writing, within 90 days following his confirmation of the steps he has taken to begin to meet the problems outlined herein, and to make periodic reports thereafter of the progress achieved."[65]

The other way in which Senate committees typically enforce the promises made at confirmation hearings is by reacting sharply and immediately when they receive an indication of noncompliance on the part of an appointee. Often this involves direct communication between the committee chairman and the appointee. The latter is reminded of his pledge to the committee, informed of the committee's continuing concern that the pledge be upheld, and, if necessary, warned that public hearings or other action may follow if evidence of noncompliance persists.

When the Commerce Committee held hearings on the nomination of John H. Reed to be chairman of the National Transportation Safety Board, it required him to promise to keep the board's deliberations free of outside political interference. Two years later the committee received information indicating that Reed had allowed the White House to pressure the board into withholding reports critical of the Nixon administration. In response, Chairman Warren Magnuson sent a strongly worded letter to Reed rebuking him and demanding that he provide the committee with complete information on the incidents involved.

A similar series of events followed the appointment of William Saxbe as Attorney General in the Nixon administration. Saxbe, like Elliot Richardson before him, was required at his confirmation hearings to pledge his support for the independence of the Watergate Special Prosecutor. In May 1974, when Special Prosecutor Leon Jaworski felt that his independence was being undermined by President Nixon's efforts to limit the prosecutor's right to go to court to enforce his subpoenas, he wrote a letter to the chairman of the Judiciary Committee indicating his belief that the President's actions were "in contravention of the understanding I had and the members of your committee apparently had at the time of my appointment."[66] The Committee responded rather angrily to this. Senator Robert Byrd remarked on the Senate floor that the President had violated "the assurances that have repeatedly been made to the Senate Judiciary Committee, that the special prosecutor would have full independence in pressing legal proceedings when the special prosecutor concluded that it was necessary to do so."[67] The Committee prepared a statement for the Attorney General reminding him of his pledge, and expressing its unanimous view that he should "use all reasonable and appropriate means to guarantee the independence" of the special prosecutor.[68] Saxbe responded with a statement in which he declared his continuing determination to fight for Jaworski's right to proceed as he saw fit.

Despite the availability of the techniques just described, Senate committees seldom resort to them. The simple reason is that there is rarely any need for committees actively to enforce the pledges they elicit from nominees at confirmation hearings. We have already examined the importance of confirmation hearings as a forum in which nominees and committees begin to form impressions of one another. In most cases, the relationship between a committee and a nominee will last as long as the latter stays in government. He and the committee will often deal with each other on important matters of mutual concern. Each from time to time will require the aid or acquiescence of the other. Broken pledges are not a very sound basis on which to construct an effective working relationship of this sort.

But this is more than a mere question of operational expediency. Confirmation pledges are also valued for reasons of principle. Nominees tend to be honorable men and women. They do not casually make promises they cannot or will not keep. Their reputations are too important to them personally and too essential to them politically to permit any disregard of promises made in a public forum.

A search of the record reveals little evidence of broken confirmation pledges. Strict adherence is the far more likely response. Elliot Richardson, for instance, thought the violation of the independence of the Watergate special prosecutor left him little choice but to resign. So too did his deputy, William Ruckelshaus. Alvin Arnett, a Nixon appointee as director of the Office of Economic Opportunity, had promised the Labor and Public Welfare Committee during his confirmation hearings that he would act to protect OEO from any efforts by the Nixon administration to dismantle it. He carried out his pledge with such vigor that he was summarily dismissed by the President in the summer of 1974. As these and many other cases indicate, the elicitation of pledges is often an effective practice of Senate committees for influencing the future actions of presidential nominees.

Delay is another tactic used by Senate committees. Since the Senate alone has ultimate control over confirmation decisions, it can simply bide its time until it has thoroughly examined a nominee and is satisfied that his opinions and intentions conform sufficiently to its expectations. Delay is sometimes used to force a nominee to take certain specified actions, to provide information, to state his policy views more clearly, or to agree to a pledge a committee has sought to elicit from him. In 1975, for example, the Banking Committee delayed action on the nomination of Philip O. Jackson to be a governor of the Federal Reserve System until Jackson appeared before the committee a second time to provide a fuller statement of his views than he had been willing to provide the first time.

Delayed action on nominations often occurs in the congressional session immediately preceding a presidential election. Senators or committees unhappy with a nominee may attempt to postpone a final decision in the hope that a new President will be elected and will nominate a different candidate for the position in dispute. This was the hope of those who forced the recommittal of Abe Fortas's nomination as Chief Justice of the United States in 1968 and of those who postponed action on dozens of President Ford's nominees in 1976. In those instances, delayed action had the effect of rejection without all the bother or pain of an out-and-out fight on a confirmation vote.

The Senate's ultimate control over nominations—the power to reject them or force their withdrawal—is not often employed. It is seldom necessary, because conflicts between the Senate and the President, or between committees and nominees, are nearly always worked out at some earlier stage in the appointment process. In this fundamental way, the confirmation process is agreement-oriented. By design and tradition, it tends to generate compromise rather than conflict. Senators derive little political benefit and even less pleasure from the rejection of a nomination. It is a step they are likely to take only when all of the compromise mechanisms available to them have been explored and exhausted. This usually occurs when there is compeling evidence of conflict of interest or unethical behavior or when the policy views of a nominee and the majority of a committee are beyond accommodation.

In the mid-1970s, for instance, committee deliberations on the nominations of Ben Blackburn to head the Federal Home Loan Bank Board, Joseph Coors as a director of the Corporation for Public Broadcasting, and Theodore Sorensen as Director of the CIA all fell into the latter category and all led to the forced withdrawal of the nominations. The philosophical and policy differences between these nominees and the committees with jurisdiction over them could not be compromised. But neither, in the committees' view, could they be tolerated.

The point that emerges here is that public policy concerns are the dominant topic in the confirmation process and the dominant factor in most confirmation decisions. The Senate considers a number of things in formulating its confirmation decisions, but no other single issue is as pervasive or as determinative as its concern over a nominee's likely impact on public policy. Even when Senators cite other reasons as their basis for opposition to a nominee—and they usually do—often that is just a disguise for their displeasure with his political philosophy or his views on important policy issues.

It is equally important to note that this deep concern with the policy implications of nominations is not limited to any specific category of offices or agencies. The Senate has a tradition of acting deferentially toward nominees to the Cabinet and to other positions in the President's immediate "family." But that tradition is not sacrosanct. It does not prevent Senators from pursuing their policy concerns wherever they may lead. In fact, some of the most extensive—and most abusive—confirmation hearings of the postwar period have taken place over the Cabinet nominations of people like Lewis Strauss, Walter Hickel, Richard Kleindienst, and Griffin Bell.

On the surface, the confirmation process seems to be riddled with inconsistency. Two successive nominations by the same President to the same position may be treated in entirely different ways by the Senate. Hearings for one may be short, perfunctory, even laudatory, with confirmation coming the same day the nomination is received. The other may be subjected to intensive scrutiny that drags on for months before some final resolution is achieved. But this is not as inconsistent as it appears. There is a logic to it, a logic rooted deeply in the concern of individual Senators with basic issues of public policy. The Senate is almost completely consistent in handling smoothly those nominations that raise no apparent policy problems and in examining rigorously those that do.

Notes

1. Joseph R. Harris, *The Advice and Consent of the Senate* (University of California Press, 1953), p. 385.
2. *Congressional Record*, 3, (July 26, 1965): 18245.
3. 1969—Judiciary—Clement Haynsworth: Associate Justice, United States Supreme Court, p. 327.
4. *Ibid.*, p. 35.
5. 1966—Foreign Relations—Nicholas de B. Katzenbach: Under Secretary of State, p. 3.
6. 1971—Agriculture and Forestry—Earl L. Butz: Secretary of Agriculture, p. 144.
7. For a good example of this, see 1976—Commerce—S. John Byington: Chairman, Consumer Product Safety Commission, pp. 110-118.
8. Interview with Samuel A. Schulhof, conducted by William Stimson, Washington, D.C., June 12, 1974.
9. 1965—Judiciary—John Doar: Assistant Attorney General (Civil Rights Division), p. 4.
10. 1966—Foreign Relations—Robert R. Bowie: Counselor, Department of State, p. 21.
11. 1966—Foreign Relations—Lincoln Gordon: Assistant Secretary of State (Inter-American Affairs), p. 22.
12. 1964—Armed Services—Daniel M. Luevano: Assistant Secretary of the Army (Installations and Logistics), p. 7.
13. 1965—Commerce—James J. Wadsworth: member, FCC, p. 36.
14. This is not exclusively the case. Senators will sometimes use a confirmation hearing to obtain information that bears on their work in another committee. See, for instance, Senator Hartke's comments at 1965—Commerce—Andrew F. Brimmer: Assistant Secretary of Commerce (Economic Affairs), p. 14.
15. 1965—Commerce—Robert L. Bartley: member, FCC, p. 36.
16. 1970—Labor and Public Welfare—Frank Carlucci: Director, Office of Economic Opportunity, p. 180.
17. 1973—Judiciary—L. Patrick Gray: Director, FBI.
18. In the history of the Republic, the Senate has refused to confirm only eight Cabinet nominations.
19. 1965—Armed Services—W. Brewster Kopp: Assistant Secretary of the Army (Financial Management), pp. 3-4.
20. Quoted in *Congressional Record*, 119 (January 16, 1973, daily edition): 5723.
21. See, for instance, 1971—Finance—William D. Eberle: Special Representative for Trade Negotiations.

22. 1970—Armed Services—Thomas H. Moorer: Chairman, Joint Chiefs of Staff.

23. 1970—Commerce—Charles D. Baker: Assistant Secretary of Transportation (Policy and International Affairs).

24. 1969—Banking and Currency—George W. Romney: Secretary of Housing and Urban Development, p. 24.

25. 1972—Labor and Public Welfare—Christopher M. Mould: Associate Director, ACTION, p. 22.

26. See Luther J. Carter, "Hickel Controversy Points Up Environmental Quality Issue," *Science*, Vol. 163, January 31, 1969.

27. See, for example, 1967—Labor and Public Welfare—Arnold Ordman: General Counsel, National Labor Relations Board.

28. 1970—Labor and Public Welfare—Sidney P. Marland: Commissioner of Education, p. 55.

29. 1964—Commerce—Nicholas Johnson: Maritime Administrator, p. 8.

30. 1969—Foreign Relations—Francis G. Meyer: Assistant Secretary of State (Administration), p. 17.

31. 1972—Finance—George P. Shultz: Secretary of the Treasury. Shultz was asked to outline the place of the Commissioner of Internal Revenue in the chain of command as the result of a recent reorganization in the Treasury Department.

32. 1970—Finance—Edward F. Zigler: Chief, Children's Bureau, Department of HEW. Zigler was questioned in detail about the relationship between his position and that of Assistant Secretary James Farmer.

33. See, for example, 1964—Labor and Public Welfare—R. Sargent Shriver: Director, Office of Economic Opportunity.

34. See, for example, 1967—Interior and Insular Affairs—Max N. Edwards: Assistant Secretary of the Interior.

35. 1964—Banking and Currency—James L. Robertson: member, Federal Reserve Board of Governors, p. 10.

36. 1970—Commerce—Charles D. Baker: Assistant Secretary of Transportation (Policy and International Affairs), p. 15.

37. 1965—Commerce—Leroy Collins: Under Secretary of Commerce, p. 4.

38. 1971—Interior and Insular Affairs—Rogers C. B. Morton: Secretary of the Interior, pp. 20–21. The Passage of PL 93-344 strengthened congressional control over presidential impoundments and virtually eliminated this as a topic of discussion at confirmation hearings after 1974.

39. 1969—Banking and Currency—Hilary Sandoval: Administrator, Small Business Administration, p. 23.

40. 1967—Foreign Relations—Rutherford M. Poats: Deputy Administrator, AID, pp. 39–40.

41. 1971—Labor and Public Welfare—Roy E. Batchelor: Assistant Director (Operations), Office of Economic Opportunity, p. 3.

42. Quoted in Susan Webb Hammond et al., "Senate Oversight Activities," in U.S. Senate, 94th Congress, 2d Session, Commission on the Operation of the Senate, *Techniques and Procedures for Analysis and Evaluation*, p. 84.

43. 1968—Public Works—Meriwether L. C. Tyler: Alternate Federal Cochairman, Appalachian Regional Commission, p. 3.

44. *Congressional Record*, 111 (February 10, 1965): 2557.

45. 1969—Commerce—Harold C. Passer: Assistant Secretary of Commerce (Economic Affairs), pp. 51–52.

46. 1972—Labor and Public Welfare—William A. Carey: General Counsel, Equal Employment Opportunity Commission, p. 1.

47. 1965—Public Works—Eugene P. Foley: Assistant Secretary of Commerce (Economic Development), p. 13.

48. 1970—Public Works—William D. Ruckelshaus: Adminstrator, Environmental Protection Agency, p. 45.

49. *Ibid.*, p. 77.

50. 1972—Labor and Public Welfare—Sidney P. Marland: Assistant Secretary of HEW (Education), p. 64.

51. *Ibid.*, p. 69.

52. *Ibid.*, p. 76.

53. See, for instance, 1966—Public Works—Ross R. Davis: Administrator for Economic Development, Department of Commerce, p. 1.

54. See 1967—Commerce—Everett Hutchinson: Under Secretary of Transportation, p. 8.

55. See 1967—Commerce—John E. Robson: General Counsel, Department of Transportation, p. 17.

56. 1972—Banking, Housing and Urban Affairs—Mary Hamilton: member, Price Commission, p. 5.

57. 1971—Finance—William D. Eberle: Special Representative for Trade Negotiations, p. 5.

58. Quoted in *Washington Post*, January 28, 1976.

59. 1969—Interior and Insular Affairs—James R. Smith: Assistant Secretary of the Interior (Water and Power Development), p. 58. See also American Public Power Association, *Newsletter*, March 27, 1969, p. 2.

60. Nominees do not always willingly make the pledges that Senators try to elicit from them. Some confirmation hearings, as a result, take on the appearance of a sparring match in which nominees try to avoid committee efforts to pin them down. Their success is dependent primarily on the intensity and unanimity of committee attitudes. If a majority of a committee supports the attempt to elicit a pledge, the nominee will have little choice but to go along. If committee members disagree among themselves, however, the nominee may be able to escape without any significant restrictions on his future freedom of action.

61. In *United States* v. *Smith* (286 U.S. 6) in 1932, the Supreme Court held that the Senate could not recall for reconsideration a nomination that had already been confirmed and forwarded to the President.

62. 1969—Interior and Insular Affairs—Walter J. Hickel: Secretary of the Interior, p. 246.

63. 1965—Commerce—William F. McKee: Administrator, FAA, pp. 61–62.

64. *Senate Executive Report, Number 1*, 89th Congress, 2d Session, 1966.

65. *Ibid.*, p. 5.
66. Letter from Special Prosecutor Leon Jaworski to Senator James East-land, quoted in *New York Times*, May 21, 1974.
67. Quoted in *New York Times*, May 23, 1974.
68. *Ibid.*

8   Senate Action on Nominations

Patterns of Approval

The formal outcomes of the confirmation process can be characterized very simply: Nominations to federal offices are almost always approved. In an average year, approximately 97 percent of all nominations will be confirmed. Another 2 to 3 percent will be voluntarily withdrawn or not acted upon. Only a handful are likely to be rejected. One could conclude from these numbers that the President nearly always has his way with the Senate, that the Senate's confirmation power is an empty weapon in a dead hand. But that is the wrong conclusion drawn from the wrong evidence.

Confirmation is a process, not simply a vote. And, as the foregoing chapters demonstrate, the confirmation process provides ample opportunity for the Senate to influence the President, his nominees, and their subsequent policy decisions without rejecting any substantial number of nominations. Senate influence is exerted in two ways, one passive, the other active.

The first occurs through what Carl Friedrich once called the "law of anticipated reaction."[1] Much of the Senate's influence over appointment decisions takes place even before nominations are publicly announced. Knowing the Senate has the power to reject his nominations, and wanting to avoid the embarrassment and political agony of that, the President normally makes an effort to check the acceptability of his nominees with key Senators before announcing them. If strong opposition appears likely, he may well decide not to make a planned nomination and to reopen the search for a more acceptable candidate. This does not guarantee good appointments, of course, but it does clear the way to confirmation. Anticipating reactions is thus a form of *conflict avoidance* in the confirmation process.

Senate influence is also exercised in the confirmation process itself. Confirmation hearings are regarded in the Senate not merely as forums for examining a nominee's integrity and qualifications but as an opportunity to explore an almost unlimited range of topics. Much of the discussion that occurs at confirmation hearings is purposive and pointed, designed to uncover differences of opinion between committees and nominees and to find ways to narrow those differences. As we have seen, Senate committees have developed a number of techniques for limiting or reducing the scope of their disagreements with nominees. On only a few occasions do those techniques fail to shrink the conflicts between a nominee and a committee to acceptable proportions. Confirmation hearings, therefore, often serve as a mechanism for *conflict resolution.*

Conflict avoidance in the selection process and confliction resolution in the confirmation process combine to make rejection a rarity. Those individuals likely to be unacceptable to the Senate are usually weeded out before a formal nomination is made. And when those who are nominated pose problems for a Senate committee, the committee has ways of resolving those problems that are less severe than outright rejection. The appointment process, like other aspects of legislative–executive relations, is part conflict, part cooperation. But the dynamics of the process allow conflict to be routinized and channeled in ways that facilitate its resolution. When it chooses to do so, the Senate is able to exert considerable influence over appointment decisions and their implications without rolling out its heavy artillery.

This is the point most frequently lost on those who assume that the confirmation power is rarely used to control or influence the executive branch simply because confirmation is denied to so few presidential nominees. The process of exercising influence is more subtle than that. It is more like diplomacy than war (though Clausewitz's dictum that "war is diplomacy carried on by other means" may well apply in the ultimate sense). Because the confirmation process is more complex and more deliberate than is commonly believed, the opportunities for using the process to influence appointment decisions and to shape the direction of public policy are more abundant and more sophisticated than the mere calling of the roll on a nomination.

Rejections

The pattern of nominee approval is normal, but not perfect. Most nominations are confirmed, but some are not. Rejected nominations, however, are not easily counted. To identify accurately the number of nominations rejected by the Senate, it is essential to include not only those rejected outright on the Senate floor but also those rejected by committee vote and those on which no formal vote is ever taken but which are withdrawn when it becomes clear that favorable action is unlikely.

The rub comes in trying to determine which nominations should be placed in the last category. A number of nominations are withdrawn in each session of Congress, but withdrawal comes for a wide range of reasons. When a new President takes office, he normally withdraws all the unconfirmed nominations of his predecessor. At other times nominations are withdrawn at the personal request of a nominee, because the administration has changed its plans or because of technical errors in the nomination papers. The Carter administration, for instance, once mistakenly nominated the brother of its intended candidate to a seat on the Council of Economic Advisers and was forced to withdraw the nomination to correct its error.[2] Even when a nomination is withdrawn because it is unlikely to be approved by the Senate, that is rarely the announced reason for the withdrawal. Usually such withdrawals are explained with the words "for personal reasons" or "at the request of the nominee." The point here is that it is hard to get a fully accurate count of the number of defeated nominations primarily because it is difficult to determine precisely how many withdrawals were, in fact, forced withdrawals.

Table 8-1 represents a determined effort to identify the actual number of rejected nominations since 1961. Included in the "rejected" column are those defeated on the Senate floor, those rejected by committee vote, and those forced to withdraw. These figures are drawn from public documents, secondary sources, and interviews with participants, but the reader should be advised that some of those in the "forced withdrawal" category, particularly some before 1970, are judgment calls. In some cases the recollections of participants produced no consensus on the real reasons for a withdrawal, and inclusion in this table was based on a weighing of the available evidence rather than clear-cut proof.

Cataloguing the reasons for nominee rejections is almost as tricky a business as counting them. Rejections occur for a variety of reasons but the real reasons often differ from the publicly stated reasons. Some nominations are rejected because of a clear and irreparable conflict of interest or undeniable evidence of illegal or unethical behavior or because a nominee quite obviously does not meet the statutory qualifications for the position to which he is nominated. These, however, are not the most common reasons for Senate rejection.

Table 8-1. Major Nominations Rejected, 1961–1977

YEAR	TOTAL	REJECTED BY FLOOR VOTE[a]	REJECTED BY COMMITTEE VOTE	FORCED WITHDRAWAL
1961	1			1
1962	0			
1963	0			
1964	0			
1965	1			1
1966	0			
1967	0			
1968	1 [b]	1		
1969	3	1		2
1970	2	1		1
1971	0			
1972	0			
1973	3	1	1	1
1974	6			6
1975	7		4	3
1976	10 [b]		2	8
1977	6		2	4

a Includes votes on recommittal.
b Does not include nominations allowed to expire at the end of a presidential administration.

SOURCES: *Executive Proceedings of the Senate; Daily Digest of the Congressional Record; Congressional Quarterly Almanac;* and interviews.

Most rejections result from policy or philosophical dissensus between a nominee and a majority of a Senate committee or a majority of the full Senate. A nominee's policy views or his political philosophy have a way of conditioning the environment in which his nomination is considered. If his views on important policy issues are not controversial and do not arouse any significant concern on the part of the committee reviewing the nomination, then the committee is unlikely to be very demanding in its expectations in other areas, like conflict of interest or formal qualifications. If, on the other hand, a nominee's policy views are a source of concern to some committee members, they will in all probability be very aggressive in their scrutiny of the other criteria, looking for additional evidence to use in building a case against the nomination. A committee's reaction to a nominee's policy views thus affects the scope and intensity of its examination of his previous record, his financial holdings, and his personal integrity.

Potential problems that may be overlooked when there is policy consensus loom much larger when there is not.

The folklore about the appointment process has long held that Senate opposition to nominees is usually "political," that is, Senators from one party tend to vote against only nominations made by a President of the other party, and party politics is the primary reason for those votes. Partisanship, of course, is a pervasive influence in the appointment process, as it is in most other aspects of legislative–executive relations. But partisanship alone does not account for all or even most of the opposition that presidential nominees encounter in the Senate.

The quantitative evidence on this question is crude but nevertheless revealing. It is crude because most Senate rejections result from inaction rather than action, and few footprints are left behind for tracking the sources of opposition. One indicator, however, of the patterns of Senate opposition to nominations can be drawn from recorded confirmation votes on the Senate floor. There are not a great many of these, but enough perhaps to provide some sense of where opposition comes from. In the period from 1961 through 1976, there were sixty-three nonunanimous recorded confirmation votes on the Senate floor.[3] On these recorded votes, 24.2 percent of the individual votes opposing confirmation were cast by Senators of the same party as the President. Penetrating further, we find that a "conservative coalition" often appears in confirmation votes, as it frequently does in votes on legislation. In the years from 1961 through 1968, for example, more than 35 percent of all votes opposing confirmation were cast by Senators of the same party as the President, the vast majority by Southern Democrats voting against Kennedy and Johnson nominees.

This same phenomenon emerges from using the Rice Index of Likeness, a simple measure of the similarity in voting behavior between two groups. This index is calculated by subtracting the percentage of "yea" votes cast by one group from the percentage of "yea" votes cast by the other and then subtracting the result from 100. The index ranges from 0 to 100, with 0 representing total dissimilarity in voting behavior and 100 representing perfect similarity.[4] Again for the period 1961 through 1976, we find an average Index of Likeness for all Democrats and all Republicans on confirmation votes of 72.8. This indicates considerable similarity in the confirmation voting behavior of the two groups. If we break out the vote of Southern Democrats, however, an interesting pattern emerges. The average Index of Likeness for Northern Democrats and Southern Democrats is 67.4, but the average Index of Likeness for Southern Democrats and Republicans is 82.7. In other words, the confirmation votes of Southern Democrats are more like those of Republicans than those of Northern Democrats. Quite obviously, party politics alone does not account for all the opposition that nominations encounter on the Senate floor.

If opposition to nominations is "political," as the folklore holds, it is political only in a particular sense. Senators may be more likely to support nominations made by a President of their own party because they are likely to feel a stronger sense of philosophical kinship to him than to a President of the other party. But there is nothing in the evidence from Senate floor votes or in the transcripts of confirmation hearings to indicate that blind partisanship is the primary source of Senators' confirmation decisions. Partisanship may have a constraining effect on Senate responses to nominees, but it is a weak constraint and is often trespassed when other considerations intervene.

Hence the conventional view that Senators' confirmation decisions are often "political" is correct only if one is willing to accept a definition of "political" that encompasses more than mere party partisanship. The Senate's response to presidential nominations is political in the sense that its confirmation decisions are part of a larger fabric of relationships between the President and the Congress. Politics, as Harold Lasswell noted long ago, is a question of "who gets what, when, how."[5] Those concerns pervade the confirmation process as they do most other aspects of legislative–executive relations. Confirmation decisions are part of the struggle between the two branches and within the Congress itself for control of the direction and substantive activities of the federal government. The division of forces in this struggle is political, but it is not always simply partisan. Support and opposition often coalesce across party lines rather than behind them. They do so because Senators' concerns with policy issues and with the needs of their constituents and their personal sensitivity to ethical questions usually supersede their concern for party unity or party loyalty.

The Confirmation Process in the 1970s

Table 8-1 shows a notable increase in the number of nominations rejected by the Senate after 1972. These figures are not anomalous. They are simply the most visible indicator of an important set of changes that took place in the way the Senate handled its confirmation responsibilities after that date. Faced with a Republican President willing to challenge them both politically and institutionally, the Democratic members of the Senate started in the early 1970s to effect a general tightening of Senate confirmation procedures and to engineer a more assertive Senate role in confirmation decisions. They did this in several ways.

They began by extending the confirmation requirement to a number of important positions in the executive branch. Many of these, in fact, were positions within the Executive Office of the President: the members of the Council on Environmental Quality, the Director of the Office of Telecommunications Policy, the Director of the Energy Policy Office, the Executive Director of the Council on International Economic Policy, and the Director and Deputy Director of the Office of Management and Budget. In general, these changes were undertaken to give the Senate a role in appointments to positions with an expanding influence on policy development and implementation. The Senate Committee on Government Operations pointed this out in its report on a bill requiring the confirmation of the Director and Deputy Director of OMB:

> The Committee does not take issue with the President's requirement for an institutional aid to assist him in exercising management and control over the executive branch. It believes, however, that such requirement must be balanced with the Constitutional role of the Congress in the formulation and finalization of national policy.[6]

Also in the early 1970s a number of Senate committees undertook a reexamination of their confirmation procedures and began to institute changes designed to make those procedures more comprehensive, more rigorous, and more consistent. The new procedures they adopted included such things as formal waiting periods between the time a nomination was received and the date of final action, the requirement that nominees fill out detailed financial statements, and the use of written questionnaires to explore a nominee's policy views prior to his confirmation hearing.[7] The policy questionnaires are perhaps the most notable of these new procedures. They force nominees to think through their views on important issues before a confirmation hearing and augment the committee's opportunities to examine and dissect those views when the nominee comes before them. The Senate Commerce Committee was the leader in introducing a number of these procedural changes, and its chairman in this period, Senator Warren Magnuson, once pointed to the value of such prehearing questionnaires in providing committee members with "a basis on which to determine a nominee's commitment to carrying out the intent of the Congress in enforcing the... statutes within his or her jurisdiction and [an opportunity] to pursue focused lines of questioning at the nomination hearing."[8]

But the most compelling evidence of changes in the Senate role in the appointment process is the increase in the number of rejected nominations. After 1972 the Senate became tougher in its scrutiny of nominees and less reluctant to reject those it found wanting.

Most of the new assertiveness revealed itself in committee action rather than floor votes. That is not surprising, given the fact that floor action in the confirmation process is rarely more than a ratification of committee action. In the years from 1960 through 1978, the full Senate has reversed the confirmation judgments of its committees on only five occasions. A nomination that is doomed to defeat rarely makes it to the Senate floor. If there is a case to be made against a nominee, it is usually made in committee. And if the case is strong enough, the nomination usually terminates with a negative committee vote or withdrawal under fire. Committees have always been the primary decision-making forum in the confirmation process, and in the 1970s Senate committees became more aggressive in the exercise of their confirmation responsibilities.

In absolute terms, the number of rejected nominations is not large, even after 1972. But the infrequency of actual rejections belies the significance of those that do occur. Defeated nominations have a deterrent effect on the President in the same way that speeding tickets have a deterrent effect on automobile drivers. The deterring power of defeated nominations is far more salient and pervasive than their numbers would indicate. They are acts of both explicit and implicit political communication. Explicitly, a rejection says to the President, "The defeated nominee was not up to our standards." But implicitly a rejection says, "These are our standards; keep them in mind in making future nominations."

In defending the structure of the appointment power in the *76th Federalist*, Alexander Hamilton wrote that "the possibility of rejection would be a strong motive to care in proposing."[9] That appears to be both the intended and the real impact of the increased willingness of Senate committees to reject unsatisfactory nominees. They have forced the President to take heed, to improve his own efforts to find nominees whose qualifications and policy views do not violate the parameters of acceptability that Senate committees have begun to establish and enforce.

These changes occurred in the 1970s for a number of reasons. In part they resulted from the efforts of the Senate to beef up its staff and information support resources in the late 1960s and early 1970s. The Senate in that period became far better equipped to make the inquiries and investigations that are essential to a comprehensive examination of presidential nominees. The growth in congressional staff and support services in that period was nothing short of remarkable. In the ten years from 1965 to 1975, Senate standing committee staff personnel increased in number from 509 to 1,277.[10] The total number employed on Senators' personal staffs increased from 1,749 in 1967 to 2,600 in 1975.[11] Authorized personnel of the Congressional Research Service grew from 219 in 1965 to 703 in 1975.[12] Similar growth occurred in the General Accounting Office and in two newer support agencies that did not exist in the 1960s, the Office of Technology Assessment and the Congressional Budget Office.

In the appointment process, the impact of this was significant. Most Senate committees were able for the first time to divide up staff duties in a way that permitted one or two staff members to assume responsibility for all the nominations referred to each committee. Committee staff members with responsibility for nominations could keep in regular contact with the departments and agencies where nominees would serve and with the White House personnel office. This same staff person usually interviewed the nominee, informed him of the committee's expectations with regard to conflicts of interest, and aided him in preparing for confirmation hearings. He might also be used to conduct an inquiry into the nominee's background, his credentials and qualifications, his relevant policy views, and his relationship with the interest groups with whom he would have to deal as a government official. If there appeared to be a problem with the nomination or strong opposition from one or more interest groups, the staff person could arrange a meeting between the nominee and the committee chairman for the purpose of examining the scope of the conflict and attempting to arrange a resolution.

The growth in Senate staff and resources was felt in other ways in the appointment process. Substantial staff assistance became available to all Senators; a responsive staff was no longer a perquisite reserved only for committee chairmen. In the 94th Congress, for instance, all members of the majority party chaired at least one subcommittee and thus were able to hire their own subcommittee staffs. Senate Resolution 60 (1975) permitted Senators to hire up to three staff aides to help them with their committee work. Even minority members acquired increased staff assistance as a result of their arrangements with committee and subcommittee chairmen, the augmentation of their personal staffs, and the resources of the minority conference and the minority policy committee.[13] The pervasiveness of staff support thus allowed any Senator who was troubled by a nomination to conduct his own inquiries. He did not need to rely on the committee with jurisdiction over the nomination. If he was unsatisfied with the scrutiny given a nomination by the committee or with the positions taken by committee members, he could engage in his own crusade against the nomination. It was not uncommon in this period or afterward for a junior Senator, in some cases one who was not even on the responsible committee, to lead the opposition to a nomination.[14]

This increase in staff and resources has contributed significantly to the ability of the Senate to play a more assertive role in the appointment process. But it accounts for only part of the change. Resource improvements are as much effect as they are cause. The Congress improved its resources largely because it had abundant incentives to be more independent and skeptical in all of its relations with the President. The Senate's role in the appointment process changed because the environment in which legislative–executive relations were conducted changed.

Several factors appear to have contributed directly to the stiffening of the Senate's backbone. One is the impact of "sunshine" legislation and the attitudes that produced it. Senate acquiescence to presidential appointments, particularly bad ones, was less comfortable for Senators than might previously have been the case. When committee decisions were made behind closed doors, usually without any record of individual votes, responsibility for the approval of poorly qualified nominees was harder to affix. But as the committee decision-making process became more open to public and media attention, Senators were forced to face the consequences of their confirmation votes. Also more open to public view was information about individual nominees. This was particularly true of information that pertained to conflicts of interest. In the past, the financial statements of nominees were routinely kept secret. Following the lead of the Commerce Committee, however, many Senate committees changed their attitude and began either to publish these statements in confirmation hearings or to make them available to press and public in committee offices. Again, the effect was to force Senators to examine this information more closely since it was a visible part of the public record.

Another factor that induced, perhaps forced, the Senate to take a more aggressive posture in the appointment process was the growing influence of groups within the population whose interests, as recently as the mid-1960s, were barely represented by any effective national organizations. Public interest, consumer, environmental, and minority groups became very active in the appointment process. Few important nominations escaped the notice of these groups, and their growing influence added a new dimension to Senate decision-making on nominations. Their participation in the confirmation process had the effect, in E. E. Schattschneider's words, of "expanding the scope of conflict." And, as Schattschneider noted,

> . . . the outcome of every conflict is determined by the extent to which the audience becomes involved in it. That is, the outcome of all conflict is determined by the scope of its contagion. The number of people in any conflict determines what happens; every change in the number of participants, every increase or reduction in the number of participants affects the results.[15]

The presence of groups such as these contributed to a substantial increase in the number of "controversial" nominations. With the upsurge of consumer, environmental, minority, and public interest groups, both sides of important public policy questions were aggressively and consistently represented in the confirmation process for the first time. Nominees whose political philosophies were one-sided or whose records showed any hint of insensitivity to minority groups, to consumers, or to the public interest were unlikely to get through confirmation hearings without a challenge from one or more of the groups that represented these diffuse interests. That was not often the case before 1970.

Journalists also became a factor of some significance in the confirmation process during this period. As more confirmation hearings became controversial (hence newsworthy), newspapers came to be a frequent source of information affecting the outcome of confirmation decisions. The discovery by investigative reporters, for instance, that G. Harrold Carswell had made segregationist remarks in a political campaign in Georgia in 1948 greatly fueled the opposition to his nomination to the Supreme Court. In 1974 President Ford was forced to withdraw the nomination of Andrew E. Gibson to head the Federal Energy Administration after the *New York Times* revealed that Gibson had a ten-year separation contract with an oil company that paid him $88,000 a year. The combination of aggressive public interest groups and an energetic investigative press had a twofold impact on the confirmation process. First, it significantly increased the range of information available to Senate committees to use in making judgments on presidential nominees. And second, it created a new set of pressures, forcing Senators to be more exacting in setting confirmation standards and more deliberate in applying them.

Fundamental to any explanation of these changes in the Senate's use of the confirmation power is the fact that the appointment process is not an isolated aspect of legislative–executive relations. The relationship between the President and the Congress is an intricate fabric, of which the appointment process is but one thread. Changes in the appointment process in the 1970s reflected changes that occurred across the entire range of powers for which the legislature and the executive share responsibility. At the same time that the Senate was asserting its own will with regard to presidential nominations, the Congress passed a budget reform act and a war powers act. As the Congress was limiting the President's discretion in selecting his own subordinates, so too was it limiting his discretion in claiming executive privilege, in reorganizing the executive branch, and in making administrative rules and regulations. The pendulum swung significantly in legislative–executive relations in the 1970s, and the changes in the confirmation process were part of that broader movement.

Politics was the source of much of this momentum. While some turning away from the presidential dominance of the postwar period was probably inevitable, the change was hastened by the election of Richard Nixon and the subsequent tensions of a divided government. Some measure of friction is inherent in our system of separated institutions and shared powers. When it exists, co-partisanship between the President and congressional majorities acts as a kind of political lubricant, reducing the friction. When the President and Congress are partisan opponents, however, conflicts are harder to manage. Disagreements over specific policies often turn into struggles over institutional prerogatives. Frequently this results in efforts formally to restate the limits of institutional powers and to restructure institutional relationships. The early 1970s were just such a period.

In our system, the products of political conflict often survive the conditions that produced them. Changes in political institutions and in their relationships with one another develop their own roots, and those roots continue to hold even after the seeds from which they sprang have disappeared. There can be no doubt that political disagreement between a Democratic Congress and two Republican Presidents provided the momentum for much of the internal restructuring that took place within the Congress and for many of the formal alterations that occurred in its relationship with the White House.

But neither should there be much doubt that these institutional adjustments of the 1970s will remain in place and in effect long after the dissipation of the conditions that produced them. Congressional staff resources will not be reduced back to the pre-Nixon level; public interest groups and investigative journalists will not disappear; and Senate committees will not quickly discard their more comprehensive confirmation procedures. Presidents may well be more successful in getting their nominees approved when the Senate is controlled by their own Party, but Presidents—regardless of party—are very likely to find that they no longer have the full line of credit the Senate was once willing to extend them.

The Senate's Dilemma

The Senate confirmation process operates under no consistent or clearly articulated set of public expectations. This is not to say that no expectations exist, only that they are diverse and often contradictory. An extensive reading of the comments of participants in the appointment process, the writings of academic political scientists, and the exhortations of newspaper editorialists reveals two predominant streams of thought with regard to the Senate's exercise of its confirmation power. On the one hand, the Senate is expected to exercise vigilance in ensuring the quality, competence, and integrity of presidential appointees. On the other, it is expected to defer to the President's right to select his own subordinates in order that he may be held accountable for the operation of the executive branch.

The dissonance of these expectations places the Senate in a crossfire. If it is too assertive in applying what it collectively believes to be appropriate standards for presidential appointees, it is criticized for interfering with the President's right to run the government. But if it is too deferential to the President, challenging only the very worst of his nominations, it is criticized for being a rubber stamp, for not effectively carrying out its responsibilities in the appointment process. It is a classic case of "damned if you do, damned if you don't."

Much of the contemporary character of the confirmation process stems from the ambiguity of the constitutional mandate and the legacy of practical experience that history has passed down to the modern Senate. But it also stems from the uncertainty and the disagreements that infect current discussions of the confirmation power. Lacking consensus on the criteria it should apply in judging nominees or the rigor with which it should apply them, the Senate has been free to define its confirmation power expansively.

As a result, the confirmation process has developed into something neither intended by the Founding Fathers nor consciously designed by the collective decisions of this or any previous generation of Senators. Instead of exercising the confirmation power as a straightforward, mechanical review of the qualifications of presidential nominees, the Senate has used it as an adjunct to its other institutional interests, predominantly in such matters as oversight, constituency representation, and public policy development. In simple terms, there are three reasons for this.

The first is the difficulty in defining evaluative criteria for judging the acceptability of nominees. For its entire history, the Senate has been plagued by a lack of agreement over the standards that ought to be applied in making confirmation decisions. There is broad agreement that nominees ought to be competent, honest, and free of conflict of interest. But there has rarely been much agreement on what those terms mean or on the stringency with which they should be applied. The Senate has had some limited success, particularly recently, in developing *procedural* standards to govern the confirmation process, but it has never been successful in establishing *substantive* criteria to guide confirmation decisions. Its confirmation decisions have been described as ad hoc, inconsistent, and political. And they have been all of those things, primarily because of the confounding elusiveness of the objective standards necessary for them to be otherwise.

A second reason for the contempary character of the confirmation process is a factor discussed earlier: the unusual access and leverage that the confirmation power provides to Senate committees in their dealings with future appointees. For Senate committees, the chance to examine the policy views of nominees, to prod them for information and ideas, to inform them of committee attitudes, to instruct them with regard to legislative intent, and to sensitize them to constituency concerns is simply too good an opportunity to pass up. Committees, of course, may have frequent occasion for future interaction with presidential appointees. But never again will they have the leverage to flush out information or impose their own priorities on those individuals that the confirmation power provides.

Finally, and perhaps most important, the contemporary confirmation process takes its shape from the strength and persistence of the Senate's primary interests in matters other than the act of confirmation itself. The character of the confirmation process is affected in very large part by the fact that confirmation is a minor, not a major, Senate function. Senators know that their constituents pay far less attention to their confirmation decisions than to the way they handle more fundamental policy issues. The people of New Hampshire, for instance, probably could not care less about the make-up of the Civil Aeronautics Board. But they do care about the inadequacy of commercial air service in northern New England. It is not surprising, therefore, that Senator Norris Cotton of New Hampshire invariably used the opportunities provided by confirmation hearings on CAB nominees to press the case for better air service in his state. Indeed, policy and constituency interests of this sort dominate the confirmation process.

None of this is anomalous. The logic of the confirmation process is the prevailing logic of congressional activity. The confirmation process is not a side track, it is part of the main line. The objectives that Senators pursue—things like sound public policy, re-election, and institutional influence[16]—are the objectives that shape their actions in the confirmation process. Their confirmation decisions flow from the same patterns of organization and power and reflect the same fundamental concerns that color every significant aspect of Senate activity. Policy and constituency considerations dominate the confirmation process because they are the dominant concerns of the Senate and because the confirmation process provides useful and often unique opportunities for expressing and implementing those concerns.

Notes

1. Carl Friedrich, *Constitutional Government and Democracy* (Ginn, 1950), pp. 49, 398.

2. See "Wrong Brother 'Nominated' as Carter Adviser," *Washington Post*, March 24, 1977.
3. This figure includes votes on cloture and recommittal, where those votes constitute final Senate action on a nomination.
4. For further explanation, see Stuart H. Rice, *Quantitative Methods in Politics* (Knopf, 1928), pp. 209–211.
5. Harold Lasswell, *Politics: Who Gets What, When, How* (Meridian Books, 1958).
6. Senate Report 93–237, p. 6.
7. See note 5 for Chapter 5, p. 117–118.
8. *Congressional Record*, 122 (March 22, 1976, daily edition): S3882.
9. Jacob E. Cooke (ed.), *The Federalist* (Meridian Books, 1961), No. 76, p. 513.
10. U.S. Senate, 94th Congress, 2d Session, Temporary Select Committee to Study the Senate Committee System, *The Senate Committee System*, p. 200.
11. Harrison W. Fox, Jr., and Susan Webb Hammond, "The Growth of Congressional Staffs," in Harvey C. Mansfield, Sr., (ed.), *Congress Against the President* (Praeger, 1975), p. 115.
12. *Ibid.*, p. 116.
13. The staff resources available to minority Senators were further increased early in 1977 as part of the committee reorganization package adopted by the Senate (S. Res. 4).
14. Senator Thomas Eagleton of Missouri, for instance, though not a member of the Foreign Relations Committee, was the leading figure in the opposition to the nomination of Peter M. Flanigan as Ambassador to Spain in 1974. The committee chose to take no action on the nomination, and it was subsequently withdrawn.
15. E. E. Schattschneider, *The Semisovereign People* (Holt, Rinehart & Winston, 1960), p. 2.
16. See Richard F. Fenno, Jr., *Congressmen in Committees* (Little, Brown, 1973), for an enlightening discussion of the objectives of members of Congress.

III

Shaping Appointment Decisions: Other Participants

We have now told the beginning and the end of this story but have left out the middle. Anyone attempting to track an appointment decision is well advised to look first at the White House and last at the Senate. But in between the trail is far less definite, far more variable. The White House is the hub of the appointment process, but its dominance of appointment decisions is far from total. As the timing and salience of appointment decisions vary, so too do the range of participants in them and the character of their interaction.

No two appointment decisions are ever exactly alike. As a former Attorney General once said of judicial appointments, "each is a little drama of its own." The participants in appointment decisions may vary widely, but those most likely to seek a role fall into four categories: agency personnel, special interest groups, political party organizations, and (outside of their formal roles) members of Congress.

Why do these groups seek out opportunities to participate in appointment decisions? For two reasons primarily. First, because they recognize the connection between presidential appointments and public policy, and they want to influence policy decisions by first influencing appointment decisions. And second, because appointments are a substantial capital resource in the political market place, and a certain status (or "clout") accrues to those who appear to influence their distribution.

Participation in these personnel decisions by the groups examined in this section is a frequent, but not (we should be careful to note) a constant, characteristic of the appointment process. A good many presidential appointments are made with little significant involvement of political actors outside the White House and the Senate committee with confirmation responsibilities. But when these outside groups do take an active part in appointment decisions, they can have a substantial impact on the manner in which those decisions are made and on ultimate personnel choices. An examination of the role they play is essential to complete this portrait of the appointment process.

Journalistic accounts of the appointment process often picture the President as a besieged figure at the center of a political maelstrom, trying to protect his appointment prerogatives from a host of alien influences. Such a picture is only occasionally accurate. More often, in fact, the White House invites participation in selection decisions. Increasingly in recent years, the Senate has invited participation in confirmation decisions as well. They do this because it is good

politics. It helps in anticipating and even co-opting potential opposition to appointees. It helps in winning the support or obligation of
important political actors. And it helps in identifying the best available candidates for demanding government jobs. Most important appointment decisions are the product of some mixture of these objectives.

Four variables seem to have the strongest bearing on who can or
will participate with the Senate and the White House in any single
appointment decision. The first is *salience*. The more important an
appointment to the fortunes of a set of political actors, the greater the
likelihood they will attempt to influence an appointment decision and
the greater the likelihood their concerns will be heard. Trade unions
will be more influential than farmers' organizations in Labor Department appointments, for instance, and vice versa in appointments in
the Agriculture Department.

The second factor is *resources*. Influence is more likely to accrue
to those who have demonstrable political support, money, access, or
political leverage that they can bring to bear on a particular appointment decision than to those who do not.

Strategies are another important determinant of appointment
decision outcomes. In politics, as in poker, how you play your cards is
almost as important as the cards you have to play. Careful assessment
of, and approach to, the real decision points in the appointment process can maximize the influence even of those groups whose resources
are less than abundant. Similarly, those who have resources but do
not marshal them effectively may squander their opportunities.

Last among these persistent factors in appointment decisions is
the shape of the political terrain. As political conditions vary, so too
do the opportunities available to different sets of political actors.
Changes in administrations or in the popularity of an administration,
changes in the chairmanship or membership of a Senate committee,
scandals, shifts in the national mood, or secular changes in American
politics can alter the environment in which appointment decisions are
made. In so doing, they may limit the opportunities available to some
actors while expanding those available to others.

The following chapters propose no simple equation of the appointment process. Their objective, in fact, is to do just the opposite:
to demonstrate the awkward politics that precede appointment decisions. I shall examine the sets of political actors who participate most
often in those decisions and attempt to indicate the conditions under
which their participation is likely to have an impact on the outcome.

9   Political Parties

It is axiomatic that Presidents prefer to nominate political executives from their own party. Co-partisans are generally the people who provide the bulk of a President's electoral support; many of them will share or respect his political philosophy and programmatic goals. Some Presidents, primarily those who have won narrow electoral victories or who face sizable opposition in Congress, will find it necessary or useful to fill some of the posts in their administrations with members of the opposition party. For the most part, however, they will rely on the members of their own party; in this passive sense, membership in the President's party is an influential factor in the selection process.

But the distinction between party identification and party organizations is important. While it is generally true that affiliation with the President's party is an important consideration in selection decisions, it does not follow that party organizations at the state and national level are themselves a powerful influence on the selection of presidential nominees. There are times when the influence of the party organizations may reach significant levels, but as a rule they are not a determining influence.

Party organizations are usually most influential in the early stages of a new administration. Before the selection process is fully organized, the party is the primary generator of names of potential candidates. The organizations themselves are strongest in election years, and the President is likely to feel a sense of obligation to party loyalists and to perceive a need to unify party factions. As I. M. Destler notes:

> The president is likely to choose the key men before he has taken the oath of office and personally experienced the problems of controlling "his" government. In this hectic pre-inaugural period, he will probably have little feel for (or acquaintance with) the type of men he will need to fight his bureaucratic battles. But he will likely be more sensitive than ever before or after to the uses of appointments to appease particular politicians or segments of his natural constituency.[1]

Even in the days preceding and immediately following the inauguration of a new President, however, the influence of party organizations on important selection decisions is very much a product of the preferences of the President and the people to whom he has delegated responsibility for staffing his administration. They may give the national committee a significant and visible role, as Eisenhower did, or they may shut it out of the selection process almost completely, as Nixon and Carter did.

In the postwar period, party organizations have tended to be most influential in filling lower-level and honorary positions (commissions, boards, minor ambassadorships, etc.) and least influential in the selection of candidates for policy-making or important administrative positions. It does not overstate the case to say that the role of party organizations in the contemporary appointment process is at most peripheral.

Recent administrations have used state and national party organizations primarily as clearance points in the appointment process. During the selection process, the White House personnel office will usually check with the national party committee to determine that a candidate under consideration is not vigorously opposed by any substantial group within the party.[2] In those instances where the statutes creating a position contain party affiliation requirements,[3] the national committee is likely to be asked to verify the candidate's party identification.

The state party organizations are often called upon to perform the same kind of clearance, to ensure the acceptability of the candidate to party activists in the state of his residence or the state where he will work if appointed. In fact, this clearance function in the states is not always controlled by the formal party organizations. It may well be dominated by a congressman, a Senator, the Governor, or some other person who has acquired the right to act as state party liaison with the White House.

Almost without exception in the postwar administrations, party organizations have complained about their lack of access to the appointment process, about the failure of Presidents and their staffs to pay appropriate heed to party recommendations and party prerogatives. The "Taft wing" of the Republican party felt left out of the Eisenhower selection process and forced a meeting with Eisenhower to seek some participation in appointment decisions.[4] Richard Nixon encountered strong criticism from within his own party for his perceived failure to clean out Democratic officeholders and replace them with loyal Republicans.[5] The Democratic National Committee unanimously adopted a resolution criticizing Jimmy Carter for his administration's failure to consult with party officials in making federal appointments.[6]

Most of these criticisms are little more than bluster, however. The fact is that modern political party organizations are powerless to force their way into the appointment process and have little recourse but to accept the role the President and his staff are willing to grant them. When they are dissatisfied—and they usually are—complaining is about all they can do. Occasionally the complaints will bring a response. At various times, for instance, in response to party protests, Richard Nixon ordered his personal staff to find positions on honorary boards and commissions for ten Republicans from each state[7] and to exercise more vigilance over the party affiliation of government consultants.[8] But these were small potatoes compared to the real prizes in the appointment process. Major appointment decisions continued to be made with little reliance on the party organizations.

Several things account for the relative unimportance of the party organizations in filling executive positions. Primary among these is the nature of the party organizations themselves. The center of gravity in the American party system remains at the state and local level. The national organizations are little more than amalgams of a wide range of sectional and functional interests. Their raison d'être is the winning of elections, not effective governance, and certainly not executive recruitment. They are neither programmatic nor policy-oriented to any significant degree.

The national party organizations do not possess an effective capability for recruiting candidates for important appointive positions. When the Republicans came back into power in 1969, for instance, the patronage office at their national party headquarters was headed by an obscure retiree who supervised a staff of two secretaries and one part-time typist.[9] The national committee was neither prepared nor organized to play a significant role in staffing the first Republican administration in eight years.

The fundamental cause of the diminished postwar role of party organizations in the appointment process is the growing gap between the personnel needs of the federal government and the personnel resources of the political parties. As Americans have become less willing to identify with one of the two major political parties, the ability of those parties to serve as the primary link between politicians and voters has deteriorated. As a result, parties have become progressively less likely to serve as the entryway into government for talented people. A Brookings Institution study in the early 1960s recognized this in noting that "party organizations are based on a substantially different substructure of American society than that from which political executives are recruited."[10] White House personnel aides have long been aware of the inadequacies of political parties as sources of potential presidential appointees. Dan Fenn has said, "It is a rare guy who comes up through a party or campaign organization who can be Assistant Secretary of Defense for Procurement."[11] And Frederic Malek indicated that "the kind of guy we're looking for doesn't hang around party offices."[12]

The organized personnel operations of recent administrations have developed, in part, as a response to the inability of the parties to provide adequate assistance in meeting the staffing needs of the modern presidency. The contact networks of businessmen and professionals that these personnel operations employ are a direct replacement for much of the work once done by party officials. It is ironic but true that the development of a full-time White House personnel staff has further reduced the necessity of relying on party organizations as sources of candidates and has thus been a prime factor in the declining importance of the party organizations as participants in the selection process.

Notes

1. I. M. Destler, *Presidents, Bureaucrats, and Foreign Policy: The Politics of Organizational Reform* (Princeton University Press, 1972), p. 288.
2. Even where party opposition exists, the President may decide to disregard it. Lyndon Johnson, for instance, went right ahead with his decision to nominate a Republican, Stanley R. Resor, as Under Secretary of the Army in spite of the opposition he received from the Democratic National Committee. See *New York Times*, December 26, 1965.
3. Many of the statutes creating multimember boards and commissions require that no more than one-half plus one of the members be affiliated with the same political party.
4. See Chapter 2, p. 17.
5. See *New York Times*, February 24, 1969.
6. *New York Times*, April 2, 1977.
7. See John S. Saloma III and Frederick H. Sontag, *Parties: The Real Opportunity for Effective Citizen Politics* (Vintage Books, 1973), p. 198.
8. Dom Bonafede, "Nixon's first-year appointments reveal pattern of his Administration," *National Journal*, 2 (January 24, 1970): 187.

9. Saloma and Sontag, *Parties*, p. 197.

10. Dean E. Mann, with Jameson W. Doig, *The Assistant Secretaries: Problems and Processes of Appointment* (Brookings, 1965), p. 273.

11. Quoted in Saloma and Sontag, *Parties*, p. 199.

12. Interview with Frederic V. Malek, Washington, D.C., June 19, 1974.

10   Departments and Agencies

No one has a more compelling interest in the process of filling executive vacancies than the people working in the departments and agencies where those vacancies occur. Theirs is a dual concern. On the one hand, they are anxious to ensure that the new appointee with whom or for whom they will work is a cooperative and competent individual. They don't want to be stuck with a political hack who happens to be a friend of the President or a friend of the Speaker of the House. They want someone with the training, knowledge, and sensitivity to make a positive contribution to the work of the agency.

Their second concern relates to policy. Federal agencies are not simply neutral implementers of government policy who follow as closely as they can whatever marching orders they get from the President and the Congress. Every agency has its own traditions, norms of behavior, and policy predispositions. Hence there is some natural suspicion when a new appointee comes on board. Incumbent personnel are wary of those who are appointed as agents of the President to "shake up" an agency or those whose policy views are not in accord with prevailing thinking in the agency.

For both reasons, agency and department personnel keep a close eye on the appointment process. The federal columns in the Washington newspapers and the pages of the *Federal Times* abound with rumors and leaks about upcoming appointments. To protect their own interests in the appointment process, agency personnel—particularly agency heads or their designees—routinely seek to be active participants in the appointment process.[1] In fact, they are often very important participants in that process, but the impact of their participation is inconsistent.

Agency heads are usually the conduit for agency participation in the selection process. The role an agency head plays may fall into one of four categories. He may *control* the selection process for a position in his agency. He may *share responsibility* with the White House personnel office in finding a candidate. He may have only the power to *veto* a candidate selected by the White House. Or he may have *no role* at all in the selection process. The second category, in which the agency head and the White House share responsibility for finding a candidate, is the most common, but cases persistently occur in each of the other categories as well.

A number of factors affect the ability of an agency head to participate effectively in the selection process. By far the most important of these is the President's management style. Some Presidents feel that management responsibility should be centralized in the White House and, with it, control over the selection of administration appointees. The Nixon administration made some efforts to set up this kind of managerial system in the early 1970s. Other Presidents feel that management is a responsibility that the President shares with his agency heads and that both, therefore, should play a part in personnel selection. This philosophy colored the selection process in the Kennedy, Johnson, and Ford administrations. Still other Presidents, Eisenhower for instance, prefer a decentralized system where agency heads are held responsible for the work of their agencies and are thus delegated substantial authority for personnel selection. None of these systems is pure. There are variations within each in the mixture of participants in selection decisions. But in general terms, the President's management preferences establish the conditions under which agency heads can influence the outcomes of those decisions.

The role of a department or agency head in the selection process may be the product of an agreement he reached with the President at the time he joined the administration. Some make no such agreements, but others have been able to get the President to promise them a free hand in selecting their own subordinates. President Kennedy, for instance, sought to enlarge the White House role in agency appointments, but he had to make exceptions to that policy in order to recruit Robert McNamara and Dean Rusk into his Cabinet.[2] McNamara, particularly, sought assurances that he would be free to staff his own department.[3]

An agency head's ability to participate in selection decisions is also affected by his standing in the Washington community—his personal prestige. If the President has great faith in his judgment or if he is highly regarded by others in the administration, it will be difficult for the White House to ignore or contravene his personnel recommendations.[4] If he is also well regarded in Congress, if he has developed a positive relationship with important interest groups, or if he has support in the press or among the public, his bargaining position in the selection process will be further fortified. In Washington parlance, he will have "clout." Each administration has its strong figures: John Snyder (Treasury Secretary under Truman), George Humphrey (Treasury Secretary under Eisenhower), Robert McNamara (Defense Secretary under Kennedy and Johnson), Henry Kissinger (Secretary of State under Nixon and Ford), Joseph Califano (HEW Secretary under Carter), J. Edgar Hoover (FBI Director under eight Presidents). People like these rarely have difficulties with the White House in securing control over the selection of their own subordinates.

An agency head's control over any particular selection decision will be affected by the interest that other political actors have in that selection decision. The more salient the position at the time it becomes vacant, the less likely it is that the agency head will dominate the selection of a new appointee. If, for instance, it is a position whose incumbent will play a prominent role in the development or implementation of controversial policies, other political actors will take a strong interest in it. Often they become competitors with the agency head for control of the selection process. If they have access to the President, he may well be thrown into the role of arbitrator between the interests of the agency head and the concerns of other sets of political actors.

A well-publicized example of this occurred in 1969. The new Secretary of HEW, Robert Finch, had selected Dr. John Knowles of Massachusetts as the person he wanted to be Assistant Secretary of HEW for Health and Scientific Affairs. He passed that recommendation on to the White House so that the President could announce Knowles's nomination. When the likelihood of Knowles's selection became known, however, the American Medical Association, with the support of key members of Congress, sought to intercede in the selection process to prevent the nomination. Because this was the top health position in the federal government, it was of particular importance to the AMA, and its salience fired the intensity of the association's desire to participate in filling it. In this particular case the AMA prevailed, and the Knowles nomination was never sent to the Senate.[5]

External pressures on the President may affect an agency head's influence in selection decisions even for positions that are not particularly salient. Occasionally someone who is personally close or politically important to the President will seek an appointment for himself or a friend to a particular position. That is no problem for the White House if the head of the agency where the position is located is willing to go along with the appointment. Merit is rarely much of a factor in appointments of this sort, however, and agency heads will sometimes resist these political placements in their agencies. Toward the end of his administration, Gerald Ford nominated Patrick Delaney, a young member of the White House staff, to a seat on the Securities and Exchange Commission. Delaney's primary "qualification" was that he was the son of the Chairman of the House Rules Committee. Roderick M. Hills, the Chairman of the SEC, vigorously and publicly opposed the nomination.[6] Hills lost the battle but won the war. The Delaney nomination was sent to the Senate, but it expired at the end of the 94th Congress without being approved.

A starker case of the impact of outside pressure on the role of an agency head in the selection process occurred in 1977. After his election, Jimmy Carter had asked Jack Eckerd, a Ford appointee, to stay on as Administrator of the General Services Administration. Eckerd agreed on the condition that he would be free to select his own deputy. Shortly after that agreement was made, the President was importuned by Speaker of the House Thomas P. O'Neill, Jr., to appoint Robert T. Griffin, a GSA employee and an old friend of the Speaker, as Deputy Administrator. In previous weeks, Carter had irked O'Neill by announcing nominations of people from Massachusetts without first informing the Speaker's office. Anxious to make up for that, he agreed to make the Griffin appointment. Eckerd, unhappy over Carter's apparent reneging on a pledge, resigned and left Washington.[7]

There are a number of reasons for the strong interest an agency head will normally take in appointments to positions in his own agency. He wants to have people under him who are competent and knowledgeable, whom he feels he can work with comfortably and effectively, and who share most of his views about the fundamental objectives of the agency. He is eager as well to bring people into leadership positions in the agency who will have a positive effect on the morale of the career personnel. He wants people who will be able to handle sensitive relations with congressional committees, interest groups, and other agencies. Furthermore, he is likely to feel that he has a better vantage point than the White House personnel office for sizing up the agency's needs and judging the qualities of potential appointees.

The agency head's objectives and those of the White House do not always fully align. The White House has to be concerned with the representative quality of administration appointments; this is not a compelling concern for most agency heads. The White House is often anxious to find positions for women and members of minority groups; most agency heads will be more concerned with the experience and proven ability of potential appointees than with their sex, race, or ethnic heritage. The President, as the appointing authority, is the focus of political pressures that an agency head often doesn't feel and may not even clearly perceive. Thus there is considerable potential for conflict between the White House and the heads of executive agencies in the appointment process.

This potential conflict, however, is remarkably well controlled. If the President and his agency heads have bases for disagreement over appointments, they also have strong incentives to work out those disagreements amicably and privately. Improving cooperation between agencies and the White House was, in fact, one of the most important reasons for the postwar establishment of presidential personnel staffs. Douglas Bennett, director of Gerald Ford's personnel staff, said "One of the very important things that the [director of the White House personnel office] has to have is very strong relationships with the cabinet, very strong personal relationships with the cabinet. . . . It's a very important factor."[8] Frederick Malek, who headed the Nixon personnel staff, wrote of the cooperative nature of this relationship:

> While the recruiting staff was centrally run from the White House, the largest number of presidential appointments were not to White House slots but to posts in the subcabinet. Naturally, each cabinet officer or other agency head had to be deeply involved in the process and had to retain the right of final selection because he or she was held directly accountable to the President for the performance of his or her organization and had to deal with the new appointees on a day-to-day basis. Consequently, our White House recruiting staff treated the agency heads as clients, consulting at every step and providing service, much as a successful corporate staff might work with the line divisions of the company. In addition, we encouraged each agency to develop a professional recruiting capacity to handle the many positions below the assistant secretary level.[9]

The term "working relationship" probably best characterizes the normal interaction between the White House and the agencies in the matter of appointment decisions. There are conditions, as described here, that may lead to short-term alterations in that characterization, but for the most part subcabinet nominations are the result of a cooperative effort by the agency and the White House to find an individual who is satisfactory to both.

Notes

1. Occasionally efforts are made by lower-level agency personnel to in-fluence appointment decisions. The American Foreign Service Associa-tion, an organization of professional diplomats, has long sought to limit the practice of placing people with political connections but little diplo-matic experience in ambassadorial positions. In 1974 the AFSA publicly opposed President Ford's nomination of Peter M. Flanigan to serve as Ambassador to Spain. See "The Diplomats Protest," *New York Times*, October 1, 1974.

   Internal, though less organized, opposition also arose on the nomina-tion of John F. Lehman, Jr., to be Deputy Director of the Arms Control and Disarmament Agency in 1975. See Rowland Evans and Robert Novak, "'The Network' Fights a Nominee," *Washington Post*, April 21, 1975.
2. See Arthur M. Schlesinger, Jr., *A Thousand Days* (Fawcett Crest, 1965), pp. 145–148.
3. On the variety of arrangements existing between recent Presidents and the chairmen of the FCC and FTC, see James M. Graham and Victor H. Kramer, *Appointments to the Regulatory Agencies: The Federal Com-munications Commission and the Federal Trade Commission, 1949–1974*, printed for the use of the Senate Committee on Commerce (GPO, 1976).
4. See "Executive Recruiting—Washington Style," *Dun's*, 99 (June 1972): 98.
5. See Rowland Evans and Robert Novak, *Nixon in the White House* (Ran-dom House, 1971), pp. 59–60; and John H. Knowles, "Man the A.M.A. cut down: Personal account of the campaign that blocked his nomina-tion," *Life*, 67 (July 11, 1969): 34 ff.
6. See *New York Times*, June 11, 1976.
7. See *Washington Post*, February 11, 1977.
8. Interview with Douglas P. Bennett, Washington, D.C., January 10, 1977.
9. Frederic V. Malek, *Washington's Hidden Tragedy: The Failure to Make Government Work* (Free Press, 1978), p. 70.

11   Interest Groups

Interest groups vie for a role in appointment decisions for precisely the same reason they try to influence other political decisions. They recognize that the interests shared by their members may well be directly affected by the outcome of those appointment decisions. They want to help shape public policy in those issue areas that concern them, and they know that participating in the choice of the decision-makers is a means to that end. Their motivation is self-interest. Securing the selection of sympathetic decision-makers reduces a group's chances of suffering from adverse public policy decisions.

Interest groups pervade the appointment process, but they vary in size, in resources, and, consequently, in their ability to influence its outcomes. A few groups have roles in the appointment process that are guaranteed by statutes. The law creating the Railroad Retirement Board specifies, for instance, that "one member shall be appointed from recommendations made by the representatives of the employees and one member shall be appointed from recommendations made by representatives of the carriers."[1] In making nominations to the National Science Board, the President is directed by statute to give due consideration "to any recommendations which may be submitted to him by the National Academy of Sciences, the National Association of State Universities and Land Grant Colleges, the Association of American Universities, the Association of American Colleges, the Association of State Colleges and Universities, or by other scientific or educational organizations."[2] Similar language appears in the statutes creating such other agencies as the Coal Mine Safety Board of Review[3] and the Federal National Mortgage Association.[4]

Another group, the American Bar Association, has a consistently important role in the appointment of federal judges, but that role is traditional rather than statutory. Since 1945 the ABA has been called upon to evaluate the qualifications of nominees for seats on the federal bench.[5] These evaluations are available to both the Justice Department, in recommending potential nominees to the President, and the Senate Judiciary Committee during its confirmation proceedings. The ABA evaluation is important primarily in a negative sense. A candidate found to be "not qualified" is unlikely, except in the most unusual circumstances,[6] to secure a judicial appointment. The ABA, therefore, is not often directly involved in the selection of judicial candidates, but it does have a significant impact on the establishment of minimum standards of acceptability.[7]

Since few groups are blessed with a statutory role in the appointment process or even with the kind of semiformal role granted to the ABA, most must flex their political muscles in order to participate in appointment decisions. In this sort of political combat, some groups are better equipped and better positioned to compete than others. The groups most likely to be consistently influential in appointment decisions are those that have a traditional proprietary interest in appointments within a particular agency. The larger the group and the closer its relationship with the agency, the greater its potential influence in agency appointments. If a group is only one among several that regularly interact with an agency, its influence in appointment decisions will not be as large as it would be if the group were the agency's primary "client." Organized labor, for instance, has a great deal of influence in executive selection, particularly at the assistant secretary level, in the Department of Labor, where it is the primary "client," but much less influence in the selection of members of the National Labor Relations Board, where other groups with an equally large interest are also influential.

The extent of group influence depends in large part on the degree of alignment between agency functions and group interests. Where an agency's actions have a direct and substantial impact on a group, the group will make a concerted effort to protect itself against the appointment of executives who it believes are unsympathetic to its concerns. A study of business regulation by the Brookings Institution noted, for instance, that "appointments, almost unnoticed by the general public, are closely watched by regulated firms. Rarely does the President appoint, and the Senate confirm, a commissioner if the regulated industry is politically aligned against him."[8]

The number of appointment decisions dominated by a single group is quite small. Most of the time interest groups are forced to compete with other political actors for a role in the appointment process. Their ability to influence outcomes is dependent primarily on three things: the contemporary political environment, the group's resources, and the strategies it employs to maximize its impact on White House and Senate decision-makers.

A group's chances of influencing appointment decisions are enhanced if the group has traditionally supported the President's party. Labor unions, most minority groups, and consumer groups are more likely to have an impact on appointment decisions in Democratic than in Republican administrations. The reverse is usually true for business-oriented groups like the Chamber of Commerce, the Business Roundtable, and the National Association of Manufacturers. Other political conditions may also affect a group's influence. If it can demonstrate that its members were an important component of the President's electoral coalition, it may be more warmly received at the White House when it claims a right to participate in certain appointment decisions. Both labor unions and blacks felt they had the right to make such a claim after the 1976 presidential election, and they pressed it aggressively.

In most cases, the nature and scope of a group's resources are the primary determinant of its ability consistently to play a part in appointment decisions. Here the obvious usually holds: Larger groups have an advantage over smaller ones, wealthier groups have an advantage over poorer ones, groups that are well organized and competently led have an advantage over those that are not. But there are also other kinds of resources that are useful in the struggle to influence appointment decisions. Sympathetic journalists are one such resource. Newspaper columnists or reporters can help a group get its message to important Washington decision-makers. The personnel preferences of AFL-CIO leaders, for instance, are often indicated in the syndicated columns of Rowland Evans and Robert Novak.[9] William Raspberry's column in the *Washington Post* frequently publicizes black leaders' views on pending appointments.[10]

Substantive expertise is another valuable resource for a group trying to influence appointment decisions. Both the White House and the Senate committees holding confirmation hearings have to take notice when a group of professional experts passes judgment on one of its colleagues. When the ABA finds a lawyer unfit to be a judge, the AMA finds a doctor unfit to serve as Surgeon General, or the National Society of Professional Engineers finds an engineer unfit to head the Geological Survey, the affected candidates are likely to be subjected to searching reevaluation.

While a group's resources may be the primary determinant of its ability to play a consistent part in the appointment process, the strategies it employs in taking advantage of those resources have the most direct effect on its success in actually influencing selection decisions. The strategies that groups employ range widely over time and terrain, but the most common are these.

Don't Be Shy. The surest way for a group to shut itself out of the appointment process is for it to blunder into a strategy of reticence. David Wimer, who served as director of the White House Personnel Operation in the latter stages of the Nixon administration, pointed out, "We don't have to spend much time contacting industry or interest groups; they come to us."[11] Douglas Bennett, who held a similar post in the Ford administration, said that "interest groups are not bashful at all."[12] An important nomination will generate dozens of unsolicited suggestions from interest groups. A group that fails to make such suggestions may well be overlooked as the search process progresses. Suggesting candidates to the White House does not guarantee that those candidates will be selected, but it does at least indicate a group's interest and decrease the chance that the White House will nominate someone who is totally unacceptable.

Cultivate Friends Who Can Help. A group with a friend who has access to appointment decision-makers has a big advantage over groups that do not. Friends in high places can help in numerous ways: by arguing a group's case, by protecting its interests, or merely by "showing the flag." Corporations and business organizations, for instance, often sought to communicate their interests in appointment decisions through Peter Flanigan, who served on the White House staff during the Nixon administration. Civil rights groups knew that another Nixon aide, Leonard Garment, shared many of their concerns and would make them known to those involved in appointment decisions. Intellectuals often used Arthur Schlesinger to carry their views to appropriate officials in the Kennedy White House.

Cultivating friends in the Congress, especially if they are powerful friends, is also a useful strategy for groups that want to influence personnel choices. The American Medical Association found its friend Everett Dirksen very helpful in torpedoing the nomination of Dr. John Knowles.[13] Consumer groups found Senator Warren Magnuson a valuable ally in persuading the White House to make consumer-oriented appointments to federal regulatory agencies.[14] The members of the Black Caucus in the House of Representatives were the principal advocates for more black appointments in the 1970s. Congressional support can be especially important in helping a group to overcome the inadequacy of its resources.

Form an Alliance. Numbers are not the sole factor in determining who gets heard in the appointment process, but, as a general rule, larger groups are more effective than smaller ones. A common strategy for those seeking influence is to band together with other groups that share their concerns. This not only temporarily enlarges the collective size and apparent political strength of the groups involved, it also provides a greater abundance of resources: more manpower, more money, and more political skills.

The alliance strategy was adopted by more than sixty women's groups at the beginning of the Carter administration to create pressure for the appointment of women to important positions.[15] This coalition was organized by the National Women's Political Caucus, and it initiated its efforts to influence appointment decisions even before the 1976 presidential election. Letters were sent to both presidential candidates identifying sixty appointive jobs that the coalition felt should be filled by women. After the election was over, the women's coalition sent lists of qualified women to Jimmy Carter's transition team. Through frequent contact, representatives of the women's coalition were able to develop a working relationship with the transition staff, and a number of the coalition's recommended candidates were ultimately appointed to policy-level posts.

The women's alliance was also able to arrange a meeting with the President and a series of meetings with the new members of his Cabinet to discuss the importance of appointments for women and to recommend specific candidates. The coalition's effort also included a constant monitoring of the appointment process. It exercised particular vigilance over Cabinet and agency head selections to prevent the nomination of individuals who it thought were insensitive to women's rights. The coalition was active, for instance, in lobbying against the nomination of John Dunlop, who had been rumored a leading candidate for the position of Secretary of Labor. The coalition was dissatisfied with his public record in dealing with issues important to women and sought—successfully—to keep him out of the Cabinet.[16]

As a Last Resort, Go to the Barricades in the Senate. The earlier a group can participate in appointment decisions, the better. This is particularly true when a group is less interested in advocating the appointment of a particular candidate than in preventing the appointment of an unpalatable one. The strong negative reaction of an

important group or set of groups is likely to be given close consideration by personnel staffs in the White House or in the agencies. If the
target of a group's opposition can be eliminated before a formal nomination is announced, few feathers will be seriously ruffled. Neither
the President nor the affected candidate will suffer any severe embarrassment.

But groups are not always able to exercise influence in the early
stages of the appointment process. They may find themselves in a
minority; that is, their opinions about particular candidates may not
be shared by other groups and individuals with an interest in a particular appointment. Sometimes the President has a candidate he
very much wants to nominate and pays little attention to his personnel advisers or to others outside the formal selection process. And
some groups are unable to participate in selection decisions simply
because they lack access to the White House. They are not aligned
with the President's party; they have not been a demonstrable part of
his electoral coalition; and they are not on his philosophical wave
length. If they want to influence appointment decisions, they must do
so outside the White House.

The court of last resort in the appointment process is, of course,
the Senate. And for those groups shut out of selection decisions,
confirmation proceedings become the primary target of their efforts at
influence. The confirmation process is generally more open than the
selection process. There are more formal decision-makers involved,
and their final decisions are usually made in public. Confirmation
hearings provide an opportunity for interest groups to state their case
in public, and there are also abundant opportunities for them to do so,
to Senators and their aides, in private, as well.

The techniques of influence relied upon earlier in the appointment process are also applied at the confirmation stage. Groups are
aggressive in making their views known, cultivate the assistance of
sympathetic friends in the Congress, and try to magnify their influence by forming alliances. A number of Gerald Ford's nominees
were successfully opposed in the Senate by interest groups using all of
these tactics.

William Kendrick, whom Ford had nominated to a seat on the
Equal Employment Opportunity Commission, was opposed by a coalition of labor and civil rights groups. The groups thought Kendrick too
closely associated with business interests (he was an employee of the
National Association of Manufacturers) and thus likely to create a
pro-business majority on the five-member EEOC. These groups co-

ordinated their opposition to Kendrick, which was vociferous and steadfast. And they relied on the long-standing closeness of their relationship with senior members of the Senate Labor and Public Welfare Committee to get a sympathetic response. The committee declined to support the nomination.[17]

A variety of consumer groups opposed the 1976 nomination of John Byington to head the Consumer Product Safety Commission. Their objection was rooted in the belief that Byington would not be an effective consumer advocate, that nothing in his background demonstrated a sensitivity to consumer concerns. Working together and with sympathetic members and staff of the Senate Commerce Committee, the consumer groups were able to focus considerable attention on the Byington nomination. Byington was ultimately appointed to the commission, but for two years only, not for the seven-year term to which he had initially been nominated.[18]

During the Republican administrations of Richard Nixon and Gerald Ford, the selection process and the confirmation process grew to be quite distinct decision-making arenas. In large part, this resulted from differences in the patterns of access at each stage. With Republican Presidents, groups representing industry and producer interests were often treated more hospitably by the White House than by Senate committees dominated by Democrats. The reverse was true in the case of those groups representing consumer and minority interests. Thus whatever bias occurred in the selection process sought correction in the confirmation process. Those groups who found themselves consistently shut out of effective participation in the President's selection decisions had little choice but to take their case to the Senate. The gap that developed between the two main decision points in the appointment process accounts in no small part for the difficulty Nixon and Ford sometimes encountered in getting their nominations confirmed by the Senate.

The role played by interest groups in the appointment process is more often indirect than direct. They are a pervasive but inconsistent force in the outcomes of appointment decisions. Their primary impact is to condition the political environment in which appointment decisions are made, in some cases to establish the outer parameters of candidate acceptability. Occasionally political circumstances will permit a single group to dominate a particular appointment decision. But that clearly happens only in exceptional cases. White House personnel officials and members of Senate committees are usually well aware of the views of relevant interest groups, but there are many groups and many other concerned parties as well. Establishing a position of dominance is a political task of such magnitude that it usually doesn't happen. Hence interest group influence is rarely more than one among many factors that appointment decision-makers have to consider in formulating their personnel choices.

Notes

1. 45 *U.S.C.* 228J.
2. 42 *U.S.C.* 1863.
3. 30 *U.S.C.* 475.
4. 12 *U.S.C.* 1723 (b).
5. See Harold W. Chase, *Federal Judges: The Appointing Process* (Minnesota University Press, 1972), p. 20.
6. An exception occurred in the case of former Governor Thomas Meskill of Connecticut, who was confirmed to a seat on the Second Circuit Court of Appeals despite the American Bar Association finding that he was not qualified. The Senate approved the Meskill nomination in April 1975 after an eight-month delay. The final vote was 54–36.
7. Much has been written about the role of the ABA in judicial appointments. Among the most enlightening sources are Chase, *Federal Judges;* Joel B. Grossman, *Lawyers and Judges: The Politics of Judicial Selection* (John Wiley & Sons, 1965); and "Role of the Bar in Selection of Justices," *U.S. News and World Report*, June 1, 1970, pp. 84ff.
8. Roger G. Noll, *Reforming Regulation* (Brookings, 1971), p. 43. For a similar assessment see Louis M. Kohlmeier, *The Regulators* (Harper & Row, 1969), p. 48. No interest group, of course, has the power to dictate appointment decisions to the President. The Carter administration, for instance, ignored the suggestions of AFL-CIO leaders that it name John Dunlop as its initial Secretary of Labor. Carter did nominate a Secretary of Labor, Ray Marshall, who was acceptable to the AFL-CIO. The Union did not get its first choice, but it did get an appointee it could "live with."
9. See, for instance, Rowland Evans and Robert Novak, "Labor Calls in Its Chips," *Washington Post*, December 11, 1976, and *idem*, "Labor Is Upset by Rejection of Dunlop," *Boston Globe*, December 24, 1976.
10. For example, William Raspberry, "Blacks and the Cabinet," *Washington Post*, December 17, 1976.
11. Interview with David Wimer, Washington, D.C., June 19, 1974.
12. Interview with Douglas P. Bennett, Washington, D.C., January 10, 1977.
13. The Knowles case is discussed in Chapter 10, on p. 202.
14. See Chapter 5, p. 106.
15. This description of the efforts of a women's coalition is drawn from several sources: "Interest-Group Doubts Rise on Top Jobs," *Congressional Quarterly Weekly Report,* Vol. 35 (April 30, 1977); "Feminists

Critical of Carter on Jobs," *New York Times*, February 8, 1977; "Catch 22 for Women," *Washington Post*, January 16, 1977; and "Women Develop Old Girl Network," *Washington Post*, February 27, 1978.

16. "Interest Group Doubts Rise on Top Jobs," *Congressional Quarterly Weekly Report*, April 30, 1977, p. 806.

17. *Washington Post*, October 15, 1975.

18. See 1976—Commerce—S. John Byington: Chairman, Consumer Product Safety Commission, and *Washington Post*, March 8, 1976.

12   Members of Congress

In Part III we examined the behavior of Senators in their formal roles in the confirmation process. But the influence of members of Congress in appointment decisions is clearly not limited to the Senate's exercise of the confirmation power. Members of both houses of Congress, like the other sets of political actors previously discussed, are important participants at every stage of the appointment process.

That may seem a little odd, given the fact that the Senate possesses the ultimate power of approval over presidential nominations. Why isn't that an adequate forum for the expression of congressional concerns and the application of congressional influence in appointment decisions? The answer is that members of Congress have interests in appointment decisions that often cannot be effectively expressed or fully realized in the formal exercise of the confirmation power.

Members of the House, of course, have no official role in the confirmation process, but they are no less interested than their Senate counterparts in the outcomes of personnel decisions. While they do make occasional efforts to influence Senate confirmation decisions, the confirmation process rarely provides them with what they regard as adequate opportunities to participate in appointment decisions.

Even Senators often find that the confirmation process cannot accommodate the kind of role they wish to play in personnel decisions. Confirmation only allows them to react to the President's nominees, not to promote their own candidates for federal offices. Even their ability to react freely to the President's nominees is constricted by the public nature of the confirmation process. They may have serious reservations about a nominee but find themselves reluctant to oppose him publicly, because he meets all the apparent qualifications for the job for which he has been nominated. The formal confirmation process is simply too confining to afford all members of Congress the kind of leverage they would like to have in appointment decisions. So they too became active informal participants in the appointment process.

Influence-seeking by members of Congress is most often directed at the President's selection decisions. Since the vast majority of presidential nominees are confirmed by the Senate, the logical place to attempt to influence personnel choices is at the White House, where the most important appointment decisions are made. This is not an invariable pattern. Senators and congressmen, as individuals or in small groups, do try occasionally to have an impact on confirmation decisions. They testify for or against nominees at confirmation hearings. They provide information to Senate committee members that bears on their confirmation decisions. And they lobby privately to persuade committee members to support or oppose particular nominees. But these activities are not usually the principal components of the efforts of a typical member of Congress to influence appointment decisions. In pursuing this kind of influence, most of their energies focus on the White House.

Members have several incentives for their attempts to participate in selection decisions. Some are driven by their concern over an appointment's potential impact on public policy. They don't want the President to nominate people who are insensitive to the interests of their constituents, whose political philosophies they find anathema, or with whose past policy actions they disagree.

Senators from Western states, for instance, have traditionally taken the view that the Interior Department ought to be run by people from the West, because most of its operations are centered in the West. When vacancies occur in high-level positions in the department, Western Senators on the Energy and Natural Resources (formerly Interior) Committee usually take an active interest in the process of filling them. Their primary concern in this is to protect the interests of their region of the country.

In 1971 Rogers C. B. Morton of Maryland was confirmed as Secretary of the Interior, one of the very few non-Westerners in this century to hold that post. Later that year, Morton decided that he wanted James R. Schlesinger, another non-Westerner, as his Under Secretary. Western Senators on the Senate Interior Committee drew the line at this point and refused to endorse the Schlesinger nomination. Senator Gordon Allott of Colorado, the committee's ranking Republican, made it clear to the White House that he didn't think Schlesinger was familiar with the political and economic problems of the West and that he would not support his nomination. Another Senator said publicly that "the last thing we need is a damn Harvard slide-rule economist." Both Morton and the White House congressional liaison staff tried to talk Allott and the other Western Senators out of their opposition, but they were unsuccessful, and the Schlesinger nomination was never made.[1]

Patronage interests are another reason why members of Congress try to influence selection decisions. Most of them at one time or another have friends, constituents, or staff employees who seek their help in obtaining presidential appointments. Most members, in fact, encounter a constant stream of requests for aid in the search for government jobs. And nearly all of them like to demonstrate to their constituents of their colleagues in the Congress that they have some influence at the White House. One effective way to make such a demonstration is to secure a presidential appointment for someone who has sought the member's help in getting a federal job.

It is not the case, of course, that every member of Congress is intensely interested in every political job that becomes vacant. Members have neither the time nor the taste for that kind of full-scale concern. But for any single job vacancy, the likelihood is high that at least one and perhaps several members will be actively interested. They then become a central part of the field of political forces that influence and constrain the President's decision-making process.

Tactics of Influence

Because they are usually acting outside their formal roles in their efforts to influence appointment decisions, members of Congress are in much the same position as other participants in this process. Their actual influence depends on the extent and nature of the resources available to them and on the success of the tactics they adopt to bring those resources to bear on specific personnel choices. The most common and the most effective of those tactics are described below.

Congressional Recommendations. The simple act of recommending candidates to the White House is the most frequent form of congressional participation in the appointment process. This is a routine function in which virtually all congressional offices participate. The bulk of the requests that members get for help in finding federal jobs come from constituents whom the member does not know personally. These are normally treated by simply forwarding the applications and resumés to the White House with a cover letter asking the personnel staff to consider the job-seeker for any vacancy for which he might be qualified.

The number of congressional recommendations received by the White House is very large. Frederic Malek wrote that five hundred such letters were received from Congress each month during his tenure as director of the White House Personnel Operation.[2] Frank Moore, the head of Jimmy Carter's congressional liaison office, estimated that more than a thousand job requests had been received from Capitol Hill by the end of Carter's first month in office.[3]

Congressional recommendations pose problems of two kinds for the White House personnel staff. One is the logistics problem of processing and promptly responding to so many communications. Failure to handle these recommendations swiftly and politely inevitably leads to congressional disenchantment, and that disenchantment often takes the form of public criticism of the President and his staff from members of his own party.

The larger problem for the White House is to determine which of these hundreds of job recommendations are important to the members of Congress who make them. As indicated, many of these recommendations are simply a routine action by members of Congress providing a service for constituents. But not always. Some of the individuals whom members of Congress recommend are people close to them, people they sincerely and actively want to help, people they think are highly qualified for federal jobs. To the White House personnel and congressional liaison staffs falls the task of separating the sincere recommendations from the routine. Malek indicates the importance of this:

> [R]oughly three-quarters of the recommendations were coming from the members of Congress and a good portion of the others from other elected officials, and we wanted to have some sense as to, really, how important it was to the member of Congress. If, for example, a Senator or a Congressman in either Party was making a recommendation, many times they would be making a recommendation just as a courtesy to a constituent who said, "I want a job."
>
> In other cases, they would be making a recommendation based on some very deep personal conviction that this person was highly worthy and they would feel very strongly about it, in which case, it would be of high political value to the President to try to respect the judgment and recommendation of that particular member of Congress.[4]

The character and frequency of these congressional referrals is suggested by the memorandum reproduced here. It is from John W. Macy, Jr., Lyndon Johnson's chief personnel aide, to Lawrence F.

O'Brien, who headed Johnson's congressional liaison staff, and it indicates the phone calls received in a typical week from members of Congress interested in selection decisions.

THE WHITE HOUSE
WASHINGTON

February 1, 1965

MEMORANDUM FOR HONORABLE LAWRENCE F. O'BRIEN

Subject: Congressional calls, week of January 25, 1965

January 25

Congressman Carl Albert — inquiring as to what was being done to find "something suitable " for Lester Johnson and what the possibilities might be for Federal employment for Victor Wickersham.

Congressman Ken Hechler — recommending consideration of George Revercomb, a present FCC staffer, for the Republican vacancy on the FCC.

Senator Douglas — recommending Michael Greenbaum, a Chicago mortgage banker, for the remaining vacancy on the Home Loan Bank Board and Stephen Gilman, an official of the All—State Motor Club, for Director of the Travel Service in the Department of Commerce.

January 26

Congressman Carl Albert — recommending John Lewis Smith, now Chief Judge of the General Sessions Court of the District of Columbia for promotion to the vacancy on the District Court — he described Smith as a friend of many years who enjoyed the respect of the entire community.

Congressman Wilbur Mills – referring William A.
Anderson, Jr., a young friend who is a graduate
of the University of Arkansas and the Harvard
Business School and presently employed by
Eastman Dale investment house in New York; apparently Anderson is interested in government
service even if it is on a part–time and volun-
tary basis.

Congressman Jack Brooks – complaining about the
attitude of the Bureau of the Budget on his ADP
legislation and urging consideration of
George Landegger's son for a junior position
in the government.

Senator Javits – reacting to my inquiry concerning
Seymour Siegal, the manager of STATION WNYC
for the FCC vacancy. He described Siegal as a
clean fellow who had done a fair and able job at
WNYC but not up to the quality of Ken Bartlett,
the Dean of Broadcasting at Syracuse, who is
Javits' candidate and who is "uniquely qualified" for the job.

January 27

Congressman Sweeney – thanking me for his constituent, one Charles Dexter.

Congressman Claude Pepper–recommending Clarence
S. Smith, career man with the Home Loan Bank
Board for the remaining vacancy on the Board.

Congressman Hale Boggs – referring James J.
Morrison of New Orleans as a Federal judicial
prospect.

Congressman Bingham – recommending William Car-
lebach, with the Department of Commerce in New
York for a Federal position and questioning
the Federal practice with respect to absence

from Saturday work by Federal employees on the basis of religious belief.

January 29

Senator Dirksen called to reiterate the following recommendations: For the CAB, former Congressman Thor Tollefson who is "good as gold." For the FPC, Robert Dolph, who has been described "clean as a whistle" by the State Attorney General and Governor and given a good send-off by the Chief Justice of the State. For the FCC, John Patterson, recently a member of the Maritime Commission.

Congressman James Morrison recommending a Miss Eppley, a career employee of the FCC, for the existing vacancy.

Senator Ted Kennedy endorsing Robert Griffin for GSA.

John W. Macy, Jr.

Each administration devises its own method for determining how much weight should be given to a congressional recommendation. During Dan Fenn's tenure on the Kennedy personnel staff, for instance, the standard rule of thumb was that it took at least three letters or calls from a congressional office recommending a particular candidate to indicate that a member was really serious about getting a job for that candidate. Fenn noted, however, that even the "rule of three" was not always a perfect indicator. Once, after receiving three strong letters from a congressman pleading for an appointment for a constitutent, Fenn called the congressman personally to get additional information and found, to his surprise, that the congressman didn't even recognize the constituent's name.[5]

If a member of Congress is anxious to obtain a presidential appointment for a particular individual, he is not likely to be shy about making the depth of his interest known at the White House. Instead of simply making written recommendations, members will sometimes undertake a vigorous campaign to persuade the White House to nominate their candidates for particular jobs. Two examples illustrate the pattern these campaigns may follow.

The first took place in 1972 when a vacancy occurred on the Federal Communications Commission. For a number of years prior to that time the Senate Commerce Committee had been urged by spokesmen for minority groups to do something about the fact that no black person had ever been a member of the FCC. By 1972 Senators John Pastore and Howard Baker had come to regard black representation on the FCC as a very important matter, and they sought to persuade Richard Nixon to nominate Benjamin Hooks, a black resident of Tennessee, to the Commission. Senator Baker described his role in that selection decision this way:

> I had the privilege of serving as ranking minority member of the subcommittee. Senator Pastore, of course, is chairman. At some point that I can't quite identify, Senator Pastore and I discussed the question of the possibility of the appointment of a black to the FCC.
>
> He expressed the viewpoint, and I thoroughly concurred, that there ought to be an appointment, and that it should be an early appointment, quickly made.
>
> We arranged, the two of us, to go to the White House to discuss this with the White House, because, after all, the appointments are made by the President, and while the advice and consent of the Senate is required, it is not the appointive authority.
>
> We found a sympathetic ear at the White House. We came back and set ourselves about the business of trying to find appropriate candidates. A number of names were submitted. I set about looking for the name of someone who would qualify in Tennesee. . . .
>
> Judge Hooks' name was developed by me and submitted first to Senator Pastore who, of course, did not know Judge Hooks. . . .
>
> The recommendation was made to the President; the President saw fit to make the appointment.[6]

The second example occurred in 1976. A change in presidential administrations always produces a flurry of personnel-related activity on Capitol Hill. Congressmen and Senators of the new President's party regard the transition as an appealing opportunity to push for administration jobs for their friends and employees. Several characteristics of the Carter transition made it especially ripe for this kind of activity. Jimmy Carter, of course, was the first Democratic President in eight years, and the overwhelmingly Democratic membership of the Congress was poised and waiting for his arrival. Because of substantial increases in the size and professionalism of congressional staff during the previous decade, there were in the Congress a good many experienced and competent staff members who were interested in transferring their skills to the executive branch. In fact, the professional staffs of the 94th Congress may have more closely resembled a "government in exile" or a "shadow government" than any other group in America's history. Further heightening the sense of anticipation on Capitol Hill was the knowledge that Carter had few personal contacts in the capital and would clearly need to fill his administration with people who were familiar with the intricacies of politics and government in Washington. Members of Congress, savoring the prospect of having their former employees in important positions in the executive branch, were happy to make personnel suggestions to the new President.

Circumstances of just this sort surrounded Carter's selection of an Assistant Secretary of the Treasury for Tax Policy, the most important tax-related job in the Carter administration. Several important members of Congress—most notably Russell Long, the Chairman of the Senate Finance Committee, and Al Ullman, the Chairman of the House Ways and Means Committee—sought to persuade Carter to select Laurence Woodworth for the post. For the previous thirteen years, Woodworth had served as staff director of the Joint Committee on Internal Revenue Taxation and was widely regarded on Capitol Hill as the Congress's most knowledgeable expert on tax policy. Long and Ullman pushed his candidacy for the Treasury post because of his expertise but also, no doubt, because they recognized that their working relationship with him would improve the chances for legislative-executive cooperation in the development of federal tax policy.

Both Long and Ullman made their strong support for Woodworth known to leading figures in the new administration. So too did Senator Herman Talmadge, the second-ranking Democrat on the Finance Committee. Long apparently discussed the appointment at length with W. Michael Blumenthal, Carter's nominee to be Secretary of the Treasury. Early speculation within the Carter transition staff had been that Joseph Pechman of the Brookings Institution was the likely nominee for the tax policy post. But early in 1977 Laurence Woodworth was nominated by the President and readily confirmed by the Senate. Given the strong and unanimous support of key members of Congress, both actions were virtually inevitable.[7]

Quid pro Quo.   In terms of their influence in personnel selection decisions, members of Congress have an advantage that rarely accrues to other participants in the appointment process. The President often needs their support to enact or defeat legislation. On those occasions when the President's need for support coincides with a position vacancy in which a member of Congress is interested, obvious opportunities arise for the President to defer to a congressman's personnel recommendation in exchange for his support on a policy or procedural matter: a classic *quid pro quo* situation.

There is, of course, no precise way to calculate the frequency with which such situations occur. There are few incentives for partners in this kind of a bargain to admit its occurrence publicly or to divulge the terms of trade. The popular perception of the selection process as an open market in which appointments are used primarily to "buy" votes on important legislation is clearly a gross distortion. The costs of being caught at that sort of game are considerable, and so too, therefore, are the risks of playing it. There are also too few positions under the President's appointive jurisdiction and vacancies occur too rarely to provide him with everyday opportunities to use appointments as side payments in the process of legislative bargaining. The difficulty is further compounded by the activism, of other non-congressional participants in the appointment process to whose importunings the President must also respond.

In a more subtle and selective fashion, however, the appointment process does sometimes intersect with the legislative process. While the President cannot create legislative majorities simply by offering appointments in exchange for congressional votes, his appointment powers do allow him occasional tactically significant opportunities to curry favor among key legislators or to change the outcome of a legislative vote that is likely to be extremely close. "Politics," as Jacob Arvey was wont to say, "is the art of putting people under obligation to you."[8] Deferring to congressional influence in appointment decisions is one way in which Presidents do that.

When Lyndon Johnson was trying to push his legislative program through a Congress with cantankerous Democratic majorities, he often found it useful to heed the personnel recommendations of members whose help was essential to him. The nomination of Hamer Budge to the Securities and Exchange Commission in 1964, for instance, resulted almost entirely from Johnson's efforts to woo the support of Charles Halleck, the House Minority Leader, for important segments of his legislative program.[9]

In the same year, Johnson was able to mitigate the opposition of the House delegation from North Carolina to the Economic Opportunity Act by promising them *not* to appoint Adam Yarmolinsky, a framer of the bill, to a position in the Office of Economic Opportunity if the bill passed. The North Carolina congressmen objected to Yarmolinsky's "left-wing background" and were reluctant to support the creation of an agency in which he was likely to be given important responsibilities.[10]

Richard Nixon's White House also found it politically expedient to appoint or reappoint individuals who had the strong support of strategically located members of Congress. When Robert Finch, the Secretary of HEW, sought to replace Robert Ball as head of the Social Security Administration, Congressman Wilbur Mills took up Ball's defense at the White House. Ball stayed on the job.[11] Senator James Eastland made it clear that his support for a bill to create several new federal judgeships was conditioned on the retention in office of an Eastland crony serving as a U.S. Attorney in Mississippi.[12] Glenn W. Sutton, a close friend of Senator Russell Long, was appointed to the chairmanship of the U.S. Tariff Commission at a time when a set of important administration tax proposals were under study by the Senate Finance Committee, which Long chaired.[13] No President in the postwar period has failed to find some opportunities to make appointments that inspired support for parts of his legislative program.

Anticipated Reaction.   Inasmuch as the White House has a profound interest in making appointments that will not be defeated in the Senate confirmation process or otherwise engender negative reactions in Congress, a great deal of effort goes into the task of determining, prior to nomination, what the congressional response to a nominee is likely to be. If confirmation appears problematic or if key members of Congress register strong objections, one potential nominee may be dropped and another substituted. "There is not much sense," Harry Flemming once noted, "in sending up an appointment that's going to cause a fight."[14] To prevent that from happening, recent administrations have carefully organized the selection process to allow regular probing of the anticipated congressional reactions to planned presidential nominations before announcing the names of their nominees. This institutionalized form of conflict avoidance provides members of Congress with substantial opportunities to influence selection decisions.

How does the White House determine the likely reaction to a planned nomination? One way, of course, is simply to listen to the signals that regularly emanate from the Congress. The reaction to an administration's recent appointments can provide some sense of the likely reaction to future ones. In authorizing new agencies or new positions, members of Congress often give indications of the kinds of people they expect to see appointed to those positions. Some members even make a point of explicitly stating their expectations about, and thus their likely reactions to, certain types of nominees. Shortly after Gerald Ford took office, for instance, he received a letter from the chairman of the Senate Commerce Committee, Warren Magnuson, that included the following indications of congressional sentiment regarding nominations to the Federal Trade Commission:

> The Federal Trade Commission is unique among independent government agencies, charged as it is, with the responsibility for enforcing fair competition in the marketplace as an alternative to regulation. It appears to me, as it does to many of my colleagues, that the appointment to fill the FTC vacancy should logically go to a nominee qualified by training, experience and dedicated commitment to the vigorous enforcement of our antitrust laws.
>
> As I have indicated to you previously, I do not consider it the function of the Senate to dictate to the President the names of those whom it feels he shall select for high executive office, even for the regulatory agencies which have historically been perceived as arms of Congress. I do think it appropriate, however, that the Senate play an active role in working with you to develop the criteria to be applied in making such selections, and it is in that capacity that I urge you to fill this vacancy with an outstanding trust buster.[15]

Another way in which the White House sizes up probable congressional reaction to a nominee is by selectively leaking the names of the candidate or candidates under most active consideration. If there are pockets of opposition in Congress, they will usually identify themselves rather quickly in their efforts to gun down a nomination that displeases them. When word leaked out that the Nixon administration was considering the nomination of Paul H. Nitze as Assistant Secretary of Defense for International Security Affairs, there soon followed a public statement by Senator Barry Goldwater that he was "unalterably opposed" to Nitze's nomination, because Nitze was identified with "a group interested in bringing about our unilateral disarmament."[16]

Early in 1978 it became known that the Carter administration was actively considering the nomination of Goldie Watkins, a nuclear safety specialist from New York, to a seat on the Nuclear Regulatory Commission. Watkins was regarded by some in Congress as a probable pro-industry voice on the commission, and indications that she was being considered for the position generated vigorous statements of opposition from certain members of Congress. Representative Jonathan B. Bingham said, for instance, "I understand [Energy Secretary James] Schlesinger has sent the recommendation to the President, but I hope that the President doesn't appoint her. Schlesinger is trying to defeat what we tried to do [in creating the commission], he is trying to put in people who are the wrong kind of people—people who are responsible to him."[17]

The most important way in which the White House tries to determine probable congressional reactions to a pending nomination is simply by asking. The White House personnel staff, the congressional liaison staff, and occasionally other members of an administration call on Senators, congressmen, and congressional staff people to get their evaluations of the President's first choices for a nomination. This normally occurs as part of the routine clearance process that nearly all major nominations now undergo.

The clearance process is primarily important as a sensing device. If it picks up negative signals from the Congress, these are likely to become a factor in the final selection of a nominee. If the negative signals are strong enough (or if their source is powerful enough), they may lead to a decision not to nominate the President's preferred candidate.

In 1970, for instance, the Nixon administration had made a tentative decision to nominate Charles J. DiBona as Director of the Selective Service System. DiBona made a courtesy call on Senator Margaret Chase Smith during which he stated his strong support for the concept of an all-volunteer army. Senator Smith, the ranking Republican on the Senate Armed Services Committee, did not like the idea of an all-volunteer army, and she felt it inappropriate to appoint as Selective Service Director "an acknowledged liquidator of the system." Her unwavering opposition, coupled with the support she received from John Stennis, the committee chairman, was an insuperable obstacle, and DiBona was never nominated.[18]

In 1969 the Nixon administration had decided on Franklin A. Long of Cornell University as its candidate for Director of the National Science Foundation. But the choice ran into unexpected opposition, primarily from Representative James G. Fulton, the ranking Republican on the House Science and Astronautics Committee. Fulton was displeased with Long's opposition to the administration proposal for an antiballistic missile system, and he had a candidate of his

own for the post. When the administration shifted positions and decided not to nominate Long, Fulton claimed the credit. "I stopped
it," he said. "I take full responsibility, I have my own type of candidate and it is not Franklin A. Long."[19] Harry Flemming noted of this
affair that "the stong personal opposition of the ranking Republican on
a crucial committee has to be very seriously considered."[20]

Negative congressional reaction to a planned nomination does
not necessarily require its termination. What it does require is a
reconsideration of the costs and benefits of making that particular
nomination. The White House has to evaluate the intensity of the
negative reaction, the validity of the reasons for it, and the extent of
the political harm likely to be done by disregarding it. It adds a new
factor to the calculus of choice.

Determinants of Congressional Influence

Little is permanent or consistent about the part that members of
Congress play in the appointee selection process. Since members
have no institutionalized role in the process, they can muster influence only by maximizing the political leverage afforded them by the
circumstances of a particular appointment. Three variables have the
most direct bearing on the ability of a member of Congress to influence presidential choice in the selection process.

The Position. The first is the organizational location of the position being filled. The combination of tradition and statutory responsibilities have led the principal participants in the appointment process to regard an influential congressional role as more appropriate for
some federal positions than for others. One might well conceptualize
the positions filled by presidential appointment as a set of concentric
circles. As one moves out from the center, the likelihood of congressional interest and involvement grows.

At the center are those positions within the Executive Office of
the President and the President's Cabinet. The opinion is widely
shared in Washington that these positions constitute the President's
immediate "family" and that he should be given the broadest latitude
in filling them. Members of Congress occasionally attempt to influence the selection of people to fill these positions, but they rarely play
a dominant role because of the persistence of the view that these
positions, more than any others, are the President's responsibility.
Given the support provided him by this traditional view, the Presi-

dent is normally freer to disregard congressional advice in filling these positions than in any others within his appointment jurisdiction.

The next circle is composed of appointments to positions at the subcabinet level in executive departments and positions in the independent executive agencies. Here presidential control of appointment decisions remains strong, but somewhat more subject to congressional influence than it was in the innermost circle. Many of the subcabinet appointments are, in practice, made by department heads working in conjunction with the White House personnel office. Some department heads in each administration will be more sensitive and more sympathetic to congressional interests than others. Hence there are broader opportunities for members of Congress to participate in some of these selections than in most of those in which the President is more directly involved.

The third concentric circle is composed of appointments to the federal regulatory commissions. Since these are outside the rubric of the executive branch and not officially within the President's chain of command, they are a much more inviting target for congressional influence than positions that fall in the inner circles. Members of Congress are wont to point out that these commissions are "arms of the Congress" and thus to claim a proprietary right to take part in choosing their members. In tracing fifty-one appointments to the Federal Trade and Federal Communications commissions, James M. Graham and Victor H. Kramer found that "members of both Houses of Congress play an important role in the selection process."[21] A study of the regulatory appointments process conducted in 1976 by the Senate Government Operations Committee corroborated this: "[A]ccording to nearly every [White House personnel] advisor we interviewed, a major source of pressure for regulatory appointments came from members of Congress."[22]

In the outer circle are the senatorial courtesy positions, principally district court judges, U.S. Attorneys, U.S. Marshals, and a smattering of seats on the federal circuit courts. In selecting people to fill these jobs, presidential control is at its nadir. Members of Congress are the dominant influences in these selections, in many cases the sole influence.[23]

The first variable, then, in the equation of congressional influence in the selection process is the nature of the position being filled. While the pattern is not perfectly consistent, the likelihood of congressional influence is much greater for some positions than for others.

The Member's Political Resources.   A second important factor in this equation is the position of the influence-seeking legislator within the power structure of the Congress. In their ability to influence the choice of nominees for a particular administration job, some members of Congress will have advantages that others lack. It is generally helpful, for instance, to be a member of the President's party or, if a member of the other party, to have been a consistent supporter of the President. As David Wimer, a special assistant for personnel in the Nixon administration, noted, "those who support the administration have more influence than those who don't."[24]

Party and committee leaders in Congress have frequent opportunities to influence selection decisions, should they choose to exercise them. In the first two years of the Carter administration, Speaker of the House Thomas P. O'Neill, Jr., left his mark on a good many Carter appointment decisions.[25] As previously demonstrated, a pivotal committee chairman can often successfully claim a right to participate in the selection of officials for positions that fall within his committee's jurisdiction. When the President's party is in the minority in Congress, the ranking minority members of congressional committees may become an important source of influence in certain selection decisions.

Other factors may also enlarge the opportunities for members of Congress to participate influentially in specific personnel choices. When a member's vote on an important substantive issue is sought by the White House, he may acquire a bargaining advantage that he can apply to a nomination decision. When a nominee comes from a member's home state, that too is likely to enlarge the member's opportunities to have a say in the selection process. There is some natural reluctance on the part of the White House to nominate any individual who is offensive to his own representatives in Congress. When Richard Nixon sought to replace Robert M. Morgenthau as U.S. Attorney for the Southern District of New York in 1969, for instance, Senators Jacob Javits and Charles Goodell, both Republicans, intervened and blocked the removal. "I want to make it very clear," Javits said, "that if I say no, they can't appoint anybody."[26]

One other advantage that improves a member's chances of influencing selection decisions is his ability to gather support from other members. There is strength in numbers, and the member of Congress who can demonstrate that he speaks for many of his colleagues is likely to be listened to more attentively at the White House than one who appears to speak only for himself. Frederic Malek once indicated that the key to Everett Dirksen's influence in the selection process was his ability to enlist the support of his Republican colleagues for the positions he took.[27] Senator William Proxmire, on the other hand, frequently expressed unhappiness with presidential nominees during the 1970s, but his unwillingness or inability to muster support for his views among his colleagues left him without much significant influence on selection decisions.

The Political Environment. Nothing guarantees congressional influence in presidential selection decisions. The final choice is the President's, and if he decides to disregard congressional suggestions, disappointed congressmen have little recourse in the short run. Thus the President determines the extent to which the views of members of Congress will be weighed in making personnel choices. But the President's freedom to make that determination is not a constant. At least two significant factors in his political environment have an impact on his freedom in making personnel choices.

The contemporary political line-up is one of them—an important one. A President facing unsympathetic majorities in Congress will more often feel the need to defer to congressional advice on appointments than will one who deals with a Congress dominated by his own party. In the latter case, support for the President's policy objectives, though neither automatic nor complete, will be more natural than in the former; it will less often need to be "purchased" by permitting frequent congressional involvement in selection decisions. Gerald Ford, who never had the advantage of sympathetic congressional majorities, found their absence the most persistent constraint on his freedom to select personnel for his administration.[28]

The other environmental factor that affects the potential for congressional influence in selection decisions is the President's "public prestige." Richard Neustadt wrote of this that "the prevalent impression of a President's public standing tends to set a tone and to define the limits of what Washingtonians do for him, or do to him."[29] In most cases, a President blessed with broad public support will be able to assert firmer control over the selection process than one who lacks that blessing. As the Watergate crisis worsened, for example, and the mandate of 1972 quickly dissipated, the Nixon administration found it increasingly necessary to grant influence in selection decisions to those members of Congress who persisted in their support of the President. Early in 1974 a Republican Senator noted the change: "We're now in a situation where the White House can no longer freely exercise its options. The Senate has revolted."[30] A Republican member of the House identified the same apparent change: "The old system just sort of collapsed. Somewhere down the line the President realized that he was in a lot of trouble. So Nixon must have decided, 'Here's how we're going to operate from now on.' "[31]

So, while it is technically true that the President can decide who will be allowed to participate in selection decisions, the political reality is that his freedom to control the selection process is greater under some circumstances than under others. The potential influence of the Congress, most of the time, is inversely related to the number of his supporters on Capitol Hill and to the scope of his popularity with the American people.

The lesson of Part III is that the President's control of the appointment process is a variable. What we have seen here is that the appointment process is less centralized in practice than in constitutional theory. Ample opportunities exist for individuals and groups without an official role in this process to play a significant part in determining its outcomes. And it is more often the President's political skills and advantages, rather than his formal authority, that determine the extent to which he can truly control personnel choices. In Part IV, I shall explore the meaning of this in terms of the overall quality of presidential appointees and the character of the process that produces them.

Notes

1. *New York Times*, March 19 and 24, 1971.
2. Frederic V. Malek, *Washington's Hidden Tragedy: The Failure to Make Government Work* (Free Press, 1978), p. 68.
3. *New York Times*, February 2, 1977.
4. U.S. Senate, 93d Congress, 2d Session (1974), Select Committee on Presidential Campaign Activities, *Presidential Campaign Activities of 1972*, Executive Session Hearings, Book 18, p. 8227.
5. Interview with Dan H. Fenn, Jr., Waltham, Massachusetts, March 26, 1976.
6. 1972—Commerce—Benjamin L. Hooks: member, Federal Communications Commission, pp. 106–107.
7. This description of the events surrounding the Woodworth nomination is drawn from discussions with members of the Carter transition staff and from newspaper accounts, especially "Hill Aide in Line for Carter Post as Tax 'Czar'," *Washington Post*, December 28, 1976.
8. Quoted in Martin Tolchin and Susan Tolchin, *To the Victor . . .* , *Politi-*

cal Patronage from the Clubhouse to the White House (Random House, 1971), p. 3.

9. Budge acknowledged this in an interview with the staff of the Regulatory Reform Study. See U.S. Senate, 95th Congress, 1st Session (1977), Committee on Government Operations, *Study on Federal Regulation, Volume I: The Regulatory Appointments Process*, p. 104. See also Rowland Evans and Robert Novak, *Lyndon B. Johnson, The Exercise of Power* (Signet, 1966), p. 388.

10. Rowland Evans and Robert Novak, "The Yarmolinsky Affair," *Esquire*, February, 1965, and Daniel Patrick Moynihan, *Maximum Feasible Misunderstanding* (Free Press, 1969), pp. 91–92.

11. Interview with Harry Flemming, Alexandria, Virginia, June 19, 1974; and Rowland Evans and Robert Novak, *Nixon in the White House*, (Random House, 1971), p. 68.

12. Evans and Novak, *Nixon in the White House*, p. 69.

13. Dom Bonafede, "Nixon's first-year appointments reveal pattern of his Administration," *National Journal*, 2(January 24, 1970): 187.

14. Flemming interview.

15. Letter from Senator Warren Magnuson to President Gerald R. Ford, October 21, 1975, from the files of the Senate Committee on Commerce.

16. *New York Times*, March 22, 1974.

17. *Washington Post*, January 26, 1978.

18. *New York Times*, February 6, 12, and 15, 1970.

19. Philip M. Boffey and Bryce Nelson, "NSF Directorship: Why Did Nixon Veto Franklin A. Long?" *Science*, 164 (April 25, 1969): 406.

20. *Ibid.*

21. James M. Graham and Victor H. Kramer, *Appointments to the Regulatory Agencies: The Federal Communications Commission and the Federal Trade Commission* (GPO, 1976) p. 382.

22. U.S. Senate, 95th Congress, 1st Session (1977), Committee on Government Operations, *Study on Federal Regulation, Volume I: The Regulatory Appointments Process*, p. 153.

23. Seats on the U.S. Supreme Court are difficult to fit into this categorization. In recent decades, the Congress has not played a substantial role in the selection of nominees to the Supreme Court. The Senate, however, has traditionally been more stingy in affording confirmation to Supreme Court nominees than to those in any other category. Of the 137 Supreme Court nominations made since the beginning of the Republic, 26 (19 percent) have been rejected by the Senate. It may well be that the assertiveness of the Senate in the confirmation of Supreme Court nominees accounts for some of the congressional timidity in their selection.

24. Interview with David Wimer, Washington, D.C., June 19, 1974.

25. Among these were the nominations of Monroe McKay to the 10th Circuit Court of Appeals, John McGarry to the Federal Elections Commission, Charles Ferris to the Federal Communications Commission, and Robert T. Griffin to the General Services Administration.

26. Bonafede, "Nixon's first-year appointments" (note 13 above), p. 186.
27. Malek interview.
28. Bennett interview.
29. Richard E. Neustadt, *Presidential Power* (John Wiley & Sons, 1960), p. 87
30. Dom Bonafede and Andrew J. Glass, "Haig revamping staff, shifts in patronage policy likely," *National Journal Reports*, 6 (April 6, 1974): 507.
31. *Ibid.*

IV

Conclusion

In the preceding pages, I have sought to answer the question: How does the appointment process work? I have examined the way presidential appointees are selected and confirmed but have had little to say about the quality of those appointees or about what, if anything, can be done to improve their quality. It is time now to ask a different question: How well does the appointment process work?

The principal function of the appointment process is to fill positions in the executive and judicial branches with individuals of high character and exceptional talents. It is, above all else, a system of personnel recruitment, and in Part IV I shall evaluate it as such. But the appointment process serves other purposes as well. It is, for instance, one of the primary tools of administrative management, an essential instrument for presidential control of the federal bureaucracy. And it is also a filament in the larger process of democratic representation, a vehicle for integrating the interests of various social, political, and demographic groups into the administrative and policy-making processes. The manner in which the appointment process contributes to the performance of these functions will also have to be considered in our evaluation.

Instead, therefore, of simply asking the single question, How well does the appointment process work?, I shall focus my inquiry in this final section on three somewhat narrower issues. First, has the appointment process been used to fill federal offices with individuals of consistently high quality? Second, has the process contributed to the sound and coherent administration of public policy? And third, has its operation facilitated and encouraged the representation of a diversity of interests in the administrative and policy-making processes?

13 The Quality of Presidential Appointees

If the ultimate test of any process is the quality of its products, then the caliber of presidential appointees ought to be the prime criterion against which we evaluate the appointment process. But in attempting to do this we run into an immediate problem: It is exceedingly difficult to assess the quality of presidential appointees. Useful yardsticks are hard to find and harder still to apply.

The problem is objectivity. There is often little agreement on what constitutes successful performance in executive offices, just as we earlier noted little agreement on what qualifies candidates for appointment to those offices. Presidential appointees are the subject of judgments by their superiors, their peers, the White House staff, members of Congress, interest groups, journalists, and so on. But rarely is there consensus among all these groups on the quality of any single appointment. A President may be pleased with an appointee who is a resourceful budget-cutter. That same characteristic, however, may lower the regard in which he is held by an interest group served by his agency. Journalists may view another appointee as superb because he is a visible and articulate spokeman for human rights. But his peers in his own department may object strongly to his tendency to make policy pronouncements, however humane, without first clearing them with departmental policy-makers. Even appointees who build a highly favorable reputation during their terms of service often become the subjects of retrospective criticism. Economic advisers, Secretaries of Defense, and treaty negotiators are particularly susceptible to historians' slings and arrows.

Because any appointee will probably have to please a number of disparate observers of his performance, few receive unanimous accolades. Most end up pleasing some groups and displeasing others, earning what could best be described as mixed reviews. Reputations develop from an accumulation of subjective judgments. Many appointees (often, ironically, those from whom little was expected) come to be regarded as excellent public servants; others are viewed as adequate; and some quickly demonstrate that they are hopelessly out of their depth. Even those charged with overseeing the White House selection process have readily recognized the uneven results of their efforts. Frederic Malek, for instance, wrote of the group of appointments made by Richard Nixon after his reelection in 1972:

> The end result was mixed, hardly surprising in view of the political factors that came into play. While a number of outstanding people were recruited to the new team and a certain political balance was achieved, there were also a number of substandard appointments. The quality of some of the appointments, plus the delay in filling positions, resulted in a slower start in the second term and a less effective government than had been expected.[1]

Similarly, Dan Fenn indicated some of the inadequacies of John Kennedy's appointments to the regulatory commissions:

> I can recall at least five who were considerably less than bright; at least three, including a chairman, who were primarily interested in keeping everything as calm and quiet as possible both inside and outside the agency; perhaps five whose devotion to the consumer was so slight as to be undiscernable; maybe eight who showed no evidence of having a new idea in the past quarter century. (Obviously some people are showing up in several of these unhappy categories.)[2]

Given the difficulty in establishing criteria for appointment and the vagaries of the appointment process itself, this variation in the reputations of presidential appointees should come as no surprise. We begin to understand some of the reasons for this inconsistency when we examine more closely the difficulties administrations encounter in attempting to find and appoint the "best person" for a particular job.

Let us suppose, for the purpose of illustration, that the President of the United States has put us in charge of locating a person to fill an important position in his administration. The only guidance he has given us is to find the "best person for the job." How do we proceed?

Before answering that question, we should note that Presidents do not always instruct their personnel advisers to find the "best person" for a job. Often they provide no instructions at all and pay scant attention to the selection process. Sometimes they instruct their aides not to find the "best person" but to find a person with a certain kind of political appeal, a union leader, for instance, or an Irish Catholic, a

Southerner, or a woman. Or they may already have a person in mind, perhaps a personal friend or a crony of the Senate majority leader. Hence an administration may nominate an individual whom it does not regard as the "best person" for a job because it has chosen to use that particular appointment for other purposes. But for the sake of this illustration, let us continue with the assumption that we are looking for the "best person" for this particular job.

The first step, of course, is to define the term "best person." An immediate problem is encountered. There is rarely any precise agreement among those familiar with a particular position on what characteristics its occupant ought to possess. As John Macy and Matthew Coffey, personnel aides to Lyndon Johnson, have noted, "Each executive position was looked upon as a unique and complex array of responsibilities that could not be clearly specified."[3]

The range of difficulty in defining the "best person" for a job varies from position to position. For some positions, at least, certain criteria can be specified. Heads of professional agencies like the Geological Survey or the National Institute of Mental Health are usually expected to have the terminal degree in a discipline relevant to the agency's jurisdiction. But even where these threshold criteria can be identified, the larger problem remains of defining the attitudinal characteristics appropriate for a specific position. These are considerably harder to pin down and ultimately derive from the subjective determinations of those overseeing the personnel search.

Efforts to define the "best person" for a job are further complicated by the fact that such a definition is rarely static. Today's criteria for the "best person" may be inadequate tomorrow. Early in an administration, when a President is trying vigorously to push new programs through the Congress, his greatest need is for political executives who can lobby effectively for those programs on Capitol Hill. Later, when most of his legislative energies are spent, a President needs executives who have the managerial ability to see to the efficient implementation of those programs. It is the rare case when a single individual is the "best person" for both tasks.

Still another problem in defining the "best person" is that the definition process is often collegial. Our view of what is "best" may not be shared by others who are interested in this position and whose political support may be essential to the success of this appointment. If we fail to consider their expectations at this early stage of the appointment process, we may well have to face their reckoned opposition—and that of their congressional friends—later on.

Even after we have settled on some definition, however subjective, of what the "best person" for the job looks like, we are still a long way from appointing that person. The next problem is to find him. The easy part of this is to find someone who satisfies certain hard criteria: an M.D., an urban specialist, an aggressive prosecutor, and so forth. The hard part is finding individuals who meet the "softer" criteria for a job, people with political sensitivity, thick skins, good interpersonal skills, and loyalty to the aims of an administration. In evaluating these, we will probably have to rely on the opinions of third parties who know the potential candidates far better than we do.

This poses yet another problem. It factors several layers of bias into our selection procedures: the biases of those who choose the references and the biases of the references themselves. Because it is so important to expand our search beyond our own range of friends and acquaintances, there is probably no alternative to this. But in relying on third parties, our search for the "best person" for the job becomes in reality a search for the "best person" known to our network of contacts.

There is still another problem in finding the "best person": Few known test tracks exist for high-level government service. No job outside of government requires quite the same combination of talents and attitudes that many government positions require. One presidential personnel adviser suggested the uncertainty that pervades this part of the process:

> How in the world do you tell? We had [one Cabinet officer] who had been governor of a large state and president of a big corporation. He was politically astute. And he was a disaster in the cabinet. Then we had [another] who was a professor, no significant administrative experience, and few prior contacts with the clientele of his department. He turned out to be an effective administrator, a good politician, and one of the President's most trusted advisors.[4]

So there is also an element of guesswork in the search process. We simply have to try to guess intelligently whether the qualities an individual has demonstrated in the private sector can be transferred with him to the public sector. We often have to make our decision on the basis of reputations that people establish in a line of work not completely analogous to that for which we are considering them. It doesn't always work out the way we would hope. As Theodore Sorensen observed of John Kennedy's initial round of appointments, "noted men rarely equal their reputations—some are better, some are worse."[5]

We should point out that, while many of the difficulties inherent in finding the "best person" for a job still prevail, more progress has been made in this area in recent years than in any other aspect of the selection process. Search procedures are still imperfect, but they are vastly more systematic and comprehensive now than they ever were in the period before 1960.

Suppose now that we have established some criteria for this position and, further, that we have found a person who seems to meet those criteria fully. We then face yet another problem: to get him to take the job. Temporary public service can make arduous demands on those who undertake it: Families have to be uprooted, the hours are long and full of potential frustrations, financial sacrifices can be large and painful. In spite of this, Americans have been remarkably generous in their willingness to interrupt their private careers and private lives for periods of public service.

For some people, however, the personal or financial sacrifices are too great to bear. The people who are most attractive to presidential recruiters—not surprisingly—often have very high incomes and substantial investment portfolios. "Our problem," David Wimer said in 1974, "is to get people who are earning $350,000 a year to come to work for $38,000."[6] But salary differentials are only part of the problem—not always, in fact, the most serious part.

Attractive candidates also turn down offers of presidential appointments because their private careers are at a crucial stage where interruption would be unwise; because they are not convinced of their ability to function successfully in a political environment; and, perhaps most frequently, because they have family or personal problems that would only be aggravated by the burdens of public service.[7]

Some federal jobs are more attractive than others. The reluctance of potential candidates is easier to overcome when the position under consideration is a Cabinet post, an important ambassadorship, or a seat on the Supreme Court. Recruiting is harder for some of the less glamorous positions in the independent agencies and the sub-cabinet. The task then becomes, as Frederic Malek describes it, "to capture the candidate's interest by selling the challenges of the post in question, the broad responsibilities, the opportunity to grow, the President's possible need of his services, and the like."[8] While the salesmanship usually works, every administration suffers the frustration of identifying some uncommonly talented people it is unable to lure away from their successful careers in the private sector.

Of the impediments to attracting the "best people" for appointive offices, one has loomed larger in recent years than heretofore. That is the development and application of stricter conflict of interest requirements. Every addition to these requirements and every increase in the rigor with which they are enforced shrinks the pool of potential candidates from which presidential appointees can be drawn. This may well be a reasonable price to pay for improving the appearance of equity and fairness in government decisions. But it also limits our options in searching for the "best person" for a job in a particular field, because it disqualifies some people with extensive experience and demonstrated competence in that field. Douglas Bennett pointed to this as the biggest problem encountered by the Ford administration in recruiting the kind of people it wanted. Bennett estimated that as many as 15 percent of the candidates it considered had to be eliminated for conflict of interest reasons.[9]

If we can successfully negotiate the tasks of defining the "best person" for our job, finding that person, and getting him to accept the job, we still have to get him confirmed by the Senate. This, too, is a complicating factor. But the complication usually comes earlier in the process than this narrative suggests. Most nominees are approved by the Senate. But often the demands of the confirmation process have to be anticipated in advance and considered at the time we establish the criteria that define the "best person" for the job. Inevitably we must look not for the best person in some absolute sense, but for the best person whose confirmation by the Senate can be safely assumed. This may well have a significant effect on the criteria we establish to guide our search, for the person who best fits the President's needs may simply not be acceptable to important elements in the Senate. If we are to get our candidate confirmed—and, of course, we can't appoint him if we don't—we have to factor Senate concerns into the search process from the outset.

If this search for the "best person" sounds tortuous, that's because it *is* tortuous. At every step of the process there are obstacles, often formidable obstacles, to the appointment of the best-qualified and most competent individuals. These obstacles are not insurmountable. The process often produces appointees who serve the public with honor and distinction. But it also produces some appointees whose service is less distinguished and, occasionally, less honorable.

Given the problems inherent in defining, finding, recruiting, and confirming the "best people" for each position, these mixed results are not surprising.

Because of the difficulties and uncertainties that hinder White House efforts to select appointees of the highest quality, every administration appoints some people who fail to cope adequately with at least some aspects of their jobs. They turn out to be too thin-skinned, they make statements that are impolitic, they are clumsy managers, they fail ever to gain the confidence of their departments, and so on. Every administration has its spectacular successes and its ignominious failures. Most appointments fall somewhere in between. The question we need to address here is whether there are systematic pathologies in the appointment process, whether poor appointments result directly from some inherent and remediable flaw in that process.

Mediocre appointments tend to occur in one of two ways. The first, to get at the truth of it, we ought to call bad luck. Predicting performance in public office is an inexact science. Sometimes candidates who look exceedingly well qualified fail to live up to their apparent qualifications. They lack the dimension that distinguishes success in the public sector from success in the private sector. The inadequacies of their public service cannot realistically be blamed on the appointment process, for every evidence was that they were highly qualified for the jobs to which they were appointed. Some appointees simply don't live up to expectations.

But mediocre appointments also occur in a second way: from the conscious selection of mediocre candidates. Here the blame is easier to assess (though perhaps no easier to remedy). We have seen that the White House does nominate and the Senate does confirm some people who are not the best qualified for their jobs, who in fact may have no particular qualifications at all. This usually happens because the circumstances at the time of appointment dictate a selection based on considerations other than merit.

The scenario is often the same. The vacant position is one of little concern to the President or his staff. Some person or group to whom the White House would like to pay off an obligation or do a favor in the hope of future return has expressed an interest in the position and has a candidate in mind. The White House investigates and finds that, while the candidate has no particular qualifications for the position, he appears to be harmless, and the position is one in which he could do little harm in any case. The decision is made to go ahead with the appointment on the grounds that the political benefits to the President justify the cost of putting a mediocrity in office. The Senate subsequently confirms the appointment, usually because it shares the President's indifference about the position and sees no reason to interfere with the political transaction that has taken place. Traditionally this chain of events has been most likely to occur in appointments to minor ambassadorships, to presidential boards and delegations, and, until recently, to federal regulatory commissions. Occasionally the pattern applies to other major positions as well.[10]

Not much can be done about the bad luck that sometimes infects appointment choices. In fact, we should probably note that the luck is not always bad. Appointees who appear initially to have few qualifications for their jobs or who encounter significant criticism from certain quarters during the appointment process sometimes perform far more capably than anticipated. A notable example is Walter Hickel, who was the butt of heated criticism from environmentalists at the time of his nomination but whose performance as Secretary of the Interior demonstrated considerable sensitivity to environmental concerns. The simple truth is that luck, good or bad, is an inevitable factor in the process of personnel selection.

The more perplexing question is what, if anything, can be done about the poor appointments that occur when the mediocrity of the candidate is known to some or all of those involved in choosing him. The apparent solution is to demand that the White House and the Senate be more vigilant, that they push vigorously to make merit the prime consideration in all selection decisions. But saying it obviously won't make it so. There may be some ways in which the quality of appointees can be made a larger factor in appointment decisions, and I shall suggest some of these shortly. But it is probably idle dreaming to expect that merit (whatever that may mean) can ever become the sole criterion in appointment decisions. Other, more political concerns and opportunities are too pervasive.

The President cannot fully avoid these and in many cases won't want to. While his critical role in the appointment process provides him with the chance to raise the overall quality of presidential appointees, it also provides him with other political opportunities that may tug him in different directions. He may be willing to sacrifice quality to expediency if it will help to get his legislative program enacted, if it will improve relationships with important interest groups, if it will overcome bad feelings between the White House and a Cabinet officer, if it will quiet the critics in his own party, and so forth. A President makes hundreds of personnel nominations every year. Not all of those, in his view, are crucial to the success of his administration. And if he can improve his political position by holding his nose and nominating a mediocrity (who happens to have been a law school classmate of a congressional committee chairman, for instance), that is a calculated choice he may be willing to make. Strengthening the support of that committee chairman will be more important to the President and to the primary objectives of his administration than will the quality of a deputy administrator in some small agency in the backwaters of the executive branch. This kind of appointment may lower the performance capabilities of that agency, but that is part of the cost the President is willing to incur for the benefit he derives in return.

The Founding Fathers envisioned the Senate as the principal guardian against lousy appointments of this sort. But individual Senators have political interests in the appointment process, as the President does. And they too are willing to disregard the meager qualifications of an individual appointee when there are other political benefits at stake. Instead of acting to ensure the consistent quality of presidential appointees, the Senate is often a leading culprit in forcing political considerations to the forefront of the appointment process. Ralph Dungan, an important participant in personnel decisions in the Kennedy administration, said of regulatory appointments, for instance:

> In my years of involvement in the appointment process, the most untoward, unconscionable, immoral. . . . pressures came from [the Congress], not in terms of maintaining high standards, but in terms of getting "my friend" appointed to such-and-such commission representing this, that, or the other industry.[11]

To reap full political value from their appointments, Presidents will often feel compelled to disregard substantive qualifications for other considerations. They are willing to do that simply because the quality of their appointments is not their primary concern. Other administration objectives often have higher priority, and, if appointment decisions can be made to serve those other objectives, any President will be sorely tempted to take full advantage of their political utility. The occasional supersession by these political considerations is the primary source of mediocre appointments.

Because the appointment power is a shared power, because those who share in its exercise are concerned with goals other than

the high quality of appointees, and because appointment choices can
be used to help accomplish those goals, it is inevitable that the substantive merit of individual appointees will sometimes be sacrified to
other objectives. In that sense, the character of the contemporary
appointment process probably does lead, inherently, to some appointments of poor quality. We may be able to improve on this situation, but we cannot fully eliminate it. No system of appointment that
is integrated into the political process and that employs open and
democratic decision procedures can ever be completely free of non-
merit considerations or of the inconsistencies in quality that result
from them.

An appointment process could probably be designed that would
lessen the intrusion of political factors and heighten the importance of
merit in personnel decisions. It is unlikely that our political environment would permit the construction of such a system, however. Practical concern with the appointment process and its outcomes is too
broad, and our allegiance to democratic norms too ingrained, to permit the limited participation that such a system would require. Hence
the paradox: Radical reconstruction would be necessary to get the
political bugs out of the appointment process, but radical reconstruction is not politically feasible.

Ours is a political government. It is unlikely under any circumstances that a nonpolitical appointment process could be grafted onto
it. It may be possible within the existing process to alter the balance
somewhat between political and merit considerations, and I shall
shortly suggest some ways to do that. But the political nature of the
appointment process is a fundamental reality, and its pernicious effect
on the substantive quality of presidential appointments cannot be
easily or fully remedied.

Notes

1. Frederic V. Malek, *Washington's Hidden Tragedy: The Failure to Make Government Work* (Free Press, 1978), p. 79.
2. Dan H. Fenn, Jr., "Dilemmas for the Regulator," *California Management Review*, 16 (Spring 1974): 89.
3. John W. Macy, Jr., and Matthew B. Coffey, "Executive Recruiting and Management Information in the White House," *Society for the Advancement of Management Journal*, 35 (January 1970): 8.
4. The source of this statement requested that it not be attributed by name.

5. Theodore C. Sorensen, *Kennedy* (Bantam Books, 1965), p. 288.

6. Interview with David Wimer, Washington, D.C., June 19, 1974.

7. This paragraph is based on interviews with presidential personnel aides from several administrations.

8. Malek, *Washington's Hidden Tragedy*, p. 72.

9. Interview with Douglas P. Bennett, Washington, D.C., January 10, 1977.

10. For a fulsome illustration of this process, see the case of Richard A. Mack, as described in James M. Graham and Victor H. Kramer, *Appointments to the Regulatory Agencies: The Federal Communications Commission and the Federal Trade Commission* (GPO, 1976), pp. 99–110.

11. U.S. House of Representatives, 94th Congress, 2d Session (1976), Committee on Interstate and Foreign Commerce, Subcommittee on Oversight and Investigations, and U.S. Senate, Committees on Commerce and Government Operations, *Quality of Regulators* (joint hearings), p. 63.

14   Administrative Management

The President is the central figure in the governing process in the United States. His responsibilities, both formal and assumed, pervade our decisions about how to govern ourselves and our efforts to implement those decisions. We expect our Presidents to provide leadership in defining the policy options available to us, making the appropriate choices among those options, and transforming those choices into effective government action. We do not expect the President to govern us, but we do expect him to provide much of the guidance and the leadership we need to govern ourselves.

It is axiomatic that no single individual can make all the important policy choices and administrative decisions in a government as large, active, and heterogeneous as ours. To develop new ideas and then to put those ideas into effect, American Presidents are heavily dependent on the men and women in the executive branch of the government. But, as students of public administration have so convincingly demonstrated, neither the President's ability to command the loyalty of those men and women nor their willingness to offer it is automatic. Election to the presidency only provides an individual with the chance to lead, it does not guarantee him facility or success in doing so.

Because the political executives who link the President to the limbs of government are so essential to effective leadership, the right to appoint those executives is a weapon of fundamental importance in the arsenal of presidential power. By appointing loyal and resourceful executives the President can significantly enhance his ability to lead. Incoherent or haphazard exercise of that power, however, can have just the opposite effect. So, to maximize the utility of their appointment powers, Presidents need to harness them to their broader leadership needs.

But do they, or can they? Much that we have seen in this study would seem to indicate that firmly tying the appointment power to presidential leadership needs is easier said than done. To do that, and to do it consistently and effectively, would be possible only if the

President had something approaching absolute control over the appointment process. But we have seen throughout that the President's control of the appointment process is far from complete. Appointment decisions do not—cannot—reflect only his administrative needs. The effects of this are revealed primarily in two ways.

First, the President does not command the complete loyalty of his own appointees. While it occasionally happens that a person is appointed without full knowledge of the process of his selection, most political appointees are acutely aware of both the identity of their political patrons and the reasons they were chosen. If they were appointed at the behest of a member of Congress, the leader of an interest group, a member of the White House staff, their natural reaction is to retain a lingering sense of gratitude and allegiance to the person or group who sponsored their appointment. Or if they were chosen for some obvious reason—to appeal to moderate Republicans, to represent big labor, to mollify feminists—that reason often remains a principal guide to their subsequent decisions and actions.

There is an ironic twist to this as well. Even when an appointee is selected without significant input from outside the White House, when there is nothing in the process of his appointment to divert his full loyalties from the President, he still may not be effective in pursuing the President's purposes within the agency to which he is appointed. He may be held suspect by the personnel of that agency precisely because they view him as the "President's man." If he is seen as an emissary from the White House, carrying the President's flag and acting as his eyes and ears, he may well be shut out of just the decision-making processes he was sent to infiltrate. The political executives and the senior civil servants already at work in an agency are much more likely to welcome a new appointee on whose appointment they were fully consulted than one who, in their view at least, was forced on them to improve their responsiveness to the White House. Hence the appointees most likely to be loyal to the White House may also be those least likely to have an impact on agency decision-making processes.

A second effect of the nature of the appointment process is that it contributes to what Hugh Heclo has labeled "a government of strangers."[1] Administrations are constructed after Presidents are elected, not before. The teams of administrators we place in each department are drawn from no common source, and their political bonds, even in the best of circumstances, are tenuous. They lack the unity that might be provided by a programmatic political party, by a set of consistent and clear selection criteria, or by any other coherent frame of reference. Instead the tendency is to chose each member individually, often at different times, usually for different reasons, and frequently with different sponsors or supporters. The ad hoc nature of the contemporary appointment process guarantees this result. Just as each selection decision rotates on its own axis, so each appointee arrives with his own kit bag of abilities, attitudes, loyalties, and commitments. Dan Fenn suggested this in discussing the regulatory appointments of the Kennedy administration:

> Recently I went through about twenty-five regulatory appointments where I felt I knew pretty well what had happened. I separated them into different categories: appointments determined by the quality of the man; appointments that were congressional "musts" . . . ; appointments made to solve a personnel problem in another agency; those where there were some personal ties of friendship or association with the White House staff (in some cases, friendships that developed during a campaign); and those who fell into a minority group. Granting some overlaps, including one man who clearly fell in two groupings, I found that eleven were in the "quality" file, five in the "congressional must" group, seven in the "personal friendship" group, two "personnel problems" elsewhere, and two minority appointees. . . .
>
> What conclusion can we draw from all this? An interesting one to my mind. Given the fact that the road to appointment as a regulatory commissioner is such an uncertain one, that men and women were selected for very different reasons even within the framework of one administration, never mind over the course of several, it is hazardous indeed to generalize about these people. I know one commissioner who wanted to be a judge, one to be a senator, one to reshape his agency, one to stay on until he retired, one to become a public figure, one to help the consumer, one to have a nice, quiet, presitigious job. They had different aspirations, different reasons for being there, different views of the job, different friends and associations, different career goals and paths. Consequently they faced different dilemmas and . . . different pressures.[2]

The diversities imposed by the appointment process are not the sole source of administrative incoherence in Washington, but they are a prime cause. Heclo notes:

> To the normal confusions of pluralistic institutions and powers in Washington, the selection process contributes its own complexities. . . .

Political forces intervene from many quarters, and their interests in
political appointments often bear little relation to presidential needs
or to qualifications required for effective performance by public executives.[3]

There is little planning or foresight in this process. We construct
teams of political executives in much the same way that a tinker might
build an engine: with available but unmatched parts. And like the
tinker's engine, our administrative machinery often sputters along
inefficiently when its gears fail to mesh.

Another source of administrative incoherence related, at least
indirectly, to the appointment process is the problem of high turnover in administrative offices. Many presidential appointees depart
before they have time to master their jobs. On regulatory commissions, in the Cabinet, in the subcabinet and the independent agencies, they come and go with depressing frequency. Personnel change
is one of the few real constants of political life in Washington. And its
effect on the work of government is fiercely apparent.

When an appointee leaves a job, two things normally leave with
him. One is his staff, often along with his network of subordinates.
Noncareer employees tend to follow their patrons. Often they have
little choice, for a new appointee will want to hire his own staff and fill
subordinate positions with his own loyalists. The higher the rank of an
appointee who resigns, the more profound the effect of his resignation. When a Cabinet secretary departs, for instance, it is not unusual
for the under secretary and most of the assistant secretaries to leave
soon as well, sometimes voluntarily, sometimes not. Departures from
appointive positions in the executive branch often have these elon-
gated ripple effects.

The second thing a departing appointee takes with him is his own
unique set of interests and priorities. We expect new appointees to
bring fresh ideas and objectives with them when they come into
government; we should not be surprised that they take these with
them when they leave. Priorities and commitments are hard to institutionalize. Successive appointees to the same position are unlikely
to have exactly the same views about what they should be doing and
how they should be doing it. And when turnover is substantial, this
constant shifting of gears and directions can wreak havoc on the administration of public policy.

In their study of Economic Development Administration programs to create minority jobs in Oakland, Jeffrey Pressman and Aaron Wildavsky strongly suggest the disabling impact that such midstream resignations can have. They quote from an EDA internal report:

> The departure of [EDA Administrator, Eugene] Foley in the Fall of 1966, followed shortly thereafter by a number of key staff people who had helped run the program in its first year, marked a dramatic shift in emphasis of the Oakland program. . . . When the Oakland program was placed in normal agency channels in Washington, its priority and singular importance diminished.[4]

The twin problems of short tenure and high turnover gained wide recognition in the 1970s. Anthony Downs wrote:

> High level federal personnel change so fast that almost no major federal program is ever initially conceived of, drafted into legislation, shepherded through Congress, and then carried out by the same officials. Therefore, no program is ever perceived in the same way by those who put it into effect as by those who invented it.[5]

A panel of the National Academy of Public Administration pointed out in a report on the implications of the Watergate scandal that

> . . . the rapid movement in and out of key positions, in and out of different agencies, and in and out of government would be intolerable in most private enterprises. . . .
>
> [M]any observers have set one or two years of experience in such posts as essential before an incumbent is prepared to pay good dividends. Former Commerce Secretary Maurice Stans, for example, said: "A business executive needs at least two years to become effective in government, to understand the intricacies of his programs, and to make beneficial changes."
>
> A secondary effect is the impact of this turmoil upon the career personnel, upon their ability to maintain some degree of operating continuity, let alone contribute to policy decisions, and upon their morale. As one career man in the OMB said: "The top management of this place is like a carousel. I don't know from week to week who my next boss will be."[6]

The question, of course, is whether anything can be done about the problem of short tenure within the context of the appointment process. The answer is probably not much. The Kennedy administration usually inquired of potential nominees whether they would serve a full term and often dropped from consideration those who indicated they would not.[7] The Carter administration emphasized this concern repeatedly during the transition period and required each nominee to pledge to serve for the President's full term. Yet even these efforts could not adequately stem the tendency of appointees to depart at their own convenience. It is unlikely that there is much more that a President can do. Clearly there is no effective way to enforce a pledge of the sort Carter required or otherwise to compel a person to stay in public service when he or she no longer wishes to do so. The appointment process is simply not the place to remedy this problem.

Recent administrations have been fully cognizant of the existence of these problems of nonresponsiveness and incoherence and of the obstacles they pose to effective presidential leadership in the governing process. Each has sought to develop a management strategy to cope with these problems. And without exception, appointments have been regarded as a key component of these strategies. But the problems are large and cannot be overcome merely by the more effective exercise of the appointment power. The appointment process is too diffuse, too open, too subject to the play of extraneous forces to lend itself perfectly to the managerial needs of American Presidents. The principal difficulty is simply this: The process of governing involves more than managing the bureaucracy. It is a political as well as an administrative task, and every President ultimately feels compelled to use his appointment powers for political as well as administrative purposes. As he employs them in pursuit of both objectives, he renders them an imperfect instrument for the accomplishment of either. The more an administration factors political concerns into its appointment decisions, the less value the appointment power has in producing responsiveness and cohesiveness in the executive branch. But the converse is equally true. The more single-minded the President becomes in adapting appointment powers to managerial concerns, the more difficult it will be for him to secure political support for the policies he favors.

The trick, of course, is to find politically appealing appointees who happen to be loyal and competent managers. But is is not an easy trick to master. Such people are hard to find and harder still to fit into the right position at the right time. As a result, no President ever escapes some measure of criticism for his handling of the appointment power. If he concerns himself aggressively with management needs, he is criticized (usually from outside the executive branch) for being a poor politician. If his appointment decisions are structured to curry political favor, he is criticized (usually from within the executive branch) for producing administrative discontinuity. This dilemma will not soon be remedied, at least not as long as the appointment process continues to have both political and administrative utility. Presidents will constantly be torn between one direction and the other, rarely finding it possible to move in both directions at the same time.

Notes

1. See Hugh Heclo, *A Government of Strangers* (Brookings, 1977).
2. Dan H. Fenn, Jr., "Dilemmas for the Regulator," *California Management Review*, 16 (Spring 1974): 89–90.
3. Heclo, *Government of Strangers*, p. 110.
4. Jeffrey L. Pressman and Aaron Wildavsky, *Implementation* (University of California Press, 1973), p. 49.
5. Anthony Downs, "The Successes and Failures of Federal Housing Policy," *The Public Interest*, No. 34 (Winter 1974), p. 134.
6. Frederick C. Mosher et al., *Watergate: Implications for Responsible Government* (Basic Books, 1974), pp. 69–70.
7. U.S. Senate, 95th Congress, 1st Session (1977), Committee on Government Operations, *Study on Federal Regulation: Volume I, The Regulatory Appointments Process* (committee print), p. 125.

15 Balance and Diversity in Presidential Appointments

The representative quality of presidential appointments is important because it bears on the legitimacy of government decisions. The executive and judicial branches may not be "representative" branches in the way the Congress is intended to be. But they are equally powerful in making decisions that affect our lives. If those decisions require us to do things we find distasteful, they are at least easier to swallow when we know they were made by people who understood our interests and cared about them. But when hard decisions are made by strangers or by known antagonists, we may begin to question not only the substance of the decisions but also the right of an "unrepresentative" body to make them. When an all-white Supreme Court validates the practice of "separate but equal" educational systems or when a regulatory commission made up of industry sympathizers imposes regulations that inflate consumer costs, disenchantment may focus on the legitimacy of the decision-makers as well as on the substance of the decision.

No presidential administration can ever be perfectly representative of the vast array of social and political groups that compose the American population, or even of that segment of it that the President may regard as his own constituency. There are too many groups demanding too many offices, and there are too few offices to meet the demand. Most presidents have sought to staff their administrations—or at least the most visible positions in their administrations—with people possessing a diversity of religious, ethnic, occupational, and geographical backgrounds. Some have even made special efforts to search out appointees from groups whose members had previously been absent from positions of policy or administrative responsibility. But these efforts failed, for most of the postwar period, to meet the expectations of some of those groups that had consistently found themselves underrepresented at the highest levels of the executive branch. Most notable among these groups were blacks and women, and it is worth a short diversion to explore

the reasons for their underrepresentation in presidential administrations.

The first reason is that the appointment process has traditionally
been dominated by white males. White male Presidents have created
personnel staffs composed primarily of other white males who have
done the bulk of their recruiting through predominantly white male
contacts in the government and in the private sector. That they
should come up with a majority of candidates in their own image is
probably only natural.

Second, there has been a persistent shortage of women and
minority group members in what we might call the "on-deck circle"
for presidential appointees.[1] Women and minorities are underrepresented in the places where administrations normally seek candidates
for federal jobs: in corporate leadership positions, in presitigious law
partnerships, in state government hierarchies, on university faculties,
and at the senior levels of the civil and foreign services. The absence
of women and minorities from this "on-deck circle" has posed a particular problem for those administrations eager to appoint more of
them. It has forced them to weigh the costs and benefits of passing
over white male candidates whose paper qualifications are often
superior in order to increase the number of female and minority
political executives. An administration that wants to make its appointments on the basis of merit criteria but also wants to bring
women and minorities into the government thus faces a painful dilemma. Demands for merit appointments and demands for female
and minority appointments (which, ironically, often come from the
same source) are inherently contradictory. If appointments are made
solely on the basis of demonstrable, substantive qualifications,
women and minority groups will continue to be underrepresented in
the public sector, because they have not had adequate opportunities
to develop their qualifications in the private sector or in lower-level
positions in the government. But if sex and ethnicity are to be prominent considerations in appointment decisions, then the "best person"
for the job (at least in the way we normally define the term) will
sometimes be passed over.

There often are good reasons for the appointment of women or
blacks or members of other minority groups even if their apparent
qualifications do not place them at the very top of a list of potential
candidates. The diversity and symbolic value of an administration's
appointments are important considerations, just as their quality is.

But the pursuit of one objective often encumbers accomplishment of the other. This simply reflects the persistent cross-pressures that beset a President in attempting to take full advantage of the opportunities that the appointment process provides.

A third reason for the traditional underrepresentation of women and minorities has been their lack of political influence. We have seen throughout this study that those who have political resources and make effective use of them are often able to influence individual appointment decisions. Those who lack such resources or use them poorly frequently get squeezed out of the decision-making process.

Blacks, for instance, have had few resources to bring to bear on appointment decisions. They have been most effective when they have been able to win the support of, or form alliances with, powerful white politicians sympathetic to their efforts to increase the number of black appointees. The situation cited earlier in which the combined efforts of black groups and Senators John Pastore and Howard Baker led to the appointment of a black Federal Communications Commissioner is a case in point. But blacks have often been unsuccessful in winning this kind of support and in translating it into influence in the appointment process.

Women have had a resource which the minority groups lack, and that is their numbers. Their political weakness has resulted from their inability to organize effectively to take full advantage of that resource. Until the early 1970s, there was little female participation of any consequence in the appointment process. Efforts to increase the number of female appointments resulted almost entirely from the personal commitments of Presidents or members of their personnel staffs, not from political pressure exerted by organized women's groups.

When the number of minority and female appointments began to increase, the growth was a direct result of the better organization and the developing political sophistication of these groups. We recounted earlier the efforts and the successes of a coalition of women's organizations attempting to influence Jimmy Carter's initial appointment decisions. The growth that occurred in the number of female appointments was the result not of any substantial alteration in the operation of the appointment process, but rather of a change in the relative political strength of the actors who compose its environment. Women and, to a lesser extent, blacks have come to recognize the political nature of the appointment process and have worked to improve their own ability to be effective participants in it. Their growing influence reflects—as one would expect in a political process of this sort—their growing political acumen.

The two principal ways in which people attain national political office in the United States are through appointments and elections. And for most of the postwar period covered by this study, the two recruitment systems performed about equally well (or equally poorly) in bringing women and minorities into important federal positions.[2] When the new consciousness about black civil rights emerged in the 1960s, its impact was felt in the appointment and the electoral processes at about the same time. The first black Senator since Reconstruction, the first black Cabinet officer, and the first black Supreme Court Justice all took office within twenty months of each other. Black representation in the executive branch kept pace with the slow increase in black membership in the Congress in the 1960s and then surpassed it in the 1970s.

For women the pattern was similar. The percentage of women in policy-making positions in the executive branch and the percentage in Congress were roughly equal until the flowering of the women's movement in the 1970s. After that the number of women remained relatively stable in the Congress but grew significantly in the state legislatures and in the executive branch.

What all of this seems to indicate is that the appointment process has performed no worse, and perhaps even slightly better, than the electoral process as a vehicle for integrating previously excluded groups into decision-making positions in the federal government. Since both are political processes, their similarities in this regard should not surprise us. Neither operates independently of the political forces at work in its environment. When a particular group increases its political strength, we should expect it to be more successful in gaining both elective and appointive office. And, in general, that is what happened with both women and blacks in the period after 1964.

But the two processes are not entirely alike. Decisions in the appointment process, because they are made by elites, reflect changes in elite attitudes more quickly and more directly than do decisions in the electoral process. Not surprisingly, then, increasing elite support for the integration of minority groups into our political life[3] has tended to affect appointment decisions more rapidly and more comprehensively than electoral decisions.

If the paucity of female and minority appointments has resulted from a bias in the appointment process, it is a political and not a structural bias. The outcomes of the appointment process reflect the interests and the strengths of the political actors who participate in it. Changes in the field of participants or in their relative influence invariably generate changes in the outcomes. Previously excluded groups have begun to see that the same process that once seemed to work against them can be made to work for them as they learn to participate more fully and more effectively in it. The change has begun to come, and will continue to come, through changes in the political arena rather than in the formal operation of the appointment process itself.

Notes

1. I am indebted to Thomas E. Cronin for this analogy.
2. One encounters innumerable frustrations in trying to determine with precision the number of female and minority appointments made by any particular presidential administration. There are few reliable sources of information on this. Each administration periodically makes such figures available, but, in order to put the best face on them, they frequently lump major and minor appointments together. Hence, summary figures on black presidential appointees are likely to include Schedule C stenographers along with Cabinet assistant secretaries.

   The statements in this section are based on figures collected from a variety of sources, some of them of uncertain reliability. As a result I have refrained from the use of precise numbers and focused instead on trends. Data for the identification of trends was drawn from the following sources: "Memorandum for the President: Statistical Highlights, on the President's Appointments, 1963–1968," from John W. Macy, Jr., to President Lyndon B. Johnson, September 18, 1968 (LBJL); Memorandum from Bob Faiss to Jim Jones, December 10, 1968 (LBJL); Dom Bonafede, "Nixon's first-year appointments reveal pattern of his Administration," *National Journal*, Vol. 2 (January 20, 1970); *idem*, "Nixon personnel staff works to restructure federal policies," *National Journal*, Vol. 3 (November 12, 1971); Dom Bonafede and Andrew J. Glass, "Haig revamping staff, shifts in patronage policy likely," *National Journal Reports*, Vol. 6 (April 6, 1974); "Women, Blacks Register Gains in Carter Posts," *New York Times*, February 6, 1977; "Interest-Group Doubts Rise on Top Jobs," *Congressional Quarterly Weekly Report*, Vol. 35 (April 30, 1977); "Women Develop Old Girl Network," *Washington Post*, February 27, 1978; and unpublished data provided by presidential personnel aides.
3. See the surveys cited in Thomas R. Dye, *Understanding Public Policy*, 3d Ed. (Prentice-Hall, 1978), pp. 44–45.

16   Toward Better Presidential Appointments

The appointment process has never lacked for critics. And, almost without exception, its critics have believed that the best way to enhance the quality of presidential appointees is to rearrange the procedures or realign the roles of the participants in the appointment process. Some have suggested a contraction in the number of positions requiring Senate confirmation.[1] Others have suggested a centralization of the nominating authority within the executive branch[2] or of the confirmation authority within the Senate.[3] Still others have proposed that candidates for appointment be formally reviewed by "nonpartisan panels of experts" in their fields.[4] If they lack consensus on the specific changes necessary to improve the appointment process, the critics are nearly unanimous in their view that structural reform is the essential means to that end.

Changes in the formal operation of the appointment process can make a difference. In this book I have catalogued a number of recent changes in both presidential selection and Senate confirmation. By nearly all accounts, these have led to overall improvements in the quality of presidential appointees. But changes in the formalities of the appointment process are not a panacea for the lingering unevenness of its outcomes. Formal procedures are only one part of the complex equation from which appointment decisions result; the motivations and constraints of the people empowered to make those decisions are an equally important element of choice. If procedures are inadequate or outmoded, good intentions will not always be enough to produce good appointments. But if decision-makers lack the freedom or the will to pursue highly qualified appointees, no set of procedures can fully protect them from the consequences of their own irresolution.

The reform impulse is part of the lifeblood of American politics. But it takes a peculiar shape. Our reforms are usually attempts to do procedurally what we have failed to do willfully. We develop new decision-making procedures in the hope that they will compensate for our lack of resolve in exercising old ones. When the Congress could not muster the will to end a cancerous war, it passed a war powers resolution to ease its burden of conscience. When it could not find the collective courage to slow the spiraling growth of federal expenditures, it passed a budget control act to concentrate, if not relieve, the agony. Most suggestions for improvement of the appointment process fall into this same sad category.

There will no doubt be future opportunities to refine and perfect the procedures by which we make appointment decisions. The things we have learned to do rather well in the last two decades we can probably learn to do even better as new skills and technologies develop. But there is nothing wrong with the contemporary appointment process that requires radical surgery. Important improvements have taken place in the way we select and confirm presidential appointees, and, with a few exceptions, our procedures are fundamentally sound. We have seen that the contemporary appointment process can produce appointees of the highest quality *when careful and persistent efforts are made to select appointees of the highest quality.* The inconsistencies that still occur in the quality, responsiveness, and diversity of presidential appointees result less now from flawed appointment procedures than from the uncertainty of human judgments and the vagaries of human motivation. The key to better appointees is not a further restructuring of the appointment process but an invigorated commitment to quality on the part of the people who control that process.

Everyone has his own idea of what constitutes a good appointment, and there is ample disagreement about this. We often hear the call for appointments based on "merit." But merit, like beauty, lies in the eye of the beholder. It is an elusive term, hard to objectify. Clearly there is no general, consensual definition.

But we need not yield to despair. If there is no precise consensus on the meaning of the term "merit," there is at least some general agreement on the characteristics that are most desirable in presidential appointees. Three of these stand out; two of them deal with individual appointees, the third with appointments in the aggregate.

The first is *substantive qualifications*, meaning simply that an appointee ought to be familiar with the material issues that are relevant to the position he will assume. His substantive qualifications should be abundant, not minimal. His training, experience, and ideas should make the appropriateness of his appointment self-evident. And his preparation ought to extend beyond his knowledge of technical matters to an awareness of, and sympathy for, the concerns of those who will be affected by his government actions. He should be affirmatively qualified for the position to which he is nominated, not just barely qualified.

The second criterion is what we might call *administrative competence*. Not every appointee is selected to head a large department or agency. Many perform staff rather than line functions. But all must possess some talent for defining, attacking, and completing a task. Appointees, whatever their prior experience or native brilliance, will be less than fully successful in government if they lack the ability to administer their own responsibilities and to oversee and encourage the work of their subordinates effectively. Administrative competence means several things: responsiveness to the overarching objectives of the incumbent administration, toughness and persistence in dealing with elements of the "permanent" government, and a full range of managerial skills, including the ability to relate means to ends, to make decisions, and to handle interpersonal relations with sensitivity. We expect presidential appointees to be skillful and creative in managing the government's business, yet we often pay scant regard to their preparation or propensity to perform in that fashion.

The third criterion is *diversity*. We earlier noted the relationship between the aggregate composition of an administration's appointments and the perceived legitimacy of its actions. Perhaps it is true that a white male can make decisions that fully serve the interests of blacks or women. Perhaps it is true that a corporate executive appointed to a regulatory commission can make decisions that fully protect the interests of consumers. But it is immensely difficult to convince women, blacks, or consumers that that is the case. What is essential here is not a perfect representation of all the major interests or groups in American society among each administration's appointees. The cross-cutting of interests would make that a practical impossibility in any case. The objective, instead, should be an appointment process in which diversity and balance are regarded as highly important objectives—not merely as ways to curry short-term political favor, but as crucial building blocks of effective representative government. If the formal participants in the appointment process are dogged in their pursuit of balance and diversity, the numbers will take care of themselves.

If these are the characteristics we most desire in presidential appointments, the question then becomes: How do we achieve them or, more specifically, how do we achieve them more consistently than is currently done? An immediate temptation is to suggest that the appointment process can best be improved by depoliticizing it, by insulating appointment decisions from political pressure. But it is not at all clear that such a solution is possible or even desirable.

Our best hope for improving the substantive qualifications, the administrative competence, and the diversity of presidential appointees lies not in trying to eliminate the politics from the appointment process but rather in trying to encourage one kind of politics as we discourage another. Cronyism, secrecy, and political tit-for-tat represent a kind of politics that rarely enhances the quality of presidential appointees. But broad participation, honest partisanship, and democratic decision procedures are quite another kind of politics, and to the quality of presidential appointees they can add a great deal. The goal of better appointments is well served by efforts to curb the former kind and extend the latter.

For the effective operation of the appointment process, no better prescription has ever been written than that which appears in the *76th Federalist*. Hamilton recognized that the "advancement of the public service"[5] was most likely to occur when both the President and the Senate play a vigorous and independent role in the appointment process. The President, in Hamilton's view, should be "interested to investigate with care the qualities requisite to the stations to be filled, and to prefer with impartiality the persons who may have the fairest pretentions to them." The Senate, for its part, should be equally assertive in providing, through "discussion and determination," a "considerable and salutary constraint upon the conduct" of the President.

Hamilton envisioned an appointment process in which the formal participants have a keen interest, in which decisions are made on the basis of careful consideration of individual qualifications, in which the President's choices are constantly subject to the vigorous collective review of the Senate. These three ingredients are as much the keys to the quality of appointees now as they were when Hamilton first considered the question.

But they are hard to institutionalize. Achieving them is more a matter of will than of procedure (though sound procedures may aid the application of the will). In the end, we can expect the overall quality of presidential appointees to improve only when the people who control the appointment process develop a commitment to excellence that they are willing to pursue even in the face of what may be formidable pressures to do otherwise.

The Role of the White House. Effective recruitment and selection of appointees is a time-consuming process. Recent experience indicates that Presidents have neither the time nor the desire to involve themselves deeply in the details of this process. Most of the operational responsibilities are delegated, therefore, to the White House personnel staff. But a President who cares about the quality of his appointments, as all Presidents should, cannot afford to divorce himself from the selection process altogether. He can and should be involved in several integral ways.

The President has to set the tone. He should consult frequently with his personnel staff at the beginning of his administration and at frequent intervals thereafter. He needs to provide his personnel aides with clear statements of the kinds of people he wants in his administration. This will give the personnel staff a set of operational parameters to guide their own activities. And, if the general criteria established by the President are clear enough, they can help to thread together the separate appointment decisions through which his administration is built, thus providing some coherence to a process from which it is often absent.

But simply suggesting parametric criteria is not enough if the President's personal ideas are to be fully imposed on the selection process. The President must also consult directly on each important appointment. He and his personnel aides need to discuss the specific characteristics they seek in a nominee and to probe together the prevailing political constraints on their selection decision. The President's views are important in these specific decision-making situations because of the uniqueness of his personal perspective. No one else sits where he sits; no one else has his vantage point; no one else can sense his concerns as clearly as he can. The more direct the guidance he provides, the more precise the personnel staff can be in recruiting candidates who conform to the criteria he suggests.

A close working relationship between a President and his personnel staff is important for other reasons as well. For one thing, it is likely to increase the President's faith in that staff and his willingness to rely on it. As this becomes known throughout Washington, the personnel staff will become the focus of activity in the selection process. Indications of concern and suggestions of possible candidates will be directed at the personnel staff rather than at the President or at other members of his administration. Relationships with Congress, with interest groups, and with the national committee of the President's party can be centrally managed through the personnel office.

All of this contributes to the comprehensiveness, the political sensitivity, and the consistency of the work of the personnel staff. With the full and recognizable support of the President, the ability of that staff to serve the President proficiently is greatly enhanced. When he fails to provide that support, when he fails to make it clear that the personnel staff is his sole agent in the appointment process, he invites circumventions of that staff, short-cutting of routine selection procedures, and ad hoc relationships with political actors interested in appointments. In undermining the control of the personnel staff over selection decisions, he diminishes its value to him and the measure of consistency and coherence it can bring to appointment decisions.

Perhaps the most important effect of active presidential involvement in selection decisions is simply that it demonstrates his belief that these are important decisions. By devoting some of his scarce time to the selection process, he lets it be known implicitly that he cares about his appointments, that he does not regard them as routine decisions to be made solely for transient political purposes. By investing his own time in these decisions, the President advertises his belief in their importance and helps to inspire others to share that belief.

The President's personal involvement in the appointment process ought to extend beyond his participation in selection decisions. He will also be well served by taking the time to meet individually with his nominees, perhaps to offer them the nomination directly, to discuss the reasons why they were chosen, and to offer some guidance on the objectives they ought to pursue once in office. The President might even attempt to meet occasionally with subcabinet and agency appointees, individually or in small groups, after they have been in office a while, to discuss matters of mutual interest.[6] For most appointees a brief handshake and an autographed picture are the extent of their personal relationship with the President. For all of their government service he is a distant personage, rarely more than a peripheral factor in the daily performance of their jobs. This contributes to the difficulty Presidents encounter in achieving loyalty and responsiveness from those who work in the agencies and departments of the executive branch. Presidential efforts to personalize relationships with subcabinet and agency appointees might well help to overcome some of that difficulty. Those officials who are responsible for acting in his name would no doubt welcome occasional opportunties, even in a group meeting, to hear and discuss his views directly.

That it is possible to do these things without tying up great amounts of presidential time or attention is perhaps best indicated by the fact that some Presidents in the past have in fact done them. Lyndon Johnson, for instance, played an active role in all phases of the selection process and attempted to meet personally with as many of his nominees as he could. He thought it important to do so. But other Presidents have not shared his willingness to devote adequate time to the appointment process despite their repeated iteration of its importance. If a President is anxious to fill his administration with talented people and to fortify his personnel choices against external pressures, he can serve his own purposes in no better way than by personally involving himself in the appointment process.

Even if he takes a keen interest in personnel decisions, however, the President will still have to rely heavily on the White House personnel staff. The personnel staff institutionalizes the President's role in the appointment process. Since the initial development of a formalized personnel staff in the White House, its role has been to locate candidates who meet the administration's needs and fit its image, to subject them to a series of security and political clearances, and then to persuade them to come aboard. The procedures that have evolved since 1961 are well adapted to the performance of these responsibilities. By and large, Presidents have been well served by their personnel staffs. Their contributions to the quality of presidential appointments can thus be improved primarily by doing better what they already do rather well: carefully defining the requirements for individual positions, searching widely and aggressively for qualified candidates, ensuring the ethical integrity and political acceptability of those candidates, persuading the best of them to join the administration, and facilitating their transition into their new jobs.

The most important responsibility of the personnel staff is, in the words of Douglas Bennett, to "keep its eye on the ball."[7] The ball in this case is the substantive quality of presidential appointees. The personnel staff has to be sensitive to the impact of an appointment on the constituencies affected by it and to the political concerns it generates. And it needs to keep the President appraised of those things. But the principal task of the personnel staff should be to minimize interference with the President's efforts to get the best possible people into his administration and into positions where their skills can be most effectively utilized.

As we indicated earlier, it is not always possible, or at least not always politically prudent, to do that. But the personnel staff can enlarge the opportunities for doing it by making substantive qualifications, administrative competence, and diversity the prime considerations in its recruitment operations and by seeking highly qualified people with minimal political liabilities. The President's most effective defense against diversionary political interventions in his selection decisions is to preempt the initiative by coming up with candidates whose qualifications are undeniable.

The personnel staff is of most value to the President when it strives to hold the line for quality. At the very least, the decision to submit to external pressures and nominate a candidate who would not otherwise have been the President's first choice should come only after highly qualified candidates have been located and a devout effort has been made to convince other participants of their merits. As Frederic Malek has noted:

> There are certain steps... that can and should be taken to limit the damage from unqualified appointments without giving up entirely the pursuit of political support and party unity. The most effective is to ensure that qualified and appealing candidates are discovered and presented as alternatives for all important positions. It is much more difficult for a chief executive to justify a truly substandard appointment... when the quality differential with the alternate is vividly apparent.[8]

The Role of the Senate. The Founding Fathers envisioned the Senate's role in the appointment process as essentially negative. Its principal responsibility, in their view, would be to act as a check against bad appointments. But over time, and in recent years particularly, the Senate has demonstrated a capacity to play both a larger and a more positive role in the appointment process than that anticipated by the Founding Fathers.

The best way for the Senate to help ensure appointments of high quality is to set high standards for confirmation. Confirmation is the last quality check in the appointment process. If the Senate's standards emphasize talent, experience, and diversity, those standards will soon come to permeate every other stage of the appointment process. Knowing that Senate expectations are high, other participants will gear their own actions to accommodate those expectations. Standards throughout the process will rise to meet those established by the Senate.

We have already seen a demonstration of this in the case of regulatory appointments. Senate concern with the low quality of regulatory appointments began to grow in the early 1970s. Concern was sharpest within the Senate Commerce Committee, which had responsibility for confirmation of most regulatory commissioners. Its chairman, Warren Magnuson, and its chief counsel, Michael Pertschuk, led the committee in putting greater emphasis on the confirmation of regulatory commissioners, setting firmer substantive and procedural standards for approving them, and enforcing those standards consistently and tenaciously. All of this, in the view of the Regulatory Reform Study conducted by the Senate Government Operations Committee, led to "a much more vigorous examination of regulatory appointments than had ever occurred before."[9]

Though Senate standards should be set high and enforced energetically, they should not be so rigid that they leave no discretion to the President. Senate committees should state explicitly what they regard as the qualifications appropriate to a particular office. In most cases these should be affirmative qualifications rather than a mere catalog of disqualifiers or minimum standards. For a Nuclear Regulatory Commissioner, for instance, it might be suggested that a nominee have a broad knowledge of nuclear technology, possess substantial experience in or familiarity with the applications of that technology, and be demonstrably sensitive to both the potential uses and the potential dangers of nuclear power. In this regard the separation of roles should be quite clear: The Senate's responsibility is to set and enforce affirmative qualifications; the President's responsibility is to find his own candidates who meet them.

Presidents might regard this as an infringement on their constitutional right to make nominations. But if it is an infringement at all, it is not a disabling one. If competence, experience, and fairmindedness are the pervasive themes in the standards set by the Senate, there should be more than enough people who meet these fundamental criteria to leave the President sufficient room to select candidates who are satisfactory to him on other counts. Should he disagree with the standards set by the Senate or with their applicability to a particular candidate, nothing prevents him from going ahead with what he believes to be an appropriate nomination. That is both his right and his responsibility. If the Senate finds his candidate unacceptable, it can withhold confirmation. That is its right and its responsibility. When both institutions assertively pursue appointments of high quality, even if it leads to disagreements on the merits of some individual candidates, the public interest will be well served in the long run.

The Senate has another, equally important, obligation in the appointment process, and that is to see that standards of political equity are observed. This is a twofold obligation. The first part is procedural and requires the Senate to ensure that all interested parties have an opportunity to express their views on a nomination in a public forum and to have due consideration given to those views in appointment decisions. It is especially important that a forum be provided for those groups who do not have political access to the White House and who have doubts about individual candidates. They may provide information that helps the Senate in making its confirmation decisions. But even if they don't, even if the Senate confirms a nominee over their objections, this public participation serves several important purposes. It affirms the open, participatory nature of what should be a democratic decision-making process. It contributes to the construction of a complete public record on the nomination. And, perhaps most important, it helps to sensitize the nominee to the opinions and concerns of those who believe themselves affected by his nomination and are likely to be part of his immediate constituency should he be confirmed.

This is most likely to be accomplished by the exercise of care and deliberation in the confirmation process. Public hearings should be held on all major nominations and on nominations to lesser offices when there is evidence of disagreement over the qualifications of nominees. Sufficient notice should be provided to permit interested parties to get to Washington and to prepare their testimony. Nominations should be required to lie before Senate committees for a specified period, long enough to allow the accumulation of reactions to them. Committee decisions should be made in public by recorded vote so that each committee member will be forced to take a public position on a nomination for which he can subsequently be held responsible. No important or controversial nomination should be considered by the full Senate until it has received a written report from the relevant committee stating the committee's views on the strengths and weaknesses of the nominee.

Adherence to these procedures would, of course, slow the confirmation process to some extent. A week or two might well be added to the time that currently passes between formal nomination and final confirmation. But that is a small price to pay for improving the care and comprehensiveness of deliberation and decision. The haste that has traditionally characterized the confirmation process serves no one's purposes. It does, however, lend credence to those who regard confirmation decisions as closed and ill considered. That criticism can be redressed without great difficulty and without great cost.

The second part of the Senate's political responsibility is substantive. The Senate needs to be attentive, as the President does also, to the aggregate distribution of appointments. The image that an administration presents to the people is defined by its appearance as well as its actions. Hence the visible composition of an administration is a factor of some consequence in its ability to achieve and sustain the respect of the people and the Congress. An administration that draws heavily from certain population groups and excludes others will always be viewed with suspicion by the groups that are not well represented among its appointees. These suspicions will be difficult to overcome even if the administration is fair-minded in its actions. Appearances often prevail in spite of the reality.

The Senate can help to minimize this problem by serving as a spokesman for those groups that have been severely underrepresented in the appointment process. Sensitivity to a wide range of interests should be one of the affirmative standards applied by the senate in reviewing nominees. Sometimes, however, it will be necessary for the Senate to be even more direct. Members of the Senate may have to declare explicitly their feeling that the next nominee to a vacant position should be a woman, a civilian, a consumer activist, or a member of a minority group. If the President has not been sufficiently sensitive to the importance of representativeness and balance in his appointments, the Senate has an obligation to force his hand. When it has chosen to do so in the past, the results have normally been favorable. To do so whenever the situation warrants is part of the continuing responsibility that Alexander Hamilton suggested when he wrote in the *76th Federalist* that the "necessity of [Senate] concurrence would be a powerful, though in general a silent operation. It would be an excellent check upon a spirit of favoritism in the President."[10]

Notes

1. See Joseph P. Harris, *The Advice and Consent of the Senate* (University of California Press, 1953), and U.S. Commission on the Organization of the Executive Branch of the Government, *Task Force Report on Personnel and Civil Service* (GPO, 1955).
2. See the discussion of the Nixon administration's "Federal Political Personnel Manual" in Chapter 2.
3. A proposal introduced in 1977 by Senators Abraham Ribicoff and Charles Percy (Senate Resolution 258) would have created a Senate

Office of Nominations, which would have primary responsibility for conducting inquiries into the integrity and fitness for office of all nominees. The proposal was not acted upon in the 95th Congress.

4. See Frederick C. Mosher et al., *Watergate: Implications for Responsible Government* (Basic Books, 1974), p. 69.

5. This and subsequent quotations are from Jacob E. Cooke (ed.), *The Federalist* (Meridian Books, 1961), No. 76, pp. 509–513.

6. Several recent White House personnel aides have made efforts of this sort to personalize the relationship between the President and his appointees. A consistent policy has never been fully implemented, however.

7. Interview with Douglas P. Bennett, Washington, D.C., January 10, 1977.

8. Frederic V. Malek, *Washington's Hidden Tragedy: The Failure to Make Government Work* (Free Press, 1978), p. 83.

9. U.S. Senate, Committee on Government Operations, *The Regulatory Appointments Process*, p. 177.

10. Cooke, *The Federalist*, No. 76, p. 513.

17   What Kind of Process?

Having now examined the appointment process in some depth, we can begin to firm up several of the generalizations we have been formulating. What we have examined here is a single channel of national political behavior. In some ways it closely resembles other aspects of the governing process in America; in others it is unique. The fundamental nature of the appointment process is revealed in its most persistent characteristics.

First, the process is very broad in scope. Virtually every government agency of any significance is headed by a presidential appointee. For that simple reason, the appointment process touches the interests, often the profound interests, of a wide range of political actors. Those who recognize the direct impact of federal policies on their lives and their self-interests rarely fail to make the logical connection between government decision-makers and government decisions. They concern themselves with the selection of decision-makers because they realize that the act of selection will affect the ultimate character of policy choices. They share the view, expressed by Herbert Kaufman, that "the type of man who holds high office often determines the type of policy the government pursues."[1]

It is precisely because so many varied interests are affected by appointment decisions that they are an object of such broad concern. Despite the constitutional language limiting the exercise of the appointment power to the President and the Senate, the actual workings of the appointment process are shaped by the interaction of a wide range of groups and interests. Each attempts to exert whatever leverage it can on the selection and confirmation processes in hopes of getting an appointee sympathetic to its own concerns or, at the very least, one who is not totally indifferent to them.

We should be careful here not to understate the role that the President plays in this process. He is more than a mere participant, more even than first among equals. The President is at the hub of appointment process. Most of the final choices are his, and he is thus the primary target of the offers, threats, demands, and supplications of the other participants. The extent of their real influence in the appointment process is thus very much a by-product of their political and personal relationships with him. Though appointment decisions usually derive from negotiations and bargaining among those who share an interest in a particular office, the White House oversees those negotiations and determines the ultimate terms of trade. The appointment process is interactive, but it is also executive-centered.

A second characteristic that emerges from our examination of the appointment process is the absence of any substantial consensus on the criteria that qualify individuals for presidential appointments. We have noted that, while there are some positions with formal statutory qualifications, these qualifications are rarely very specific and apply mostly to minor offices. Beyond such nostrums as "appointments should be based on merit" or that the "best man for the job" should be sought, there is little agreement on applicable standards for evaluating the quality of personnel choices.

The absence of such standards has an important bearing on the character of the appointment process. It means, in effect, that the hundreds of major appointment decisions in each administration are made without the guidance of any rigorous decision rules. Appointment decisions are ad hoc and often ad hominem as well.

It is inevitable, where no firm decision rules exist, that decisions will result from informal processes of political interaction. With no objective criteria for determining who is the best candidate for a job or even, in some cases, an appropriate candidate for a job, ultimate personnel choices will evolve from the negotiated settlement of clashing perspectives. It is the case here, as it is wherever consensual decision rules are absent, that might makes right. And "might," in the appointment process, is the ability of any participant or set of participants to force their own concerns into the authoritative decision calculus of the President or the Senate.

This is not to suggest that merit does not enter into presidential and senatorial considerations. It is, however, only one concern among several and is often secondary to assessments of political support and opposition in the final choice of appointees. It is crucial to bear in mind that personnel decisions are made by and influenced by *political* actors, by people who are highly sensitive to the relative weights of countervailing political forces. It is only logical that political calculations should often top the list of concerns they factor into appointment decisions.

A third important characteristic of the appointment process is a relative absence of visible conflict. This is particularly noteworthy because of the irony it presents. All the elements we commonly associate with political conflict abound in the appointment process. There are a valued object (the appointment itself); several sets of politically muscular participants anxious to control that object; and few decision rules to govern their interaction effectively. We should expect a much more volatile process than we have, in fact, observed.

The absence of visible conflict is less mysterious than it seems. Conflict is not absent from the appointment process but is simply well contained. Over time, the authoritative participants in this process, the President and the Senate (especially its committees), have developed a number of procedures designed to manage the conflict that is inherent in the appointment process. These procedures are not perfect. They don't always work. Conflict sometimes explodes into public view and forces institutional confrontation over appointment decisions. But, if nothing else, this study has revealed that such confrontations are the exception, not the norm.

Opportunities for conflict avoidance and conflict resolution are woven through the contemporary appointment process. Interested participants have several access points at which they can express their concerns. The clearance procedures employed by recent administrations provide the President with an antenna for sensing potential conflict and for addressing or avoiding it. Senate confirmation proceedings are composed of several mechanisms that permit the identification of conflicts and provide ways to whittle them down to manageable proportions. The participants in this process have established in operation what would have been difficult to design on a drawing board: a relatively open and interactive method for making hundreds of important and complex decisions with only a minimum of aggravated conflict.

Conflict is fundamental to democratic regimes. Its effective management is essential to their success and survival. That this has been substantially achieved in a process as potentially conflict-laden as the appointment process is no mean feat, and we should be mindful of its importance.

A final characteristic emerging from our examination of the appointment process is its inconsistency. One of the striking things uncovered in the research for this book was the frequency with which astute journalists, congressional staff members, agency officials, and interest group employees inaccurately predicted the outcomes of contemporary appointment decisions. This is a significant reflection of the failure of individual appointment decisions to adhere to any firm or easily predictable patterns. The way a current Assistant Secretary of Commerce was chosen, for instance, may give no clue at all to the way his successor will be chosen.

Much of this unpredictability can be traced to the short-term focus that prevails in the appointment process. Interest in personnel decisions rarely extends much beyond existing position vacancies. Most of the participants in the appointment process concern themselves only with those appointment decisions under contemporary consideration, not those in the past, which are water over the dam, or those in the future, which are not yet in view. The White House personnel staff is the one notable exception to this, but its desire to impose a long-term perspective on appointment decisions often exceeds its ability to do so.

The political character of the appointment process makes a short-term focus inevitable. Political forces cluster around individual decisions. Interactions among the active participants are shaped by their perceptions of the importance of a single decision and by their access, *at the time the decision is made*, to the decision-makers themselves. Calculations and strategies of influence are based on the immediate circumstances presented by each individual decision. Those circumstances change rapidly, and the next decision will require a new set of calculations and perhaps new strategies as well.

Hence consecutive appointments to the same position can follow very different paths. An interest group that found itself shut out of the first decision may work to cultivate friends in the administration or the Congress to increase its leverage on the second. The President's standing in the public opinion polls may have declined precipitously between the first decision and the second, thereby forcing him to be more aware of the political implications of that second decision. The list of possible circumstantial variations is almost endless. That the decision process itself is also a variable, a dependent variable, should come as no surprise.

The complexity and apparent unpredictability of the appointment process is troubling to social scientists looking for definable, reliable patterns. It greatly impedes any effort to reduce the appointment process to a set of systematic generalizations. We are not the first to recognize the difficulty in this. Richard Fenno, whose discussion of the appointment process for Cabinet officers is perhaps the most perceptive ever written, pointed out:

> The process finds its underlying consistency in the fundamental pluralism of American politics. Until such time as the basic contours of

the system change, Cabinet appointments will continue to frustrate those who seek a neatly rational scheme of selection to which they can apply equally well-structured systems of prediction and of judgment.[2]

The process we have observed here can probably be abstracted only in outline form, perhaps by using what Graham Allison has called the "governmental politics" model.[3] In his study of the Cuban missile crisis, Allison presented this model in the context of bureaucratic decision-making. But it is broadly applicable to the appointment process as well.

The centerpiece of Allison's model is the notion that important government decisions are joint products, that they result from the interaction of many "players"—"players who act in terms of no consistent set of strategic objectives but rather according to various conceptions of national, organizational, and personal goals; players who make government decisions not by a single, rational choice but by the pulling and hauling that is politics."[4]

The governmental politics model suggests that the outcome of a decision-making process—that is, the character of the decision itself—rests not on the arguments that support a particular choice, nor on the routines of relevant organizations, so much as on the relative advantages and skills that participants can bring to bear on the act of choice. The perspectives and preferences of the participants differ, and so too do their skills and resources. The intensity with which participants apply their advantages varies from one decision context to the next. Hence, as Allison argues, "To explain why a particular formal governmental decision was made, or why one pattern of government behavior emerged, it is necessary to identify the games and the players, to display the coalitions, bargains, and compromises, and to convey some feel for the confusion."[5]

The governmental politics model provides no accurate basis for predicting the outcome of any particular appointment decision. It is doubtful that any model can do that. It does help, however, to reveal the important components of appointment decisions and to explain the relationships among them.

Appointment decisions derive not from decision rules, precedents, or habit, but from the cauldron of political conflict. Outcomes are determined by the way in which conflict is staged and the ways in which it is managed and resolved. To understand the nature of these outcomes and the behavior that governs them, it is essential to focus on the array of participants that surrounds each of the major decisions in the appointment process, to determine the resources available to those participants, and to identify the strategies they use in bringing those resources to bear on individual appointment decisions. That is what this book has attempted to do.

Politics—the expression and consideration of differing viewpoints—is as essential to the process of selecting government leaders as it is to the process of government itself. The appointment process is political because, within a framework of democratic expectations, it could be nothing else. Appointments matter; people disagree about them. Appointment decisions can be made only through a political process where conflicts can be expressed, considered, and narrowed to manageability. If Americans did not disagree over appointments, a political process would not be needed to make them. But people do disagree, and political procedures are necessary to forge decisions out of that disagreement. Our machinery of government is built of odd parts. Politics is the only lubricant that can make it work.

Notes

1. Herbert Kaufman, "The Growth of the Federal Personnel System," in Wallace S. Sayre (ed.), *The Federal Government Service* (Prentice-Hall, 1965), pp. 23–24.
2. Richard F. Fenno, Jr., *The President's Cabinet* (Vintage, 1959), p. 87.
3. Graham T. Allison, *Essence of Decision: Explaining the Cuban Missile Crisis* (Little, Brown, 1971), Chapter 5.
4. *Ibid.*, p. 144.
5. *Ibid.*, p. 146.

Appendix:
A Note on the Research

When once asked why he robbed banks, Willie Sutton, a master of the trade, replied, "Because that's where they keep the money." A similar principle has guided the research for this study. In searching for answers to the questions this book has raised about the appointment process, I have tried to employ the best available sources. The key word here is "available." In social science research, the best sources are often not available.

The compelling need for students of political decision-making is to get inside the heads of decision-makers. We need to find out why they do what they do: what motivates them, what constrains them, what stirs their interest to intensity. But getting inside people's heads requires a kind of analytical surgery for which the instruments of social science research are often insufficiently delicate. Most of us have little psychological training, and even if we did, it is unlikely that we could get many political actors to submit to psychological testing. There is no perfectly objective means to determine why individuals act in certain ways. Hence we have to rely on other, less efficient methods to determine the components of political behavior.

The tools of social science research provide us with three principal ways of doing this. The first of these—the most straightforward but not necessarily the most useful—is to ask individual political actors why they act the way they do. In effect, to go to the horse's mouth. Much social science research proceeds in this fashion. We ask voters what factors determined their vote. We ask Congressmen whom they rely upon for substantive information. And, as noted above, we ask bank robbers why they rob banks.

Individual actors can be important sources of information about their own actions. But sometimes they lie, not because they are evil people but for several other reasons. They may lie because they are embarrassed about their actions. Survey respondents, for instance, sometimes say they voted in an election because they are embarrassed that they didn't. Government officials sometimes lie about their reasons for acting in a certain way because they would suffer negative political consequences if the real reasons became known. Congressmen, for instance, may say they supported a bill because they thought it was in the national interest when the real reason was heavy pressure from an interest group that had made a large contribution to their last campaign. And politicians sometimes lie to curry favor and affection or to try to shape the way history regards their actions. The constant reader of political memoirs, for instance, soon learns to apply a standard discount rate to much of what he reads.

So, while going to the original source is very often a fruitful way to discern the motives that impelled certain actions, it is also fraught with hazards. Nothing guarantees accuracy in the way a decision is explained, even if the explainer was a participant in it. The search for answers must be broadened.

A second technique for determining the motives and strategies of decision-makers is to probe the views of close observers who were not themselves participants in the decision-making process. This is an especially useful approach when one can find observers who had no stake in the decision or in the success of any of the participants. Observers of this sort can be found in almost every area of government activity. Most of them are journalists.

On the whole, social scientists have made far less effective use of journalistic sources than they might have. There are, of course, some inherent problems in using journalism as source material. The task of the journalist is different from that of the social scientist; the former is less concerned with perspective, context, and explanation and more concerned with specific events and decisions. Recognizing the differences between the two, the fact remains that good journalism can be an invaluable resource for social science research.

Journalists are themselves observers of events and decisions. In many cases, they will have produced the only unofficial written record of events that occurred before a research project began. Their proximity when important decisions are made provides them with some sense of the nature of the decision-making process and the motives of the participants. Journalists may not have all the facts, and there may be biases in their reporting, but that is probably true as well even of the participants in a decision. To avoid the use of journalistic sources for that reason alone is a counterproductive form of self-denial. The contemporary reports of events and decisions are an important source of factual and contextual information for the social scientist. They should be used with some caution, but they should be used.

A third technique for discovering the factors that underlie a se-ries of decisions is to look for visible patterns in the way those deci-sions are made or in their outcomes over time. This is quite a different sort of research from the first two mentioned. It requires some perspective and some rigorous attempts at objectivity. The idea is to identify decision characteristics that develop naturally, perhaps even without the conscious awareness of the participants themselves. This has become an increasingly important kind of social science research in the last few decades. It is used, for instance, to study changes over time in issue voting in presidential elections, to assess party unity on congressional roll calls, and to examine the relationship between membership on the armed services committees and the domestic dis-tribution of defense contracts. The advantage, and thus the impor-tance, of this kind of research is that it is based on something other than the subjective judgments of those who participate in or observe events. It may be quantitative or nonquantitative depending on the nature of the data. The key criterion is not whether the data base lends itself to quantitative analysis, but whether it is comprehensive enough and rich enough to reveal the most important and persistent characteristics of a decision-making process.

If sufficient resources and opportunities are available, a com-prehensive research approach to a complex topic ought to include all three of the techniques discussed here: interviews with participants, examination of contemporary reports of events and decisions, and broadly based investigations and analysis of relevant data bases and documents. Each of the three techniques has inherent flaws. But using all three in concert allows the advantages of one technique to compensate for the disadvantages of another.

Each of these approaches has been used in doing the research for this book. The nature of the information and resources available made that both possible and necessary. A variety of useful sources were available, but none of them were sufficient in themselves to provide a clear or comprehensive picture of the operations of the appointment process.

The most important sources, because of the breadth and depth of the information they provided and because of their ready availability, were the transcripts of Senate confirmation hearings. The Senate holds public hearings on virtually every major nomination it considers. The vast majority of these are published, and those few that are not are available for inspection in appropriate Senate committee rooms. The hearings vary in length and in scope of inquiry, but in general they provide clear and (most importantly) consistent indicators of the kinds of interests and concerns that Senators bring to the appointment process. The statements of nominees, Senators, and witnesses also provide a good running narrative of appointment decisions—of who participated and of the intensity of their interest. The hearings do not paint a full portrait of appointment decisions, but they do reveal a great deal about the Senate's role in the appointment process. More than 1,200 complete hearing transcripts covering most of the major nominations from 1964 through 1978 were read in the preparation of this book.

Contemporary journalism has also been an important resource for this study. I attempted, where possible, to use journalistic accounts as original rather than merely secondary sources. And I sought to make extensive use not only of national newspapers and magazines but also of trade journals and the house organs of various independent organizations. The value of the latter is that they often pay more attention to the appointment process than do national news sources. They cover routine as well as controversial appointments. And because their reporters are more familiar with both the personalities and the issues involved in appointment decisions, reporting in these journals tends to achieve a higher level of factual accuracy and a better sense of the context in which these decisions are made.

Substantial assistance in the construction of this analysis was provided by a large number of people who had themselves participated in appointment decisions. In some cases, the contributions were indirect. I derived a great deal of useful information from reading memoirs, examining collections of White House staff papers and memoranda at presidential libraries, and culling the files of Senate committees. In a number of other cases, White House aides, Senate staff members, and appointees themselves graciously consented to talk with me about their participation in appointment decisions. Many of them were willing to talk with me on several occasions, and often at considerable length. Many of the interviews were followed up with letters and telephone conversations. These interviews and discussions were of utmost importance in filling the gaps that existed in the public record and in providing me with a sense of the competing perspectives that underlie so many appointment decisions.

Several dozen elite interviews were conducted in the course of this study. Most lasted approximately an hour. Some were slightly shorter, many were considerably longer. I sought whenever possible to interview people outside their offices and during their leisure time. This was intended both to get more time with the interviewees and to free them from the distractions of telephones, secretaries, and schedules. In most cases, that aim was achieved. When circumstances seemed appropriate and the interviewee was willing, a tape recorder was used. Most of the time, however, I took notes during the interview and then fleshed them out immediately afterward. During these interviews I used a mixture of open- and closed-ended questions. Closed-ended questions were used to probe those areas in which I thought it useful to attempt comparisons among committees or administrations. Open-ended questions were used to explore particular appointment decisions or other factors that were specific to one administration, committee, or time period. In some places in the text of this book, I have quoted individuals whose interviews were not recorded on tape. In each such case, I have attempted to give the individual involved an opportunity to read the quoted remarks to be sure that they have been accurately reconstructed.

A few final words are in order about Part II of this book on the confirmation process. The most difficult research decision I had to face in writing this book was how to make most effective use of the confirmation hearings that were the primary resource in the preparation of this section. There were, it seemed to me, two ways in which these might be treated. One was to try to draw a sample of the 1,200 confirmation hearings for which published transcripts were available and to undertake a quantitative content analysis of those hearings. The obvious advantage of that approach was that it promised to generate some hard data on what went on in those hearings, data that other scholars could examine and attempt to verify or replicate. But in my initial efforts to treat the confirmation hearings in this way, I ran into several problems that I soon came to regard as insuperable. The first was the extraordinary complexity of the endeavor. Confirmation hearings vary greatly in length, but many run on for days and in their published version for hundreds of pages. The time demands in undertaking a content analysis of even a sample of the available hearings were enormous.

A second problem was the difficulty I encountered in trying to impose a standard of objectivity. The difficulties were especially apparent in trying to define and categorize the issues raised in confirmation hearings. Over a period of more than a decade, change occurs inevitably in the content of certain political ideas and the meaning of certain political terms. Issues like "equal rights," "fiscal responsibility," and "conflict of interest" took on different shades of meaning with the passage of time. Categorizing discussions of these issues and quantifying the frequency of their appearance thus became a very slippery enterprise.

Yet a third problem with this approach was that it often seemed to me simply misleading. The frequency with which a concern was expressed in confirmation hearings did not always correlate with the salience of that concern that one perceived from a close reading of the hearings. Some issues were raised in almost every confirmation hearing: Potential conflicts of interest are perhaps the best example. Yet in the vast majority of cases these concerns were raised routinely and dispensed with quickly. They almost never had an important bearing on the outcomes of the confirmation process or on the interchange that developed between nominees and the committees that reviewed their nominations. Content analysis, in this setting at least, was simply not a sensitive enough research tool to permit these careful distinctions between frequency and salience. For that, and for the other reasons noted above, I chose not to rely on a quantitative approach to the confirmation hearings.

What I chose to do instead was to read all 1,200 of the hearings and to draw from them those variables that appeared consistently to be of greatest concern to Senate committees and to have the largest bearing on Senate confirmation behavior. I made this choice knowing full well that it would strip this part of the book of some of the "hardness" that quantitative content analysis promised to provide. I did so, however, only after concluding that content analysis could not deliver on its promise of objectivity and empirical rigor and was not an adequate tool for mining the rich lode of information that the confirmation hearings contained. While it may appear, then, that I have sacrificed "hardness" for "richness," that choice was made only after initial probing persuaded me that standard quantitative approaches would be extraordinarily difficult to apply consistently and would often produce indicators that disguised more than they revealed.

Research of the sort described here is an imperfect art. Sources are often incomplete, biased, or in conflict with one another. Findings can never be fully conclusive or universally applicable. One is always left wishing his research tools were more delicate, the data more precise, the evidence harder, patterns clearer. But they aren't.

So the quality and the value of this kind of research is ultimately as reliant on the way it is carried out as on the way it is designed: on its breadth of inquiry, on the persistence of its pursuit of objectivity, and on the skepticism with which it treats conventional or oversimplified characterizations of complex behavior. Those, I hope, are the standards by which this book will be judged.

Index

Abell, Tyler, 131n.21
Abrams, Creighton, W., 156
ACTION, 48, 171n.25
Adams, Sherman, 17, 18, 19, 20, 70–72
     passim
Administrative Conference, 10
AFL-CIO, 208, 213n.8
Agency for International Development
     (AID), 28
  Far East Regional Director of, 115
  Deputy Administrator of, 115,
     120n.24, 171n.40
Agriculture Department, 193
  Secretary of, xviii, 17, 20, 41, 118n.12,
     126, 131n.14, 136, 170n.6
Aiken, George, 127
Albert, Carl, 219
Alexander, Clifford, xx
Allen, James, 148
Alliance for Progress, 138
Allison, Graham, 276
Allott, Gordon, 216–217
American Bar Association (ABA), 20
  role of, in appointment of federal
     judges, 206–207, 208, 213n.6,
     213n.7
American Foreign Service Association,
     205n.1
American Indians. See Indians
American Medical Association, 202, 208,
     209
American Public Power Association,
     172n.59
Amtrak, 120n.25
Anderson, Harry R., 118n.7
Anderson, William A., Jr., 220
Appalachian Regional Commission, 157,
     172n.43
appointment process

defined, xii–xvi
  conflict avoidance in, xvi–xviii
  conflict resolution in, xviii–xix
  importance of, xxi
  legislative-executive relations in, 185,
     215–232
  nature of, 246
  past suggestions for improvement of,
     260
  suggestions for role of President in,
     264–267
  role of Senate in, 267–270
Arms Control and Disarmament Agency,
     152
  Deputy Director of, 205n.1
Arnett, Alvin, 167
Articles of Confederation, 91
Arvey, Jacob, 224
Association of American Colleges, 206
Association of American Universities,
     206
Association of State Colleges and Uni-
     versities, 206
Association of the Bar of the City of New
     York, 99
Atomic Energy Commission, xiv, 84, 143

Baker, Charles D., 171n.36
Baker, Howard, 157, 222, 257
Ball, Robert, 225
Bannerman, Graeme C., 125, 131n.11
Banuelos, Romana Acosta, 110
Barr, Joseph W., 118n.10
Barrett, Ashton, 119n.23
Barrett, Richard, 27
Bartlett, Ken, 220
Bartley, Robert L., 142, 170n.15
Batchelor, Roy E., 155, 171n.41

DATE LOANED

MAR 0 ..1982			